Praise for *The Modern Reader's Guide to Dante's* The Divine Comedy

"No reader could find a more clarifying prologue to a reading of *The Divine Comedy* than this perceptive, direct, and deeply informed introduction. It is as enjoyable to read as it is helpful in its purpose."
— Josephine Jacobsen, Poetry Consultant, Library of Congress (1971–73)

"Dante had Virgil, Beatrice, and Bernard as tour guides through the universe. Joseph Gallagher becomes our guide through Dante with the best short introduction to *The Divine Comedy* now available."
— Dr. Stephen Vicchio, past chairman, Department of Philosophy, College of Notre Dame of Maryland

"Joseph Gallagher opens Dante's journey to all, being at pains neither to bore nor to oversimplify. He has Erin's own way with scholarship, and his eye for the marvelous and the paradoxical should make this little volume the *vademecum* for the budding Dantista."
— Dr. Jack Furlong, founding director, the Coppin-Hopkins Classics Program in the Baltimore City schools

"In this book, Gallagher has provided a concise and valuable road map for the beginner who has always wanted to tackle Dante's great work but was afraid to try. Gallagher's precise summaries and notes on key texts make it an ideal companion volume to read beside the master work itself. This book will be very valuable for any nonspecialist who would like to take the fantastic Christian voyage with the Italian master."
— Gary Eberle, associate professor of English, Aquinas College, Grand Rapids, Michigan

"In an entertaining, vivacious, yet strictly scholarly vein, Joseph Gallagher takes us to Dante's Hell. But the trip does not end there. Following Dante's stringent intentions, Hell is only the preparation for the consolations of Purgatory and the bliss of Paradise. These, under Joseph Gallagher's wings, are finally accessible even to the most untraveled beginner. Read this summary of the whole *Divine Comedy,* and you will want to read the entire poem itself."
— Dr. Regina Soria, professor emerita of Italian and chairperson emerita, Department of Modern Languages, College of Notre Dame of Maryland

A MODERN READER'S GUIDE TO DANTE'S

The Divine Comedy

A MODERN READER'S GUIDE TO DANTE'S

The Divine Comedy

JOSEPH GALLAGHER

FOREWORD BY JOHN FRECCERO

LIGUORI/TRIUMPH
LIGUORI, MISSOURI

Published by Liguori/Triumph
An Imprint of Liguori Publications
Liguori, Missouri
www.liguori.org

Library of Congress Cataloging-in-Publication Data

Gallagher, Joseph.
    [To hell & back with Dante]
    A modern reader's guide to Dante's The Divine Comedy / Joseph Gallagher ;
foreword by John Freccero.
        p.   cm.
    Originally published: To hell & back with Dante. Liguori, Mo. : Triumph Books,
c1996.
    Includes bibliographical references and index.
    ISBN 0-7648-0494-4 (pbk.)
    1. Dante Alighieri, 1265–1321. Divina commedia. I. Title.
PQ4390.G28   1999
851'.1—dc21   99-20714

This book was originally titled *To Hell and Back with Dante: A Modern Reader's Guide to Dante's* The Divine Comedy, copyright 1996.

Frontispiece: *Allegorical Portrait of Dante,* Samuel H. Kress Collection, © 1995 Board of Trustees, National Gallery of Art, Washington, D.C.

Contents

Foreword ix

Preface xi

Catechism of *The Comedy* xv

Part 1: *Inferno* 1

Part 2: *Purgatorio* 67

Part 3: *Paradiso* 129

Appendix 203

Bibliography 215

Index 217

Foreword

THE DIVINE COMEDY's status as one of the classics of world literature perhaps obscures for us the extent to which Dante's work was not only immensely learned, but enormously popular as well. Even during the poet's lifetime, according to a probably apocryphal story told by one of Dante's commentators, children ran after the poet in the streets of Ravenna, hoping to touch the cloak of the man who had been through Hell. The power and prestige of his language were such that the Florentine dialect in which he wrote eventually became the Italian language. Phrases from his poem became idioms in modern Italian, and there is scarcely an Italian today, of whatever degree of cultivation, who cannot recite from memory verses and even pages of the text.

Not only has Dante's poem permeated the language and culture of Italy, but Italian history has in a sense permeated Dante's text. Some romantic poets took as pure eroticism the story of his love for Beatrice as a child. Patriots in the nineteenth century read Italian aspirations to national unity into the poem. Anticlericals throughout the centuries have drawn general conclusions from Dante's condemnation of particular individuals—priests or popes—in spite of his unswerving loyalty to both the papacy and the priesthood. It is as if the poem were a Rorschach test for Italy's continuing interpretation of its own identity. Both the beauty of Dante's words and his connection to his own people are inevitably lost in translation.

This is a loss for which scholarship cannot compensate. The best a scholar can hope to do is to reestablish the text in its historical context, like an archaeologist reconstructing an ancient monument from its remains. At that point, the work of interpretation begins, to explain what the stones mean. Moreover, the interpretation must be bold, given the abyss that separates our culture and values from those of the Middle Ages. It must somehow account for the poem's popularity even now and explain its relevance for a modern reader. In other words, it must translate Dante's culture, as well as his words.

As obvious as this is, bold, new interpretations of *The Divine Comedy* are rare, for they require learning, self-confidence, and a certain moral tranquillity. Joseph Gallagher possesses these qualities to a remarkable degree. He is erudite and well prepared, having done his homework without a trace of that impatience one sometimes finds in the scholarly notes of critics and poets. He has read almost everything of relevance but remains independent and uncowed by centuries of learned opinion. Where the critics seem right, he is generous in his acknowledgment; where they are clearly wrong, he is unshakeable in his opposition. This is clearly someone who has questioned authority before and who knows when to stand and when to yield.

Gallagher is most daring when he updates the poem to apply to our own times. For example, commenting on canto 14 of the *Purgatorio,* he compares the devastated countryside that Dante describes to the defoliation caused by Agent Orange in modern warfare. The anachronism shocks at first, but on reflection, nothing seems more natural or more "Dantesque" than to take the moral standards of the poem seriously and to apply them to the present. For all of his humor and good nature, Gallagher's moral standards seem as demanding as Dante's own. He is as anxious as the poet to attack the stupidity of war. He also stresses Dante's ecumenism: his sympathy for Arab thought and the absence in his poem of any trace of medieval anti-Semitism.

Most interpreters of Dante's poem have treated the theology as part of an antiquated medieval background, to be tolerated or explained away. The Italian philosopher Benedetto Croce suggested we read it as we would read science fiction, perhaps with what Coleridge referred to as "suspension of disbelief." T. S. Eliot offered similar advice in his essay on the poetry of Dante. For Gallagher, however, Dante's moral theology is the heart of the poem. He analyzes it from the inside, so to speak, and finds Dante at times too severe with the sinners depicted in the poem. Gallagher's charity brings him to the point of questioning if anyone is ever eternally damned. His compassion for sinners seems overwhelming.

Yet there is no sentimentality in this commentary. There is wit and wisdom and the serenity that comes with suffering overcome. One suspects that Gallagher has himself been to Hell and back—which makes his voice sound so much like Dante's own.

JOHN FRECCERO, PH.D.
Chairman, DEPARTMENT OF ITALIAN, NEW YORK UNIVERSITY

Preface

WHEN I WAS a child of three, the poet T. S. Eliot visited my native Baltimore and had his first meeting with novelist F. Scott Fitzgerald. Their hostess showed Eliot her copy of *The Divine Comedy* and proudly noted that she had read it. "Begun to read it," he corrected her.

When I was a man of forty I still had not seriously begun to read that masterpiece—the first truly great Christian poem, and arguably still the greatest. This, despite the specifically Catholic character of the poem and my nineteen years of Catholic education—twelve of them in seminaries. Few teachers had mentioned it. None had required or ardently urged the reading of it.

Feeling properly ashamed of my midlife situation, I finally read the whole poem—in a monastery. In the subsequent quarter of a century I have reread it numerous times, read about it widely, and taught it often. The effort to teach it has proven to me that, when it comes to mastering this masterpiece, any reader is a beginner for a long time. In fact, "you can't read it until you've read it."

There are said to be more books written about *The Divine Comedy* than about any other single work of literature (the Bible is a collection). And according to Theodore Besterman's *World Bibliography of Bibliographies,* only Shakespeare has had more lists of books compiled about him than Dante.

Such facts support Eliot's opinion that "Shakespeare gives the greatest width of human passion; Dante the greatest altitude and greatest depth. They divide the modern world between them; there is no third." In his *Western Canon,* Harold Bloom has asserted that Dante and Shakespeare do not "belong" to the Western Canon—"They *are* the Western Canon." Other Western classics gain importance to the extent that they either influenced these two geniuses or were influenced by them.

(Not everyone has received word of this eminence. A student of mine once phoned the bookstore of a famous university to ask if they had *The Divine Comedy.* The clerk asked, "Who's that by?" "Why, Dante," my student replied. The puzzled response: "Is he giving a course here this summer?")

Dante's influence has not only been on literature. I had looked at Auguste

Rodin's statue *The Thinker* for many years before I learned that it was the sculptor's version of Dante. It didn't take me quite so long to realize where composer Peter Tchaikovsky found his inspiration for *Francesca da Rimini* (*Inferno*, canto 5). Sergei Rachmaninoff wrote an opera (1906) on the same subject, and Franz Liszt composed the *Dante Symphony* (1856) and the *Dante Sonata* (1839), subtitled "After a Reading of Dante."

All of this relevance can prove a stumbling block to the reader. There is perhaps too much information about *La Comedia* (as its author called it in old Italian). By one counting, a total of 408 characters make a personal appearance in the poem. Another 426 are referred to by name. The poet also cited 112 other persons who are outside the story itself: for example, someone quoted. The six-volume Italian *Enciclopedia Dantesca* (1984) contains a total of 6,357 large pages.

First-time readers are easily overwhelmed by all the data that have been collected about all the personages and episodes mentioned so compactly in the poem. They may feel as though they are climbing Mount Everest with Mount Everest on their backs. After all, Dante was interested in everything. One early commentator claimed that Dante used the Provençal language at one point in the poem because he wanted to show that he knew something about everything—*"aliquid de omnibus."*

In addition to its fifty direct Bible references and hundreds of allusions, his poem is a storehouse of history, biography, mythology, theology, philosophy, astronomy, poetry, and the most earthy and picturesque observations about daily life in fourteenth-century Italy: fireflies shining on a summer night, flies giving way to gnats, a tailor squinting, a shepherd slapping his thigh in disgust, an ox licking its nose, a stable boy grooming a horse, a poor man selling combs, oarsmen stopping at a whistle, dust particles being illuminated by a shaft of sunlight coming through the blinds, a mother in night clothes fleeing a fire with her babe, lowlanders building dikes, and Venetians caulking damaged ships. All sorts of birds and animals are also distinctively described. The poet appears to have been that ideal writer on whom nothing is lost.

Longfellow dubbed the poem "This medieval miracle of song." Others, with understandable exaggeration, have called it Thomas Aquinas's *Summa Theologiae/Theologica* set to music. Like the great cathedral-builders of his age, and the scholars writing their comprehensive *summas,* Dante wanted to construct a colossal and audacious poem that would bring all the key elements of time and space into a luminous and integrated whole.

A reader doesn't have to share Dante's philosophy, theology, and science to stand in awe at the genius with which he used the materials at hand to build his cathedral of words. And the human nature that he plumbed so deeply and illumined so vividly has not changed that much since fourteenth-century Italy.

I believe I would have faced up to *The Comedy* much earlier if I had first read, or read along with the poem, the kind of introduction that I myself have now written. After all, even Dante had Virgil, Beatrice, and Saint Bernard for guides. I have sketched only the major structural, narrative, and poetic elements of the poem. I have not presumed any large amount of background knowledge on the reader's part.

My hope is that this guide will prompt its readers to begin mastering the masterpiece themselves.

A note on the translations in this guide: Dante quoted from Saint Jerome's Latin Vulgate Bible. The Catholic Douay-Rheims translation into English (1582–1609) was based on the Vulgate, so I have used that version in this text.

Since there have been at least one hundred English translations of *The Comedy,* and since most of these have been essentially literal ones (not poetic nor paraphrases), prose translations will tend to resemble one another. There are, for example, only a few ways to say, "In His will is our peace." For this commentary I have checked numerous prose versions, and I have inclined to forge common interpretations or to do my own version on various occasions for specific reasons—for example, greater clarity when I cite out of context. The versions I have checked most often are the literal ones of Huse, Singleton, and Sinclair.

A warning from Dante in *The Banquet:* "Nothing that has been harmoniously composed...can be translated into another language without destroying its sweetness and musicality." That is not to say that a translation cannot have its own musicality, but Dante's Italian and rhymes are supremely melodic. Reading his ideas in translation could be compared to reading the libretto of *Carmen* without ever hearing the original score. Byron called Dante "the most untranslatable of poets." More than one person, like T. S. Eliot, have learned Italian just to be able to read *La Comedia.*

A reminder: Apart from the *Inferno*'s canto 34, there are three cantos for each number from 1 to 33. Hence there is no canto 5 as such. So reference must be made to the section in which a particular canto 5 appears (for example, *Purgatorio,* canto 5, or *Purgatorio* 5). If, for some special numerical reason, reference is made, for example, to the poem's

64th canto, by subtracting 34 from 64, you know that the *Purgatorio's* 30th canto is meant. Any canto above 67 (34 plus 33) will be in the *Paradiso*.

Finally, throughout the centuries, many a reader has found *The Comedy* not just an unforgettable reading experience, but a life experience. For me, after seventeen years of working on this guide, it has proven a gratifying life experience to work with my exemplary editors, Anthony F. Chiffolo and Patricia Kossmann (again!). To them I robustly acknowledge my debt for a trinity of virtues that they embody: *fiducia, cortesia,* and *pazienza*.

Reader, may God grant that you gain fruit from your reading
(Se Dio ti lasci, lettor, prender frutto di tua lezione) (Inferno 20:19).

A Catechism of *The Comedy*

Q. Who was Dante Alighieri?

A. He was an Italian Catholic writer born in Florence under the sign of Gemini (May 14–June 13 in his day) in the year A.D. 1265. In his fifty-seventh year, on the night of September 13–14, 1321, he died of malaria in Ravenna. There, he lies buried in a Franciscan church, despite apologetic Florentine efforts to have his remains returned to the native city that exiled him for life. There's an empty tomb for him inside Florence's famous Santa Croce Church, and a statue outside it. Florence, however, supplies oil for the lamp burning at his real tomb.

Q. What does his name mean, and where did he get it?

A. Dante is probably a contraction for Durante (as in Jimmy!) and would mean "enduring"—like his reputation. Or it may mean simply "giving," as is "Wednesday's child." There was a Durante Abati who may have been his maternal grandfather. His mother was Bella Abati, who died when the poet was about thirteen.

Alighieri was a family name on his father's side. Indeed, his father, who died when the poet was about eighteen, was named Alighiero degli Alighieri. Dante's great-great-grandfather (whom the poet meets in the *Paradiso*) married a woman named Alighiera degli Alighieri.

The surname was sometimes spelled Aldighieri or Alaghieri. A document survives in which Dante spelled his name Alaghary. His early biographer, Giovanni Boccaccio of *Decameron* fame, seems to have solidified the Alighieri spelling. The name has been traced to the city of Ferrara (seventy-five miles northeast of Florence) where a Aldighieri family flourished from the 1000s to the 1200s. In Latin, Dante was called *Alagherius* and *Alagerius*.

Authorities seem reluctant to guess the meaning of the name. Some suspect a link with the Old German *Alger/Algeron* (old spear? noble spear?) or Old French *Algeron* (man with a moustache or beard) or even Algeria.

Q. Do historians know much about Dante's life and background?

A. Not very much, and some of that is disputed. In that respect he is like Homer and Shakespeare.

Q. What was the social level of his family?

A. He appears to have had a middle-class background of some nobility, though in his day his family connections were poor in money and numbers. His father was a notary who owned a bit of property.

Q. Did he have brothers and sisters?

A. He seems to have been an only child. By his stepmother, Lepa, he did have a half-brother and a half-sister or two.

Q. Did he have a wife?

A. Yes. She was Gemma Donati, and he may have been engaged to her when he was as young as twelve. From records, we know he was married to her by the time he was thirty-three.

Q. Did they have children?

A. Yes, though neither they nor his wife are mentioned in *The Comedy*. His sons were Pietro and Jacopo. He had at least one daughter, Antonia, who may be the same one who as a nun bore the name Beatrice. There may have been a third son, Giovanni. The male line died out in 1563 with the death of a Francesco Alighieri, six generations after Dante.

Q. But what of his beloved Beatrice, the heroine of his poem?

A. Though a few scholars have thought she was entirely fictional, there was a Florentine girl named Beatrice (happy-making) Portinari who was a year younger than Dante. She married Simone de' Bardi and died not long afterward at the age of twenty-four. (In *Purgatorio* 33:7, Dante speaks of her as a virgin.) Dante wrote of first seeing her when he was nine and of being permanently smitten by her beauty. They seem to have had little if any personal contact, though he wrote his first sonnet about her. Her death plunged him into destructive grief. In an early and brief work, *La Vita Nuova*, he said he hoped "to write of her what was never said of any woman." *The Comedy* fulfilled that hope (see the appendix, on *La Vita Nuova*).

Q. How did Dante spend his youth?

A. He was a student; an author of scholarly prose and poetry, though some of the poetry was not so lofty; a soldier, fighting on horse in the front lines at the crucial battle of Campaldino in 1289, when the Florentine

Guelphs and their allies decisively defeated the Ghibellines; an ambassador; and a politician. To qualify for office he joined one of the guilds, that of physicians and apothecaries, which—curiously—also included booksellers and painters. Dante told us that he drew. One source called him "an excellent draftsman."

Q. Who were these Guelphs and Ghibellines?

A. The Guelphs got their name from Welf, the founder of a princely German family; the Ghibellines got theirs from a German castle named Waiblingen. In Germany itself, the descendants of Welf became great political rivals of the family that owned the castle—the Hohenstaufens. (Through George I, the present Queen of England has Guelph ancestry. In Canada there is a university town of Guelph.)

Q. What did these German families have to do with Italy?

A. Rich in almost every way, but vulnerable on almost every side, Italy was for nearly a millennium almost always under attack: without, from Germanic tribes, Huns, Lombards, Muslims, Magyars, Byzantines, Normans, and Spaniards; within, from warring city-states and private adventurers. Over time, two centers of defense and stability emerged: the papacy and some dominant continental power.

Since 962, Holy Roman emperors had held land in Italy by conquest, donation, and feudal lordship. From 1138 to 1254, when Hohenstaufens/Ghibellines like Frederick Barbarossa and Frederick II ruled as emperors, many Italians wanted them to augment their power in Italy—against whatever local forces seemed threatening to their self-interests. The foes of such imperial influence took the name of the German rivals of the Hohenstaufen/Ghibellines, and were called Guelphs. In this power game, the Guelphs often allied themselves with papal power.

Q. What was the highest political office that Dante the Guelph ever held?

A. For two months in mid-1300 he was, in effect, the mayor of Florence and thus an important man in that most important city. Those two months had dire, lifelong repercussions.

Q. What were these?

A. First of all, he was obliged to send his best friend into exile, where he became mortally ill. After his own political enemies among the Guelphs came to power, Dante was accused of corruption, fined five thousand florins, had his goods confiscated, and was sentenced to be burned alive (in 1302). (In 1315 both he and his sons were sentenced to public decapitation.) He never saw Florence again, partly because he later rejected any compromise solutions to his situation there. Dante was not the groveling sort. He seems never to have seen his wife again, though at least some of his children later joined him in Ravenna.

Q. Was he actually guilty of any crimes?

A. Repeatedly calling himself an undeserving exile, he always denied any guilt. No evidence has ever proven him wrong.

Q. What did he do during those twenty years of exile?

A. At a time when roads were very unsafe and exile was a kind of death, he wandered about most of Italy, and perhaps outside of it, looking for patrons who could appreciate his literary talents. He wrote *The Comedy* and other works, and lectured. He was returning from a diplomatic mission to Venice when he caught his fatal illness. Dante described himself as "wandering as a stranger through almost every region to which our language reaches…a ship without sails or rudder, driven to various harbors and shores by the parching wind that blows from pinching poverty" (*The Banquet* I:3).

Q. What is his masterpiece called?

A. Simply *La Comedia* in Dante's Italian (*La Commedia* in modern Italian; *Comoedia* in Latin). Not because it is funny, but because the main character (himself) attains a happy ending—a healing vision of God—and receives a divine message to deliver. As a common man writing for the common man and woman, he used the vernacular Italian and not the Latin of scholars.

Q. How did it come to be called "Divine"?

A. Impressed by its majesty and its religious concerns, commentators early began referring to it as "divine"—as did Boccaccio in his pioneer *Life of Dante* (*circa* 1360). Some of the earliest manuscripts followed suit in their titles. Other commentators sometimes applied the adjective to Dante himself. The word first appeared in the title of a printed version in 1555. In the work itself, the author wrote that it was a "sacred" poem on which Heaven had set its hand.

Q. How long did he work on it?

A. He finished it just before his death in 1321. Some scholars say he began it even before his 1302 exile, but today most experts hold that it was mainly composed during the last ten or eleven years of his life.

Q. How long is the poem?

A. It contains 14,233 lines. (Homer's *Iliad* is 15,693 lines; his *Odyssey,* 12,110 lines; and Virgil's *Aeneid,* 9,890 lines.) These lines are spread over one hundred cantos (songs) of varying length. The shortest is 115 lines; the longest, 160; the average, 142. Though Dante liked symmetry, he was obviously not fanatical about it.

The work is further divided into three major *cantiche* or *canzoni* (canticles/song collections): the *Inferno* (4,720 lines), the *Purgatorio* (4,755 lines), the *Paradiso* (4,758 lines). Apart from an introductory canto in the *Inferno,* each major section contains thirty-three cantos, for the sum of a perfect hundred.

Q. Is each line of the same length?

A. Yes. Allowing for cases in which sounds merge because one word ends with a vowel and the next word begins with a vowel (for example, *che il = ch'il*), the reader will find eleven syllables in each line. Such a line is called hendecasyllabic, from the Greek *hen* (one) and *deka* (ten). Many lines are easily read as a sonnet line of iambic pentameter (five sets of ba/BOOM beats: cf. Wordsworth's "The world is too much with us, late and soon")— but with an extra syllable at the end: thus, *"E cad-/ di co-/ me cor-/ po mor-/ to ca-/ de."* (Actually, Hamlet's famous line is hendecasyllabic: "To be or not to be, that is the question.")

Q. Does the poem rhyme?

A. Yes, unlike the *Iliad,* the *Odyssey,* and the *Aeneid.* (Rhyme, practically unknown to the ancient Greeks and Romans, was introduced to the West with the hymns of the early Christian Church.) Dante's basic unit is the *terzine* (tercet), a three-line stanza of which the first and third lines rhyme *(aba):* for example, cat/green/bat. The rhyme of the middle line (green) becomes the rhyme for the first and third lines of the next *terzine (bcb)*. Thus, seen/glow/keen...flow/red/snow...and so on. Thus, each rhyme occurs in sets of three, and *terza rima* gets its name from having a "third rhyme," that is, a third rhyming word.

This interlocking pattern has two documentary advantages: 1) it is easy to see when a line has been dropped out; 2) it is hard to insert bogus lines. Manuscripts had both kinds of problems, and Dante knew it.

Also, every *terzine* (except the very first) looks both to the past and to the future in its rhyme. You hear a sound you've heard and a sound you're going to hear again. Each canto ends with a single line that rhymes with the middle line of the previous *terzine* and forms a quatrain: *yzyz*.

Dante is often credited with inventing *terza rima*—no earlier instance of its use is known, though there are approximations in Provençal poetry. In any case, he made it famous, and in the poem his sentences are most often three lines in length. When they are not, the sentences are six lines long or occasionally nine. In short, our poet thinks in tercets—Trinitarian units of three lines.

Q. Are there any familiar examples of "third rhyme" in English?

A. Yes: Percy Bysshe Shelley's "Ode to the West Wind" and Robert Frost's "Acquainted with the Night."

Q. Aren't there quite a few sets of threes in *The Divine Comedy*?

A. You've noticed! For Dante (at times accused of triadomania) three was a special number because it reflected the ultimate, mysterious reality of three persons in one God: Father, Son, and Holy Spirit. Spiritual writers wrote of the three ages of mankind, which successively featured the activity of one person of the Trinity. Time itself is past, present, and future. Also, a syllogism is composed of major, minor, and conclusion. Finally, Dante for various mystical reasons associated Beatrice with the number nine, the square of three (see the appendix, *La Vita Nuova*). If the first canto of the *Inferno* is regarded as introductory, each of the three parts of the poem contains thirty-three cantos, just as its basic unit of verse, the *terzine*, contains thirty-three syllables.

Q. What is *The Divine Comedy* in essence?

A. It is the story of an enlightening and purifying journey taken by a sinful poet to the next world and to its spheres of endless punishment, temporary purification, and endless bliss. It is also a love story showing how a good woman's love can save a lost man. In his story Dante spiritualized the poetic tradition of courtly love, in which a lovely, inaccessible woman is won over in silence by the brave exploits of an admirer. In this tradition, however, the result was often adultery.

Q. How long does the journey take?

A. About five and a half days: from the night before Good Friday until Easter Wednesday of the year A.D. 1300. In that year the Catholic Church celebrated its first "Holy Year," a Jubilee period stressing spiritual repentance and renewal. Dante probably visited Rome on pilgrimage during that year.

Q. So you could call the poem a travelogue?

A. Yes, and in that sense it is part of a long tradition of journey literature: Homer's *Odyssey,* the biblical *Book of Exodus,* Virgil's *Aeneid,* the search for the Holy Grail in Arthurian legend, Chaucer's *Canterbury Tales,* Cervantes's *Don Quixote,* and Bunyan's *Pilgrim's Progress.*

Q. Is it just a gripping adventure story?

A. No, it is much more. It is also a parable of political realities (corruption versus honesty); moral realities (the freedom that comes from accepting just laws versus the self-slavery of lawlessness); and mystical realities (the individual's self-absorption versus his or her trusting surrender to the Divine).

Q. Why did Dante write it?

A. In words that William Penn cited in the brochure for his Pennsylvania Colony, Dante said he wanted his poem to liberate people still living in the world from the state of misery and lead them to a state of happiness. He also wanted to praise Beatrice and the saving graces he received through her.

Q. Did he explain his plan in any other way?

A. Yes. In a letter whose authenticity is sometimes disputed, Dante wrote to his patron and the dedicatee of the *Paradiso,* Can Grande della Scala of Verona: "The subject of the work, then, in its literal sense is 'the state of souls after death'—and this is without qualification, since the whole progress of the work hinges on and about that subject. Whereas if the work is taken allegorically, the subject is this: man becoming liable to the justice which rewards and punishes, inasmuch as by the exercise of his freedom of choice he merits good or ill" (see the appendix, letter #10).

Q. Why is the work so special and so highly honored?

A. Some persons are outstanding in their intellectual qualities, others in their moral vision, still others in their emotional depths. Dante, who was eminent in all three realms of truth, goodness, and beauty, expressed himself through an astonishing array of poetic gifts rooted in imagination and verbal expressiveness. In the process, enhancing his own Florentine dialect (one of fourteen then current in Italy), he brought the melodious Italian language from its infancy to heights of perfection. For his compatriots, he is simply *Il Poeta*—a title he himself gives Virgil seventeen times in *The Comedy*. His was a "rhapsodic intellect," "a mind in love," "the most piercing intellect ever granted to the sons of men."

John Ruskin wrote of Dante, "He is the central man of all the world, as representing in perfect balance the imaginative, moral and intellectual qualities all at their highest." Thomas Carlyle called the poem Dante's "unfathomable heart song." Ralph Waldo Emerson recommended it as *the* textbook for teaching the young the art of writing well. Even Leon Trotsky urged his Marxist companions to study their Dante. Had not Karl Marx himself at the end of the preface to volume I of his *Das Kapital* quoted the maxim "of the great Florentine," his fellow exile: "*Segui il tuo corso, e lascia dir le genti* (Follow your course, and let the people talk)"? (Actually, it is Virgil's maxim, which Marx rather cheekily altered from *Purgatorio* 5:13. There Virgil says, "Come behind me and let the people talk" when Dante slows down to hear a purgatorian who is amazed at his shadow.)

Q. Do we have any manuscripts in Dante's own hand?

A. Unfortunately, no. And even the earliest manuscript copies show variations among them.

Q. Do we have any portraits of him done from life?

A. Not for sure. To his contemporary and friend Giotto has been ascribed a portrait of a young Dante painted for Florence's Palazzo di Podesta. On the occasion of his seven hundredth birthday in 1965, the United States issued a five-cent stamp bearing his unattributed likeness.

(For the same occasion, at the end of the Second Vatican Council, Pope Paul VI presented each participant with a copy of *The Divine Comedy* containing his own dedication in praise of a "marvelous man who sang marvelously *[Mirus mire concinit]*." For the sixth centenary of Dante's death [1921] Pope Benedict XV issued a brief encyclical to teachers and students of the Catholic world, lauding this "noble figure, the pride and glory of humanity" who had "learned almost all that could be known in his time." These kudos were for the author who was among the first to be placed on the *Index of Prohibited Books* for his *De Monarchia*, which challenged absolutist papal claims in the political field.)

Q. Did he write other works?

A. In addition to *La Vita Nuova*, he wrote the Latin political work called *De Monarchia (Concerning Monarchy)*, an Italian poetic/philosophical work *Il Convivio* (alias *Il Convito [The Banquet]*), and a Latin linguistic work *De Vulgari Eloquentia (On Eloquence in the Vernacular)*. The last two projects were not completed (see the appendix).

Q. Is *The Divine Comedy* a difficult book?

A. It is certainly a rich and packed book. It has been called one of the last great Gothic cathedrals. Like any great cathedral, all its treasures cannot be seized on the run. One of my favorite cartoons shows a couple leaving their idling car and dashing toward Notre Dame Cathedral in Paris. "You do the inside," says the husband, "I'll do the outside." We know how Woody Allen took a speed-reading course and then read *War and Peace* in an hour: "It's about Russia," he reported.

However densely packed, *The Comedy* moves so swiftly that critics can speak of its velocity. Though often theoretical, it contains few passages that are not vivified by delightful images. The language itself is generally clear, simple, and direct. On that score, one scholar could claim that "Dante is the easiest major Italian author to read." (How different for us from Chaucer's English, half a century younger!) As for meaning, however, Robert J. Clements asserts that "of the greatest authors of the past, Dante is the least accessible. Dante's aesthetic was obscurantism. He...challenges us to get not only one, but four meanings from his poetry...[he had] excessive disdain for the average reader...[a] desire to be less available...[and a] medieval addiction to hermeticism [where the meaning is a hermit in hiding]." For all this, even the first-time reader can appropriate many riches without garnering them all.

Q. What of translations?

A. There are more than one hundred English translations of all or parts of *The Comedy.* Robert Pinsky has recently (1994) produced a highly praised *Inferno.* He was one of twenty poets who had already translated the *Inferno* in varying styles (*Dante's Inferno*, Ecco Press, 1993). Of the entire work, both Dorothy Sayers (Penguin, 1949–62) and John Ciardi (Mentor, 1954–61) have produced skillful modern English versions available in paperback. Sayers did hers in complete *terza rima*. Ciardi rhymed only the first and third lines of each tercet, but did not carry over the middle rhyme to the next *terzine.*

Rhyming translations require the use of paraphrasing and words that are sometimes obscure (since English is a relatively rhyme-poor language). I prefer a literal translation in prose. H. R. Huse has provided a useful one in a single-volume paperback (Holt, Rinehart and Winston, 1954), which keeps notes to a minimum and brackets sections that are relatively skippable. A flavorsome unrhymed translation in tercets is C. H. Sisson's (Oxford University Press, 1980, 1993).

More recent is Allen Mandelbaum's highly recommended three-volume paperback (Bantam, 1982), in poetic prose of three-line units, with basic notes and the original Italian.

John D. Sinclair has produced a three-volume paperback version (Oxford University Press, 1939) that gives the Italian on one side and a paragraphed prose translation opposite. In addition to a minimum of footnotes, he has appended a superlative essay after each canto.

Charles Southward Singleton of Johns Hopkins University has published a six-part work now available in paperback (Princeton University Press, 1970–75). Offering, like Sinclair, the original Italian and a paragraphed prose translation, he has provided a separate volume for each of Dante's three canticles. For each there is also a companion volume giving exhaustive commentary almost line by line. Totaling 2,144 pages, this is the most thorough reference work in English.

Q. What of illustrations of *The Comedy?*

A. Michelangelo illustrated a volume of *The Comedy,* but sadly it fell from a ship into the sea. Gustave Doré (1833–83) produced 136 drawings covering the entire poem. Other notable illustrators were Sandro Botticelli (92 drawings) and William Blake (32 drawings). Raphael included Dante twice in his frescoes in the Vatican Palace's Stanza della Segnatura: he's at the bottom right of the *Disputa del Sacramento;* with Virgil and Homer he's at the top left of the *Parnaso.* (So, by a delicious irony, the poet who most famously excoriated the Vatican ends up honored twice in the most famous room of the Vatican Palace!) Modern painters like Corot, Ingres, and Delacroix also drew thematic inspiration from the Florentine.

This book's frontispiece, a painting by an anonymous Florentine of the late 1500s, was generally unknown until purchased by the National Gallery in Washington, D.C., in 1961. About four feet square, *Allegorical Portrait of Dante* shows the poet holding in his left hand a manuscript of *The Comedy,* opened to the first sixteen tercets of canto 25 of the *Paradiso.* There he wrote poignantly of his (unfulfilled) hope of returning from exile to the baptistery where he was christened, and of being crowned there with the laurel leaves of a poet. Crowned thus by history in the painting—more than two centuries after his death—Dante gazes toward the seven-story mountain of Purgatory, on which the smoke of wrath, the flames of lust, and the Forest of Eden are visible. On a lower level of the mount, the minute figures of Dante and Virgil can be distinguished. On the water at the base can be seen "the little vessel of my talents" that produced the *Purgatorio.*

The poet's right hand hangs, as if in blessing, over his native Florence, indicated by the Arno River and the great cathedral dome, eerily illumined by infernal flames rising from below. The dome had not been built in Dante's day but was there in the artist's time.

The *New and Revised National Gallery of Art* notes that by the time of the painting, "The independence of Florence...was dead. Florentine literature...was bankrupt; and Florentine painting was now only an afterglow. Yet an unknown painter envisaged this tragic symbol of the greatness of his beloved Florence and in so doing created one of her last masterpieces" (p. 184).

Here then is the masterwork written by a man separated by exile from wife and children, and under a death sentence—a man with no wealth, no high-born family connections, no fixed address, no church status, no political base, indeed with a slandered political reputation. Yet he dares to do the unthinkable: to write a work of high seriousness encompassing the whole universe—not in the obligatory Latin, but in a vulgar tongue still in the turbulent state of formation.

Part I

Inferno

In the midst of my days,
I shall go to the gates of hell.
—Isaiah 38:10

IN THE MIDST of life, you can find that, without knowing precisely how, you have lost your bearings or even your sense of meaning. Perhaps you have lost as well some precious relationship. Suddenly, you find yourself engulfed in darkness and fearful confusion, or mastered by some destructive habit or emotion. It's hell.

In a flash you may glimpse the way out. But something blocks the easy escape. (Habits start out as cobwebs and end up as cables.) You need a friend or friendly adviser to guide you awhile. If you are fortunate, some persistent and energizing love for truth, goodness, or beauty will nourish you during the crisis and lead you out of it.

In Dante's case he had to "hit bottom" and witness the full maturation of the fruits of evil *(Inferno)*. Next he had to be purified of his own slavery to the roots of evil *(Purgatorio)*. Then he would at last be able to rise to the beauty of "that delightful mountain which is the source and cause of all happiness" *(Paradiso)*.

Like the hero of many a story, Dante is graced with the help of a wise man (Virgil) and a fair maiden (Beatrice) so that he may successfully fulfill his quest for a treasure (wisdom), which he then brings back home (in his poem).

Persons in Dante's original condition feel crushed by the weight of their own existence and assaulted by what seems a hostile universe. That feeling of "being under" or of "going under" reflects the root of the word *inferno,* which means "under" or "below," as in "inferior" and "infernal."

Our English equivalent, "Hell," derives from a word root meaning "a covered place" and is thus akin to "hall," "hull," and "hole." Graves and Hell itself are holes that have been "covered over."

After his death, Christ himself "descended into Hell," according to the Christian creed. Thus even Christ had what the French poet Arthur Rimbaud called "a season in Hell."

Readers who might be repulsed by the idea of eternal punishment are free to think of Hell at least as a metaphor for the serious earthly consequences of moral abdication. This isn't difficult in a century of Nazi concentration camps and a potentially global Hiroshima.

Christian orthodoxy does not require the belief that any human being is actually in Hell. In addition, one can theoretically be "cast into everlasting fire" (as the Bible says) without necessarily having to stay there everlastingly. Some Christians have held that in the end all will be saved—fallen angels as well as human beings. Their belief is in what has been termed apocatastasis—"upset verdict."

The punishments that Dante describes in the *Inferno* should not be seen as sadistic inventions; fitting the crime as they do, these punishments are rather the ultimate and necessary flowering of the sin itself. So the reader should not think that a vengeful God "sends" people to Hell. If God's awesome love respects human freedom, serious sinners who die unrepentant will be getting the god they asked for during their lives—themselves. (God would be saying to them, "Thy will be done.") Seeing clearly the unworthiness of that disappointing divinity would be Hell. In the meantime, the behavior of such self-centered divinities helps produce Hell on Earth.

Outline of the *Inferno*

HOLY THURSDAY, April 7, to Easter Sunday, April 10, A.D. 1300

Three types of sin:
1. Incontinence: Second, Third, Fourth, and Fifth Circles. (Arch-heretics inhabit the Sixth Circle.)
2. Violence: Seventh Circle (three concentric parts: river, wood, desert)
3. Fraud:
   a. without treachery: Eighth Circle (ten "evil pouches" of Malebolge)
   b. with treachery: Ninth Circle (four concentric rings of ice)

Canto

1. Good Friday, April 8, 1300: Dante lost; three beasts; Virgil rescues Dante
2. Dante hesitates; three heavenly women; start of twenty-four–hour trip to Earth's center
3. *Hell's Gate:* the morally neutral; the gathering of the damned; Charon; Acheron
4. *First Circle:* Limbo; the unbaptized; the good pagans
5. *Second Circle:* Judge Minos; the lustful; dark winds; Francesca and Paolo
6. *Third Circle:* the dog Cerberus; the gluttonous; endless cold, dirty rain

7. *Fourth Circle:* the wolf Pluto; misers, wastrels; rock-pushing; the River Styx. *Fifth Circle:* the angry (thrashed); the sullen (submerged, bubbles)

8. *Fifth Circle (continued):* the boatman Phlegyas; Filippo Argenti; City of Dis sighted

9. *Fifth Circle (continued):* the Furies at the gate; the delivering angel; City of Dis entered. *Sixth Circle:* heretics in flaming tombs

10. *Sixth Circle (continued):* Epicurus; Farinata prophesies; father of Dante's friend Cavalcanti

11. A pause: Virgil explains the classification of sins

12. *Seventh Circle:* Minotaur, centaurs; the violent against others; the river of blood

13. *Seventh Circle (continued):* the violent against self; the tangled wood; the suicides; the Harpies

14. *Seventh Circle (continued):* the violent against God/nature; the desert, with flame flakes; the blasphemers; Capaneus

15. *Seventh Circle (continued):* the violent against nature; the sodomites; Brunetto Latini

16. *Seventh Circle,* the violent against nature *(continued):* three Florentine noblemen; the usurers

17. Man-serpent Geryon lowers Virgil and Dante to next circle

18. *Eighth Circle:* first ditch: panderers, seducers; whipped by demons; Jason. Second ditch: flatterers; immersed in filth; Thais

19. *Eighth Circle (continued):* third ditch: simonists; popes upside down in flaming holes

20. *Eighth Circle (continued):* fourth ditch: soothsayers; heads on backwards

21. *Eighth Circle (continued):* fifth ditch: grafters; boiling pitch; deceiving demons

22. *Eighth Circle,* fifth ditch *(continued):* Ciampolo of Navarre; deceived demons

23. *Eighth Circle (continued):* sixth ditch: hypocrites; leaden cloaks; two monks; Caiaphas and Annas

24. *Eighth Circle (continued):* seventh ditch: thieves; fiery serpents; Vanni Fucci

25. *Eighth Circle,* seventh ditch *(continued):* transformation of thieves

26. *Eighth Circle (continued):* eighth ditch: evil advisers; enflamed souls; Ulysses/Diomedes
27. *Eighth Circle,* eighth ditch *(continued):* soldier-monk Guido da Montefeltro
28. *Eighth Circle (continued):* ninth ditch: dividers; mutilated; Muhammad, Bertran de Born
29. *Eighth Circle (continued):* tenth ditch: falsifiers; ills of mind, body; alchemists
30. *Eighth Circle,* tenth ditch *(continued):* impersonators, counterfeiters, liars; Gianni Schicchi
31. Towering Giants: Dante and Virgil lowered into pit; frozen Cocytus
32. *Ninth Circle:* traitors. Caina: traitors to kin; ice up to neck, heads bent down. Antenora: traitors to city; faces upward; Ugolino
33. *Ninth Circle (continued):* Tolomea: traitors to guests; on backs, heads up
34. *Ninth Circle (continued):* Judecca: traitors to benefactors; under ice, except for Satan; Judas, Brutus, and Cassius

Canto I

THE 136 LINES of the first canto swiftly sketch the design for the whole poem. They cover the second longest time span in the *Inferno* and the third longest in the entire poem: namely, from sometime during the night before Good Friday, April 8, 1300, until the evening of that day. (We are given clues to these calendar specifics later on. Dante often employs flashforward and flashback.)

Taking Dante's biblical view of seventy years as the typical human life span (Psalm 89/90:10), we can figure that our poet (born in 1265) was by 1300

> In the middle of the journey of our life
> *(Nel mezzo del cammin di nostra vita),*

to cite the famous opening words of the poem. (In point of fact Dante, who lived to be only fifty-six, was seven years beyond his midpoint by 1300.)

Having lost his way, he has just spent a terrifying night in a dark, deadly wood. At dawn he finds an exit and tries to climb the sun-topped mountain ahead of him.

All day, three beasts block his way up the slope: a spotted leopard, a lion that frightens the very air it breathes, and a she-wolf that is hungrier after eating than before. This trinity of *lonza, leone,* and *lupa* can be taken to stand for the three main types of human sinfulness that keep human beings from attaining their true potential: lust (boundless desire for bodily pleasure), pride (boundless self-admiration), and cupidity (boundless yen for power and wealth).

In despair, Dante finally heads back down the slope toward the fearful wood, where the sun is silent. At this critical point midway through the first canto he sees a human figure and utters from Psalm 50/51 the first spoken words of the poem:

Have mercy on me!
(Miserere di me!)

These words will reappear in the penultimate canto of the whole poem as the penultimate Bible quotation.

The second half of this canto is almost entirely spoken dialogue—roughly the same proportion as found in the poem as a whole.

In a hoarse voice the shadowy figure identifies himself as a fellow Italian poet, the great Virgil (70–19 B.C.), who has been dead for more than thirteen centuries. In the sixth chapter of his poem the *Aeneid,* Virgil described a visit to the underworld by his hero Aeneas. Dante borrowed quite a few names and details from this chapter, which in turn echoes Homer's "next world" chapter of the *Odyssey* (Book 11).

Dante admired the poetic genius of the pagan Virgil, who was thought to have been prophesying the birth of Christ in another of his poems, *The Fourth Eclogue,* and who sang the praises of the Roman Empire. As the poet-theologian of Roman destiny, Virgil's *Aeneid* has Jupiter/God say of the Romans: "To them I have given empire without end." Dante regarded that empire as divinely willed and as being carried on in his own day in the person of the Holy Roman emperor. Our poet had come to believe that only this emperor could bring justice and peace to his chaotic and fratricidal Italy—"the garden of the empire."

This Virgil, whom Dante instantly calls his master, chides him for returning to the misery of the dark wood. When the blushing Dante blames the ferocity of the she-wolf, Virgil answers, "You must take another road...you should follow me." Dante replies, "Lead me."

Meanwhile, Virgil has obscurely prophesied the coming of another animal, a greyhound, which will drive the she-wolf back to Hell: there, in line 110, the word *inferno* makes its first appearance in the poem.

Virgil also outlines the three-part journey facing Dante:

1. to an eternal place of despairing shrieks
2. to a place where souls are contented to be in a temporary, purifying fire
3. to the dwelling place of the everlastingly blessed.

Since this last place is the citadel of that supreme Emperor whom Virgil "knew not," and against whose law Virgil was in some mysterious sense a rebel, he cannot take Dante there. But he predicts that a woman more worthy will do so.

Notes

Sometimes the three animals are viewed as the sins of youth, of maturity, and of old age. Alternatively, they are seen as the three main types of sin punished in Hell: incontinence, violence, and fraud. At the pit of Hell Dante will see its emperor with his three voracious mouths. In any case, the good hound of line 101 reminds modern readers of Francis Thompson's *The Hound of Heaven.*

Virgil, who is sometimes called "the Father of the West" because of his vast poetic influence, says that his parents were from Mantua—*montovani.* His name in Latin was Vergilius; eventually the spelling "Virgilius" became dominant. Dante uses the Italian spelling *Virgilio.* Virgil's family name was *Maro,* by which Dante calls Virgil in some of his other works. That name appears on Shakespeare's burial memorial.

Maro is, by chance, an anagram for *Roma* and *amor.* With a little ingenuity, those three words can be used to summarize the main themes of the whole *Comedy:*

1. *Maro:* nature and natural grace as embodied in Virgil
2. *Roma:* natural and supernatural authority
3. *Amor:* human and divine love.

Dante liked such word play.

\

Since Dante's word for greyhound, *veltro (ueltro)*, is an anagram for Lutero, some admirers of Martin Luther regarded him as the prophesied reformer. Whom Dante had in mind is a celebrated puzzle. Was it some generic savior, or some specific person like Can Grande (Big Dog) della Scala, a military leader in Verona, who was the chief agent of the Holy Roman emperor in Italy? This savior's birth was to be "between Feltro and Feltro." Was that a geographical location—there was a Montefeltro and a Feltre in northern Italy? Or does the phrase refer to the constellation Gemini, whose two brightest stars are Castor and Pollux, often depicted wearing felt *(feltro)* caps? The mystery persists. "Indeed, the problems that remain unsolved in our understanding of this great poetic structure are still many" (Singleton).

The opening line of the poem still reverberates: see James W. Jones, *In the Middle of This Road We Call Our Life* (HarperSanFrancisco, 1995).

Canto 2

THE SECOND CANTO is about second thoughts. Of its 142 lines, 119 are dialogue. The action covers the few minutes it would take for the dialogue to be spoken; that makes it the "shortest" canto of all. Dante had first been so desperate, and then so entranced to meet Virgil, that he instantly agreed to follow him. Now, as it grows dark, Dante thinks about his guide's reference to shrieking, pain, death, and fire. His courage fails him.

Addressing Virgil, who is leading him by an unspecified path to the gate of the underworld, Dante acknowledges that two other people had visited the other world while still in the flesh: Aeneas (the father of Silvius) and Saint Paul ("the vessel of election"). But they had special destinies: Aeneas was to be the ancestor of the Romulus who founded Rome and gave it its name; Paul was caught up into Paradise so that the faith he preached could be strengthened within him (2 Corinthians 12:3).

For Dante, as he detailed in his *De Monarchia,* both the Christian church (centered in the Roman papacy) and the Roman Empire were divinely willed partners in the world's salvation. "But I, why should I go there, and who grants it? Neither I nor any man would think me fit for this."

Virgil reassures Dante by telling him of three heavenly women who are concerned about him: Mary, the mother of Christ; Saint Lucy, a third-century martyr; and Beatrice (Portinari), a beautiful Florentine girl whom Dante had idolized but who had died in her twenty-fourth year—a decade before the action of the poem. These three women who are "behind" Dante balance the three impeding beasts who were so recently in front of him.

Medieval Christians regarded Mary as their spiritual mother. Her name, like Christ's and Beatrice's, however, is too holy to be directly mentioned in Hell. Even God is usually mentioned in paraphrase. (In medieval Siena a woman named Mary would not be allowed to function as a prostitute.)

Lucy, whose name means "light," was the patroness of good eyesight and had two churches in Florence dedicated to her. Dante wrote in his *La Vita Nuova* of eyes strained from too much weeping over Beatrice, and in *The Banquet* of overtaxing and weakening his vision. He may have been born around her feast day. He obviously had a special devotion to her.

As this poem will increasingly spell out, Dante saw in the pure and lovely Beatrice a revelation of God's own truth and beauty. As such she was a Christ-figure and an image of the ideal Church and its light-giving theology (revelation). Some regarded this identification as blasphemous.

As Virgil tells it, giving quotes within quotes within quotes, Mary noticed that Dante was in deep trouble. She alerted Lucy that "your devotee has need of you now." Lucy in turn notified Beatrice, urging her to aid the man who once loved her so much that he rose above the common crowd. Knowing of Dante's regard for Virgil, Beatrice left Heaven itself to track down Virgil in the part of Hell known as Limbo (hem; in Latin, *Limbus;* in Italian, *Lembo*). There "good pagans" spend eternity, suspended between torment and bliss.

Virgil, who seemed to know who Beatrice was as soon as she told her name, returned her extreme compliments, then wondered why she did not fear to visit Hell. She replied that "love impelled me and makes me speak." Seeing Beatrice's tears, Virgil was the more eager to do her bidding and befriend her friend.

So, Virgil now asks Dante, why do you hesitate when three such blessed women are backing you? Courage returns to Dante's heart, and he to his original decision. Now he sets out definitively on the deep and savage way to the center of the Earth.

Notes

At the start of this canto, when Dante is about to tell of his actual journey to Hell, he invokes the Muses, those womanly patrons of the arts—

how feminine this canto is!—and thus shows that his poem is now truly beginning. The first canto was therefore introductory. The *Inferno* and the other two *cantiche* (canzones/canticles/canto-groups) will comprise thirty-three cantos each, so that the total will equal a perfect one hundred. (Ten is three times a Trinity, plus a Unity; one hundred is ten times itself.)

From time to time Dante's courage will fail, despite the guidance of such an admired father figure as Virgil. On this occasion Dante revives when he realizes that significant mother figures are supporting him. These women wisely stand back awhile, allowing divine help to come to him through Virgil, the embodiment of natural reason at its best, a pagan instrument of God's grace. Like the Aristotelian philosopher Saint Thomas Aquinas, Dante was a Christian of supernatural faith who did not, however, despise the natural, the rational, or the non-Christian.

Canto 3

WITH THIS THIRD CANTO and the fearsome inscription that opens it, we enter Hell proper. There we will remain for about twenty-four hours, so that on the average each of the remaining cantos covers less than an hour.

Dante doesn't say by what route he and Virgil arrived at the gateway to the starless, woeful city of eternal pain, to the people who have forfeited the vision of truth, "the good of the intellect." Dante is understandably terrified when he reads the oft-quoted words inscribed over the unguarded gateway:

> Leave behind every hope, you who enter.
> (*Lasciate ogne speranza, voi ch'intrate.*)

Virgil assures Dante that the words don't apply to him—though they do apply, sadly enough, to Virgil.

The rest of this canto focuses on two sets of lost people: a large mass of naked souls endlessly racing around a plain just inside the gate; and a crowd of naked souls freshly arrived from every land, who gather at the far edge of this plain and wait to be ferried across a river to the farther shore and thence to their proper permanent places in the descending and contracting spiral of Hell.

Dante was a passionate man and seems to have invented the idea of a special place on the outer rim of Hell for passionless people who lived without praise or blame, and who thus never truly lived. Here they have fittingly joined that part of the fallen angels who were neither for Good nor Evil, but only for themselves. They are hateful to both God and His enemies, so that pity and justice alike despise them. They would defile Heaven; they wouldn't fit into Hell's scheme either, for they would give the wicked some relative glory.

For these wretched souls whom both Virgil and Dante disdain to identify—thus making them literally ignominious (nameless)—Dante invents the first of his "punishments that fit the crime." On Earth these self-servers refused to take a stand on any objective value. Now they are compelled to race forever behind a shifting banner. Because they lived mingy lives, they are tormented by hornets, wasps, and worms. Their greatest grief is that they have no hope of death: *"questi non hanno speranza di morte."*

Among them Dante sees "the shade of him who through cowardice made the great refusal." This anonymous soul is often taken to be the ascetic Celestine V who, by resigning the papacy in 1294, allowed Dante's enemy, Boniface VIII, to gain the papal throne. (Celestine, elected in his mid-eighties after a papal vacancy of twenty-seven months, lasted a mere five months; he was canonized in 1313.) Pontius Pilate is one of several other nominees for this guilt of great refusal.

The second crowd of souls, freshly deceased, are those who lived without reverence for God and who died unrepentant. (But at least they lived!) By an unnamed route they have gathered at the mythical river Acheron (joyless). Fed by all the blood, sweat, and tears of history, this river will flow downward under various names to form the frozen lake at the pit of Hell.

Across the Acheron the ferryman Charon, whose eyes have rings of fire and glow like hot coals, will transport this second crowd to Hell proper. (If his name truly means "lovely," it serves here as irony.) Though these damned souls are cursing God, their parents, the human race, as well as their own conceptions, divine justice has turned their fear of punishment into desire for it.

The fierce, straggly-bearded Charon notices the living Dante and orders him away. Implying that this rejection is a sign of Dante's ultimate salvation, Virgil tells Charon that Dante's presence has been decreed where Will and Power are one, so let there be no further inquiry.

Yielding, Charon departs with his human cargo. Before he reaches the opposite shore, a new crowd has collected. In the meantime, the plain shakes violently. A gust of wind and a red flash follow. Dante suddenly falls into a terrified stupor.

Notes

Dante indicates that the crowd of neutrals was vast: "I would never have believed that death had undone so many." T. S. Eliot used this line near the beginning of *The Waste Land*.

It has often been said (even by President Kennedy in a major speech) that Dante put the morally neutral in the lowest or hottest part of Hell. As we have seen, they are in neither, though they are undoubtedly in the most disgraceful part.

Canto 4

WHEN A THUNDERCLAP awakens the stupefied Dante, he unaccountably finds himself on the other side of the river Acheron and near the brink of the abysmal valley of pain. Thinking of what sights await them, Virgil turns pale with pity. Mistaking pity for fear, Dante grows even more frightened.

The two soon come to the first circle, where vast crowds of men, women, and children (*infanti* here; later in the poem, *innocenti*) throng, people who lament only by sighing, who suffer grief without torment as they live in desire for God but without hope. On the inner side of Hell's gate we saw throngs inhabiting a dishonorable Limbo. On the inner side of the Acheron we now encounter throngs living in an honorable Limbo. Dante doesn't tell us how these shades got there. They are not here for any grievous, unrepented sin, nor for lack of merit, but for lack of baptism.

"Grief seized me at the heart when I heard this," the poet tells us, "for I knew people of much worth were suspended in that Limbo." The mystery of the necessity of baptism and of faith in Christ afflicts Dante throughout his poem—though he encounters some happy surprises on this subject before his journey ends. Like orthodox Christians of his day he accepted this mystery, however painful, believing that in God's eyes it somehow could not be unjust.

The Church teaches that after His death, Christ "descended into Hell" and liberated those Old Testament figures who had an implicit faith in His coming into history. Dante wonders whether Virgil has any knowledge of this "harrowing of Hell." The latter, who died in 19 B.C., states that he had not been long in the afterlife when a mighty person came to this circle and released many spirits, including pre-Christian biblical figures like Adam, Noah, Israel, Moses, David, and Solomon. Before this, Virgil insists, no human souls had been liberated from the underworld.

The two have been walking while conversing, and now they arrive at a circle of light occupied by the world's great pagan poets—Homer, Horace, Ovid, and Lucan. Heaven itself gave them this postmortem distinction. This is Virgil's own home in the afterworld, and he is welcomed back with honor. These supreme poets, neither sad nor joyful, make Dante one of their own company—an honor which, of course, Dante is conferring on himself.

The six poets walk together, "talking of matters that were fitting for that place, but of which it is well to keep silent now." They come to a noble castle surrounded by a moat and by seven walls symbolizing the traditional natural virtues that would have adorned good pagans. Dante walks over the moat as if it were solid. Once inside the castle he sees people "with eyes slow and grave, with looks of great authority, and with gentle voices seldom used." He is shown the famous heroes of Troy and Rome, including Aeneas and Caesar; and eminent Greek and Roman philosophers, including Socrates, Plato, and Aristotle, this last being "the master of those who know." The disgraceful Limbo was full of nameless people. Here, Dante cites by name thirty-eight figures, some historical, some legendary.

At the start of this canto, Virgil had told his pupil "the long way urges us onward." Now, at its end, Dante stops his naming and gives the reason: "My long theme so drives me on, that many times my words come short of the facts." And so they leave the quiet behind them and come to a place where no light shines.

Notes

The Russian novelist Alexander Solzhenitsyn took from this canto the title of his 1968 novel, *The First Circle.*

In spite of medieval Christian hostility toward Islam, Dante honors three eminent Muslims in Limbo: the philosopher Avicenna (980–1037); Averroës (1126–98), an Aristotelian philosopher whom Thomas Aquinas referred to simply as "The Commentator"; and Saladin (1138–93), the magnanimous sultan who retook Jerusalem from the Crusaders. He was a Kurd, born (like Saddam Hussein) at Tikrit on the Tigris. Some Muslims take offense that Saladin is pointedly described as being "apart, by himself." Was he ostracized, or was he just not a mixer?

Canto 5

IT HAS TAKEN US four full cantos to get to the second circle, where Hell proper may be said to begin. For it is at this point in the shrinking spiral, which will take us to the Earth's center and Hell's core, that we encounter Minos, the legendary king of Crete. In Greek mythology Minos was a creature half-human and half-beast—an apt symbol for the dehumanizing effects of sin.

Before his horrific presence all grievous sinners who died unrepentant must now appear and confess their guilt. By twisting his tail a certain number of times, the snarling Minos shows to which of the remaining eight circles the sinner is to be sent forever. In some cases his tail hurls a sinner on his or her way. (Nothing is said about a sinner who might qualify for more than one circle.) Like Charon, Minos challenges the still-living Dante. But as before, Virgil recites his formula about Will and Power, and opposition melts.

The two wayfarers now proceed to a place "mute of all light." (We must assume that somehow the two are still able to see.) Here a hellish storm rages with tempestuous bellowing. "No hope of less pain, not to say of repose, ever comforts" the sinners here, sinners who sowed the wind of lust and are now reaping the whirlwind:

Hither and thither, upward and downward it drives them.
(Di qua, di la, di giu, di su li mena.)

Virgil points out the shades of Dido, Cleopatra, Helen of Troy, Achilles, Paris, and Tristan. "He showed me more than a thousand shades," says Dante, using a numerical phrase he will often repeat. Then he sees a man and a woman clinging tightly together and being tossed about with exceptional violence. "Who are these?" he asks. Virgil suggests that when they come closer Dante entreat them by the love that drives them. (Twelve times in this canto the word "love" appears in one form or another.)

Like doves, the couple respond to Dante's call, though it is only the woman who speaks as the noise presumably dies down awhile. She says she was born in Ravenna (where Dante will die and lies buried). Thus this Francesca da Rimini was also Francesca da Ravenna and Francesca da Polenta (to give her family name). Her present (unnamed) partner and brother-in-law, Paolo Malatesta of Rimini, was seized by love for the fair body that was taken from her when her husband killed them both. For Paolo, she herself was seized "by that love that absolves no beloved one from loving." In the end, "love brought us to one death." Caina, a place at the bottom of Hell, awaits her kindred-murdering husband, she presumes.

Dante would have known Paolo of Rimini when the latter was a captain of the Florence commune. Our poet also fought alongside Francesca's brother at the battle of Campaldino (1289). Later, the exiled Dante was the long-time guest in Ravenna of Francesca's nephew, Guido da Polenta the Younger. Dante is the only known source for the story of this tragic love affair, portrayed hauntingly in music by Tchaikovsky in his *Francesca da Rimini* (*circa* 1876).

Dante lowers his head in thought. Now it is Virgil who does the asking: "What are you thinking?"

"Alas, how many sweet thoughts, how great the desire that brought them to their woeful end." (Chaucer's Wife of Bath will similarly lament: "Alas that love were ever sin!") Using Francesca's name without being told it, Dante asks how she became aware of her fateful love. Her reply is classic:

> There is no greater pain than to recall happy times in wretched ones...but...I will tell as one who weeps in the telling. One day, for our delight, we read about Lancelot, how love [for Guinevere, King Arthur's wife] compelled him. We were alone and without misgivings. Many times that reading drew our eyes together and changed the color in our faces.
>
> But it was one point alone that overcame us. When we read that the longed-for smile was kissed by so great a lover, he that shall never be parted from me, all atremble, kissed my mouth. A Galeotto was that book, and he that wrote it. That day we read no farther.

As his mistress speaks, Paolo weeps. Overcome with pity, Dante swoons: "I fell as a dead body falls *(E caddi come corpo morto cade).*"

Notes

In line thirty-four, reference is made to evidence of a landslide. We will hear more later about this effect of Christ's visit to Hell.

King Arthur stories were quite popular in Dante's day; in them, Galeotto was a pandering go-between for Lancelot and Guinevere.

The story of Francesca and Paolo inspired Rodin's *The Kiss*. Dante doesn't say how long after their first adultery Francesca and Paolo were murdered. Some maintain it was a lengthy affair. When the lovers died around 1285, Paolo was near fifty, married to a Beatrice (!), and the father of two sons. Francesca was the mother of a nine-year-old girl, presumably by her husband.

A tradition claims that when the dashing Paolo came to arrange the marriage between Francesca and his ill-favored brother Gianciotto (John the Cripple), she was deceived into believing Paolo was to be her spouse. It was love at first sight. Her first sight of the truth, however, occurred when she woke up beside Gianciotto after their wedding night.

Though unprepossessing, her husband was reputedly valiant and able. Though the union was lovelessly arranged to confirm a peace pact between the warring lords of Rimini and Ravenna, Gianciotto came to love Francesca deeply, and wounded her fatally by a rapier thrust that was meant only for his brother. He buried them both in the same tomb.

Though it is one of the longer mini-dramas in the poem, the poet's telling of Francesca's story is a marvel of compression: the entire episode takes only seventy lines. And what a delicacy is "That day we read no farther *(Quel giorno piu non vi leggemmo avante)*"! The story surely gives one of the earliest examples of a book as an occasion of sin. In Germany alone, the Francesca story has, by one count, inspired forty-six plays, forty-two novels, and more than seventy short stories.

Canto 6

WHEN DANTE REVIVES, he finds himself already in the third circle, where gross gluttons are punished. In the previous circle the mutual self-indulgence of illicit lovers was punished. In this circle the solitary self-indulgence of those who unrepentantly ate and drank to excess is punished in a gloomy setting that grates on all the senses: the soggy ground on which they lie stinks; and hailstones, snow, and filthy rain pour down with monotonous sameness. The beastly guardian of this circle, who attacks and butchers the shades, is a three-headed dog with a greasy beard and a bulging belly. He howls so fiercely that the tormented shades, howling themselves, wish they were deaf.

In the sixth chapter of his *Aeneid*, Virgil wrote that Aeneas tossed something to this mythological demon, Cerberus ("meat-greedy"), whom Dante further describes as a giant worm. Like a true glutton, Cerberus is now distracted again from his duty by the appearance of something to eat—a handful of dirt tossed by Virgil.

Gluttons typically lie down after their heavy eating and drinking. So we find the sinners of this circle all lying flat, twisting and turning in the effort to ease their pain. One sinner recognizes Dante, sits up, and asks Dante whether he recognizes him. As Oscar Wilde's Dorian Gray discovers, evil disfigures. Dante can't recognize this fellow Florentine, who reveals that his fellow citizens used to call him Ciacco (hog).

He also reveals that "in the bright life" he was Dante's contemporary. Presuming that Ciacco, though damned, knows something of the past, present, and future, Dante asks what has caused the troubles of Florence, what its fate will be, and how some of its once promising citizens are now faring.

Ciacco blames the troubles of the divided city on envy, pride, and avarice—an evil trinity recalling the animals that thwarted Dante in the first canto. Significantly, Florence so gluts itself on envy that already its sack spills over. Before very long it will spill Dante out into exile.

Ciacco sees a temporary victory for Dante's political party but then the triumph of his enemies, thanks to a schemer (probably Pope Boniface VIII). The five "good" citizens inquired after by Dante are now among the blackest spirits in Hell. Dante will soon meet four of them. Only two good citizens (unnamed) remain alive, but nobody heeds them. Our poet will see twenty Florentines in Hell, guilty between them of nine different kinds of sins.

Ciacco pleads for Dante to speak of him to others when he returns "to the sweet world," a phrase suggesting the world as tasted by a glutton. He is the first of many whom Dante will meet in Hell who will reveal a longing to be remembered in the world of the living—as though to be forgotten was a fate worse than being remembered as damned. This sinner who never had enough of eating has now had enough of speaking. Refusing further conversation, and contorting his features, he falls back to the unsweet earth of Hell.

Virgil finally speaks, revealing that Ciacco will lie there until the Last Judgment, when he will be reunited with his once-glutted body. Dante wants to know how this reunion will affect the pain felt by these spirits. Citing philosophical principles, Virgil asserts that being more complete, souls reunited with their bodies will have more intense feelings, whether of pain or bliss.

Walking with slow steps over the foul mixture of shades and rain, the two poets come to a place for descending and encounter still another monster, Pluto.

Notes

Translator John Ciardi has described this circle as a kind of cosmic garbage dump. As repulsive as the sinners are, Dante is saddened by the misery he sees on every side. Though life was rough in strife-ridden Florence, Ciacco can still speak of the sweet and bright world he left behind.

This canto contains the first of many references to Dante's native Florence (*Fiorenza/Firenze:* "flowering"), capital of Tuscany (a word at the root of Etruscan, Tosca, and Toscanini). The city lies about 145 miles northeast of Rome. In the title to this poem, Dante describes himself as "a Florentine by birth, but not by behavior." At the time of his birth, Florence was Italy's most flourishing city and contained thirty thousand citizens within its walls and seventy thousand outside. It was arguably the greatest cultural and artistic center of Western Europe from the fourteenth to the sixteenth centuries. Among others native to it or closely linked with it were Boccaccio, da Vinci, Machiavelli, Michelangelo, Petrarch, the Medici, Fra Angelico, Cimabue, Galileo, Giotto, and Savonarola. It was Italy's capital from 1865 to 1870. Pope Boniface VIII said it had a "fifth essence" (quintessence) beyond earth, air, fire, and water that made it superior to all other cities. Dante lived at a time when Florence was erupting in all areas with a creativity born of this mysterious excellence.

By A.D. 1300 a local dispute that began with a snowball fight in nearby Pistoia had pitted "White" Guelphs against "Black" Guelphs. In general, the Guelph party in Italy was anti-imperial and usually pro-pope. (With Dante's help, the pro-imperial party, called Ghibellines, had finally been expelled from Florence in 1289.) By 1300 Dante belonged to the "White" Guelphs (who wanted to minimize all outside influence). He was exiled shortly afterward by the "Blacks" (who wanted to enhance their papal connections). His experience of exile and of a fratricidal Italy finally turned the poet into a Ghibelline, as his *De Monarchia* demonstrates. (A memory aid: Guelph and pope each have one syllable; Ghibelline and emperor, three syllables each.)

Canto 7

SINCE SO MUCH WEALTH comes out of the earth in such forms as gold, oil, and food, the pagan god of wealth, Pluto (wealth, as in plutocrat), was also the god of the underworld. As encountered now by Dante and Virgil, the god is a wolflike monster of rage, who clucks out strange words that may be a warning to Satan or about him. At a rebuke from Virgil, this bloated figure collapses in a heap, as earthly fortunes and Wall Streets sometimes do.

Thus begins the seventh canto, which will be the first to deal with two separate circles, united by a common theme: rage. The fourth circle contains communities of rage; the fifth circle punishes in its muddy marsh shades consumed with solitary rage.

The fourth circle entraps souls who misused this world's wealth in either of two ways: by hoarding it as though it were everything, or by spending it as though it were nothing. Guilty of avarice, the hoarders push heavy stones around a semicircle, where they eventually clash with the stone-pushing wastrels. As they clash, one group shouts, "Why hoard?" and the other group, "Why squander?" Then each group reverses direction and heads for another clash on the opposite side of the circle.

From the way their hair is cut in a circle at the crown, Dante recognizes many clergymen among the avaricious. Virgil agrees that this is a favorite clerical sin ensnaring even bishops and popes. This is the first explicit mention of popes in Hell and the first of many attacks Dante makes on religious figures who betray their calling.

Dante feels that he should recognize some shades in this group, but Virgil answers that these people lived undiscerning lives and have now become indiscernible themselves. They didn't know what true wealth is. He doesn't want to "squander" further words on them.

But Virgil does devote some words to the mysterious but wise working of Fortune, a kind of guardian angel who sees that worldly wealth passes from one person, family, nation, and race to another. Fortune's doings are "hidden, like a snake in the grass." Virgil is borrowing here from his own *Eclogues*. His old Latin "*Latet anguis in herba* (a snake lies in the grass)" now becomes the Italian "*occulto come in erba l'angue* (hidden like a snake in the grass)." This is the ageless "narrow Fellow in the Grass" that left Emily Dickinson "Zero at the Bone."

Following a gloomy stream of darkest purple, the two descend a rough pass to a marsh called the Styx (dreadful). Here Dante sees muddy, naked shades all enraged and beating one another with hands, feet, heads, and chests, and tearing one another with their teeth.

Virgil identifies these as people who were ruled by wrath. He points out surface bubbles and ascribes them to sullen souls who lie beneath. They are confessing in a kind of muffled hymn:

> We were sullen in the sweet air gladdened by the sun.
> Now we are sullen in the black mire.

Making a wide arc around the filthy mud at the edge of the dry land, Dante and his guide eventually arrive at a tall tower. When they first entered this fifth circle, Virgil mentioned that the stars were beginning to sink. (He seems to know such things intuitively.) So it is now past midnight as the two conclude their journey through what will turn out to have been merely the suburbs of Hell—the part outside the deeper City of Dis (Satan) proper. Within the walled city ahead of them are punished sins worse than the unwillingness to control lust, hunger, avarice, dissipation, and distemper.

Notes

In his prison-written *De Profundis*, Oscar Wilde refers to this canto in a meditation on the sin of sullenness.

Dis was the Roman name for the Greek god Pluto—lord of the underworld. Both Dis and Pluto mean "rich" and refer to the wealth that lies underground. Dante has already used Pluto to guard the circle of the avaricious and wastrels. He uses Dis as a synonym for Satan himself. (Dives, the rich man of the Gospel story of poor Lazarus, is actually a generic word for rich, from which the word *Dis* is contracted.)

Canto 8

ALL IS RAGE and frustration in this canto, during which Dante and Virgil leave the circles of outer Hell and cross the Styx to the gates of inner Hell. Within these gates are punished sins of violence and fraud—sins as cold and hard as the iron walls surrounding the city.

Dante begins this canto with a bit of backtracking and a reference to "continuing" his story. Some commentators see in this an indication that the author had been delayed for some time in writing this canto—perhaps because of his exile and the temporary absence of his manuscript.

In response to two mysterious flames signaling from the top of the wall tower, a second ferryman appears who controls this part of the one, long, descending Acheron that runs through Hell under different names (Acheron, Styx, Phlegethon, Cocytus). His name is Phlegyas, a mythical figure who was the son of Mars, and whose daughter was loved by Apollo. Unhappy about this affair, Phlegyas (inflamed) set fire to a temple of Apollo, who retaliated by killing him with arrows.

Perhaps the ferryman thinks he has caught some shades trying to escape from their proper circle. When Virgil states the true situation, Phlegyas falls into a characteristic fury. Still, Dante and Virgil enter his boat. It sinks lower only when the living Dante steps aboard.

Up to this point in the poem Dante has been wondering, weeping, grieving, pitying. Now for the first time, as he recognizes an arrogant Florentine thrashing in these waters of the wrathful, Dante grasps the true ugliness of a particular sin and directs hardhearted words to the hardhearted Filippo Argenti (whose name could be translated into English as Phil Silvers). Filippo showily shod his horses in silver. (Some say he once got away with slapping Dante, who was taunted by his friends for being overly meek—even cowardly—in his youth.)

Virgil praises Dante for his harsh words, embraces him, gives him his only kiss of the journey, and somewhat joltingly speaks words that were once spoken in praise of Christ himself—"Blessed is the womb that bore thee" (see Luke 11:27). Thus the sole reference to Dante's mother. (The story goes that prior to his birth she dreamed that her son would eat the berries of laurel leaves and change into a shimmering peacock.) In what seems an un-Christlike request, Dante would like to see further humiliation visited on this Filippo, whom Virgil pushes away as he tries to enter the boat. Soon other sinners in the water turn on Filippo and batter him, so that in fury he turns his own teeth against himself.

New sounds of grief rivet Dante's eyes on the walled city that has come into view. Within that city he sees mosques glowing with fire—this feature is a reflection of his belief that Islam was a perversion of Christianity. Virgil speaks of the eternal flames that burn within this city and gives us our first reference to "hellfire."

Quitting the boat at the city's entrance, Dante and Virgil see "more than a thousand" fallen angels hovering above the gates. (We first saw fallen angels on the plain of the morally indifferent.) Virgil indicates that he wants to speak to them privately. Restraining their rage, they summon the sage forward, but bid Dante to turn back—this man who "without having died traverses the kingdom of the dead."

Virgil reassures Dante, who has begged him to turn back too. The sage advances toward the wrathful spirits, who suddenly race back to the gates and slam them shut. Disconcerted, Virgil walks slowly back, his face stripped of all boldness.

"Even if I get angry, don't worry," says the pagan poet, who cannot directly take on these malevolent forces, despite his special warrant from on high. He tells Dante that these same spirits had once vainly tried to keep Christ from entering Hell. Even now, someone has passed again through Hell's gate and is on his way to open the city to them.

Notes

A few times in Hell Dante acts cruelly, though Virgil will eventually reprimand him for being too sympathetic. In any case, it is an unpurified Dante who goes through Hell, one who needs to reject sinful traits in his own spirit. Moreover, Dante is hardhearted only with the hardhearted.

In line ninety-four, for the first time in the poem, Dante speaks directly to his reader. Throughout his poem, in a tone of intense and dignified comradeship, he will address his reader as *lettor* sixteen times. About five other times, without the word *reader,* he will address his reader in the singular or plural. According to Eric Auerbach, "It is difficult to find anything similar in earlier European literature." (This scholar called Dante "the poet of the secular world," one who aimed to make the next world more real, but paradoxically and revolutionarily ended up intensifying the full-blooded individuality of men and women forged in this world and vividly preserved in the next.)

Canto 9

IN THIS NINTH CANTO, Virgil (a child of nature) and Dante (a child of grace) both stand helpless before infernal spirits until a messenger of grace sends them scattering and with a touch of his little wand *(verghetta)* opens the gates of lower Hell. (Reflecting Virgil's legendary role as a magician, his name is sometimes linked with the Latin word for wand, *virga*—a connection that may help account for the change of spelling from *Vergil* to *Virgil*.)

Meantime, Virgil stands perplexed, muttering to himself. As Dante's terror mounts, he indirectly asks Virgil whether he really knows his way. Referring to a legend that Dante may have invented, Virgil states that the sorceress Erichtho once sent him to the pit of Hell to summon up a spirit. That spirit was to prophesy whether Caesar would defeat Pompey at the crucial battle of Pharsalia (in 48 B.C.). "Therefore, be assured. I know the road well."

Suddenly, a trinity of demons in the shape of snake-covered women appears over the gate. These Furies, these spirits of hopeless remorse, these pursuers and punishers of unavenged criminals, are the handmaidens of Pluto's wife, Hecate (alias Persephone/Proserpina/the Moon), the queen of eternal lamentation.

The Athenian hero Theseus once tried to abduct Hecate but was imprisoned in Hell until Hercules/Herakles rescued him. The Furies now conclude that they had not made enough of an example out of Theseus. So now they invoke the demon Medusa (guardian), alias the Gorgon (terrible), whose glance of despair turns people into stones. She never does put in an appearance in this scene. (In mythology, there was actually a trinity of Gorgon sisters.)

"Don't keep looking," Virgil warns. He turns Dante around and, not trusting him to keep his eyes closed, covers them with his own hands. Dante asks those readers who possess good understanding to catch the meaning behind these "strange" verses. In this first such reference to a hidden meaning, the author seems to be warning that human reason is no match for utter despair.

Dante's ears are still open, however, and he hears a fearful sound as of a whirlwind in a forest. At this point Virgil tells Dante to look, but to bow and be silent before a powerful figure that is passing dry-shod over the Styx. This messenger, who seems full of scorn, rebukes the evil spirits and reminds them of the punishment that Hercules once inflicted on the dog Cerberus when he dragged it by a chain that skinned its neck and throat.

Like leaping frogs, the demons disappear, the messenger retraces his path without a word to Virgil or Dante, and these two poets enter the city without opposition. Inside, Dante sees a large plain full of flaming tombs. Virgil explains them as the graves of arch-heretics and their followers, each more crowded than Dante may suppose. Therein, like lies with like, and all are afflicted with varying degrees of heat.

Note

In his organization of Hell, Dante has been following a pagan classification of human sins. In such a list there would be, of course, no sins against Christian belief. Dante works these in by putting "heretics" on one of two edges: if their heresy was essentially "negative" (as in the case of the good pagans), he puts them on the rim of outer Hell. If the sin was "positive" (as in the case of the formal heretics), he stations them on this rim of inner Hell. Here are included even pre-Christian teachers of what Dante views as objective heresy: for example, the denial of immortality.

Canto 10

VIRGIL AND DANTE now pass through the area of flaming tombs. Dante asks whether the sinners here might be seen, since the lids are off the sepulchers. Virgil replies that after Judgment Day in the Valley of Jehoshaphat (outside Jerusalem), body will be joined to soul and the tombs then sealed forever. He points to the tomb where Epicurus (342?–270 B.C.) and his followers lie, now painfully aware of their error in teaching that the soul does not outlive the body. (In *The Banquet*, Dante wrote, "Of all brutal opinions, that is most foolish, vile and pestilent which holds that there is no life after this one.")

Hearing Dante speak in Tuscany's Florentine dialect, one of the damned spirits rears up from his tomb, calls him "Tosco," praises his accent, and begs him to linger awhile. At first Dante is afraid to go close, but Virgil pushes him toward the figure, whom he identifies as Farinata degli Uberti. (Dante had asked Ciacco about him in canto 6.) Like the recent angel, the spirit looks "as though he had disdain for Hell."

Since he doesn't recognize Dante, the famous Ghibelline leader asks him, a little haughtily, who his ancestors were. As Dante obliges him, the spirit recognizes some of the enemy Guelphs he had helped to defeat in the bloody battle of Montaperti (1260). Dante counters by saying that his Guelph family has learned the art of coming back (1251, 1266), but Farinata's hasn't.

At this point a second shade pokes its head above the tomb. It is the father of Dante's "first friend," the poet Guido Cavalcanti, who married Farinata's daughter—another Beatrice. (In-laws of each other sharing an eternal coffin—that would be many people's idea of Hell!) Presuming that it was his gift of poetic genius that won for Dante this trip through the underworld, the notoriously pleasure-loving and skeptical old man wonders why his ingenious son isn't with him. Dante suggests that perhaps it was because Guido lacked regard for his unnamed companion.

Because Dante answers in the past tense ("lacked"), the father cries out, "Does not the sweet light still strike his eyes?" Presuming his son dead—as he will be in four months, because of an illness contracted during a brief exile that Dante will be forced to impose on him—he swoons back into the tomb.

Dante is confused. He has been assuming that the shades in Hell know the present, since they seem to know the future. Farinata confirms this latter impression when, cold-heartedly ignoring the poignant exchange between Dante and Cavalcante de' Cavalcanti, he continues his earlier conversation and prophesies that within fifty moons Dante himself will learn in exile how hard it is to make a comeback.

Farinata then asks why the Florentine Guelphs have been so unforgiving toward the Ghibellines. Dante blames the bloodiness of the slaughter of the Guelphs at the battle of Montaperti (four thousand were killed in a single day.) Yet, replies the lordly shade, "I alone defended Florence at that time from those who wished to destroy her." (Here the word *Florence* itself occurs for the first time in the poem.)

Hearing Virgil call for him, Dante quickly asks Farinata who else is with him. The shade mentions two other disbelievers in immortality—Emperor Frederick II (1194–1250) and "the Cardinal." "Of the others I am silent," concludes Farinata as he too slips from view.

Pondering the ominous prophecy he has just heard, Dante returns to his guide. Keep those words in mind, Virgil advises, and when "you face the sweet radiance of her whose fair eyes see all things, she will explain your life's journey." Actually, it will be one of Dante's own ancestors who will perform this service—though in the presence of Beatrice. Misunderstandings characterize this entire canto, which ends with the poets heading for the center of this sixth circle.

Notes

In line 101 God is called "il Duce."

Nineteen years after his death in 1264, Farinata was condemned as a heretic. Frederick, an Epicurean, reportedly searched the Scriptures to prove that "a man is nothing after he draws his last breath." Cardinal Ottaviano degli Ubaldini, who died in 1273, was by far the greatest cardinal of his time. When people said simply "the Cardinal," they meant him. He is supposed to have said, "If there is a soul, I have lost mine a thousand times for the Ghibellines."

Canto II

THIS MOST PROSAIC CANTO of the *Inferno* provides a breather—literally, since by pausing above the seventh circle and letting their noses get used to the rising stench, the travelers will be able to breathe more easily when they resume their downward journey. They pass by the tomb of a fifth-century pope, Anastasius (496–98), whom medieval tradition unjustly thought to have been guilty of denying Christ's divinity. (To my knowledge, Dante here becomes the first known writer to put a pope in Hell by name.)

A bit cheekily, Dante the student asks his mentor to think of some way to keep them from wasting time while they are pausing. That's just what I was planning to do, Virgil retorts. What he does is give Dante a verbal diagram of what lies ahead, citing teachings from the Bible and Aristotle.

Three more circles remain to be visited: seven, eight, and nine. These punish malice as it appears in two basic forms: violence and fraud.

Violence (the seventh circle) is subdivided into injury done to one's self or one's property; injury done to one's neighbors or their property; and injury done to God's sovereignty. This last sin includes the wrongness of cursing God or denying Him (blasphemy); harm done to God's child, nature (homosexual behavior); and harm done to God's grandchild, human industry (usury). Virgil's reference to the French town of Cahors reflects its reputation as a center of money-grubbing usurers.

For its part, fraud has two major divisions: injury done against the common fellowship of humans; and injury done when some special trust is betrayed (treachery). As we shall see later, the first kind of fraud has ten subdivisions (eighth circle); the second, four (ninth circle).

Dante wants to know where the sinners he has already seen fit in. "Why are they not inside the ruddy city if God is angry with them? If He isn't angry, why are they in such a plight?"

Sharply rebuking his pupil as more than usually obtuse, Virgil recalls the philosophic tradition that views sins of incontinence as less offensive and blameworthy than others. In their weakness, human beings fail to "contain" their longing for various pleasures, but the resultant sins are not so willfully and cold-bloodedly chosen as those of malice in the strict sense (fraud) or mad bestiality (violence).

Citing again the position of the stars, Virgil indicates that it is now about 3 A.M. on Holy Saturday. "Follow me now, for I wish to go...the cliff which we must descend lies farther on."

Note

In line twenty-two, malice means both fraud and violence; in line eighty-two, it means fraud alone. The inconsistency is in the text. The chilling phrase *la divina vendetta* makes its first appearance in line ninety, when Virgil is discussing God's justice. In line sixty-six he also speaks of treacherous souls as being "eternally consumed" after death, though—as we shall see—this condition is imposed by ice and not by fire.

Canto 12

WE WILL BE IN the seventh circle, the circle of the violent, for the next six cantos. Think of yourself as crossing a dart board of concentric circles: the outer circle (canto 12) is a river of blood in which are boiled those who harmed others through violence. The middle circle (canto 13) is a wild and gloomy wood, where self-destructive souls are punished. The third, inmost circle is a scorching desert that punishes the blasphemous (canto 14), sodomites (cantos 15 and 16), and greedy moneylenders (canto 17).

Having entered the City of Dis/Satan and passed through the plain of the heretics in their flaming tombs, Virgil and Dante now descend over the rocks of a landslide. Virgil explains that Christ's descent into the first circle to liberate the saved at the time of His death caused this landslide.

As befits a circle where irrational force is punished, a monster that is half-man and half–raging bull guards the approach to the landslide. This Minotaur bites itself in rage and staggers blindly when Virgil taunts it. Run to the pass, Virgil tells Dante, while the Minotaur is distracted.

The two now arrive at a bloody river (Phlegethon: "fiery"), around whose edge thousands of centaurs run in single file, shooting with bow and arrow any shade that tries to rise above its appointed level in the boiling blood. The bloodier the shade was in life, the deeper it is now immersed in blood. Tyrants like Alexander the Great and Attila the Hun are up to their eyebrows, as is Dante's near-contemporary Ezzelino, who on one occasion burned eleven thousand people at the stake. (A three-year papal crusade finally crushed him.) Others are up to their throats or chests or feet.

At first the poets are challenged by some centaurs, who are horselike in their lower bodies but human above. Their leader is Chiron, the fabled teacher of Achilles. After uncovering his mouth by combing his beard with the notch of an arrow, he amiably obliges the travelers by providing them with Nessus as an escort. This Nessus was slain by Hercules but left behind a poisoned shirt that was given to Hercules by his own wife and caused his death.

Like the Minotaur and the other centaurs, the half-human Nessus is a symbol of the brutalizing results of violence. Pointing to a shade up to his neck in blood, Nessus explains, "That one clove, in God's bosom, the heart that on the Thames still drips with blood." The reference is to Guy de Montfort, son of the baron Simon. Simon was murdered and his corpse desecrated at the battle of Evesham in the year of Dante's birth. In revenge, Guy murdered his first cousin Prince Henry of Cornwall in Viterbo, Italy, in March 1271. Henry was attending Mass at an assembly of cardinals gathered to elect the successor of Pope Clement IV. According to a story that our poet follows, the heart of Henry was placed on a pillar on London Bridge. Its dripping blood proclaimed that his death was still unavenged.

Among these shades Dante recognizes many, but with none does he seek to converse—an unusual situation. Finally, at a shallow place in the river, Nessus carries Dante across to the edge of a wood and then returns to his own assignment.

Note

We met Minos, the judge of the dead, at the entrance to the second circle. When he was king of Crete, his wife Pasiphaë conceived a passion for a bull and then conceived the Minotaur when she hid inside an artificial cow and was impregnated by the bull. The Minotaur developed the unpleasant habit of devouring an annual tribute of young Athenians, until it was slain by Theseus (duke of Athens) with the help of Ariadne (the lover of Theseus and half-sister of the Minotaur). Involvement with bulls ran in the family. Minos himself was the offspring of a mating between Europa, a royal maid of Asian Tyre, and the god Zeus disguised as a white bull. She rode on his back as he swam to Crete. Besides then giving birth to Minos, Europa gave her name to Europe.

Canto 13

DANTE AND VIRGIL now enter the middle round of the seventh circle, where suicides are punished. It is a deadly, dense, and tangled wood with no path, no green foliage, no smooth branches, no fruit. Here the repulsive Harpies, horrid birds with women's faces, make their nests.

Dante hears moans from a tree but sees no moaner. Perhaps making fun of the rhetorical style of the spirit they are about to discover, Dante says of Virgil: "I believe that he believed that I believed" that the sounds were coming from someone hiding behind the tree. Virgil bids him snap a branch from a nearby large thorn tree. At once its trunk cries out, "Why did you break me? Have you no pity?"

"As a green log, burning at one end, drips from the other and hisses with the steam that escapes," words and blood issue from the broken branch. Dante fearfully drops it.

As if in apology, Virgil says he wouldn't have urged Dante to break a branch and discover the truth if Dante had not taken as fictional a similar situation recounted in the *Aeneid* (3:22 ff.)—as if to say, "I'll show you!" But tell Dante who you are, Virgil suggests to the wounded shade, and Dante will make amends by refreshing your fame back on Earth.

The soul describes himself as once the faithful confidant of Emperor Frederick II. As poet, scholar, and legalist, he was once the most influential statesman of his time in Western Europe. Betrayed by the envy of others, this Pier della Vigne (*circa* 1190–1249) was accused of disloyalty—some say by plotting with the pope to poison his master. After being blinded and led from town to town on an ass, he is said to have committed suicide by braining himself against a prison wall.

Virgil questions him on behalf of Dante, who is wordless with pity: how do souls become bound in these branches, and can they ever escape?

The shade says that Minos hurls them down here, where they take root at random. The Harpies feed on their leaves, giving pain and a "window" for pain at the same time—like suicide itself. At the Last Judgment the sinners will be given their bodies back, but they will not inhabit them. Rather, their once-rejected bodies will hang rejectingly on the tree branches.

At this point, a loud sound startles the group. Two naked souls are fleeing the black bitches of which the wood is full. Less serenely than Bach's "Come, Sweet Death," one soul escapes, crying, "Hurry now, O death, hurry." The other hides in a bush, where the dogs savagely tear both him and the bush.

The bleeding bush identifies itself as a Florentine who hung himself in his own home. He says that Mars, the god of war, will keep avenging himself on the city of Florence because he was replaced as city patron by John the Baptist. Mars would do even worse were he not somewhat appeased by the remains of his statue near the city's Arno River.

Note

From other sources we know that the two naked souls committed suicide of a sort by being reckless with their wealth and foolishly courting death in battle. Pier della Vigne's name was not given in this canto but was easily supplied by early commentators.

Canto 14

LOVE FOR HIS NATIVE CITY *(natio)*, which has not yet exiled him, impels Dante to gather the scattered leaves belonging to the savaged spirit of his fellow Florentine.

He and Virgil then quit the wood and come to a scorching desert void of any plant or leaf. On dry, thick sand, swollen flakes of flame are slowly falling. These flames land on many groups of naked souls, all weeping miserably, though in different positions. The blasphemers are fewest and lie supine, facing the Heaven they cursed; the usurers sit bent over like money counters; the sodomites are the most numerous and are continuously running.

> Ever without repose was the dance
> of the wretched hands, now here, now there,
> brushing off the fresh burning.
> *(Sanza riposo mai era la tresca*
> *delle misere mani, or quindi or quinci*
> *escotendo da se l'arsura fresca.)*

Dante sees an exception to the universal weeping. It is a great shade paying no heed to the fire, lying twisted and scornful, unripened by the rain. Hearing Dante ask Virgil who he is, the shade shouts the answer loudly: "As I was alive, so am I dead. Jove hit me with all his strength and killed me, but his vengeance *(vendetta)* could not have the joy of seeing me grieve."

Virgil responds with so much feeling than Dante has never heard his voice louder: "O Capaneus, since your pride remains untamed, you are punished the more. Your rage is the best torture for your fury."

Speaking to Dante, Virgil continues: This is one of the seven kings who besieged ancient Thebes. "He held and seems still to hold God in contempt, and to fear Him little."

The sage leads Dante on, warning him to beware of the burning sand. They come to a little stream overflowing from the river of blood. Above this stream the fiery flakes are somehow quenched. The stream, which Virgil finds uniquely notable, provides a safe passageway that the two now tread while Virgil summarizes the decline of the human race by a parable about a mammoth statue on the island of Crete. That island, "equidistant" from Asia, Africa, and Europe, was regarded as the center of the world's Golden Age and the cradle of Rome's own ancestry.

The material of this statue of an old man facing Rome declines in quality as it descends from the golden head. The foot of clay, too much leaned on, may represent the contemporary papacy, overly involved in political affairs. A fissure mars every part but the golden head; from this crack drip tears of blood and sorrow. These tears form the waters that the two poets have already seen in Hell (including this remarkable stream) and will form the frozen lake Cocytus at Hell's innermost core. From the top of the mount of Purgatory a final river, Lethe, will wash into Hell all memory of sin in the minds of the saved.

This Old Man of Crete, a symbol of human history and decadence, is based on a vision in the biblical book of Daniel (2:31–35), with features added from pagan sources such as Ovid.

Note

Borrowing from many sources for his supply of imagery, Dante at times clothes Christian conceptions in mythological or pagan dress. This practice can be disconcerting, since it involves mixing fable and legend with what Dante surely held as literal truths. Thus, in this canto, the pagan god Jove's punishment of a legendary figure becomes an example of divine justice as believed in by a Christian.

Canto 15

WITH VIRGIL SPEAKING but a single sentence, this extraordinary canto is almost exclusively a dramatic and moving dialogue between Dante and an

admired Florentine "teacher" of his, presumably condemned to run for-
ever in this desert for unrepented sins of homosexual behavior.

To avoid the heat, the poets have been walking on one of the banks
built like Flemish dikes on either side of the flame-quenching stream. A
band of spirits comes running along the bank and gazes at them the way
people squint at one another on a moonless night, or as an old tailor
sharpens his eye before the eye of his needle. One of the band recognizes
Dante and grasping at the hem *(lembo)* of his solid cloak cries out, "What
a marvel!"

This figure moves its arm up toward Dante. Not even the scorched
features of this shade keep Dante from recognizing an old model and
hero. Returning this rare reaching out of a shade by lowering his hand
toward the baked visage, Dante uses the respectful form of *you* to ask
incredulously, "Are you here, Ser Brunetto?" (*Ser* was the title used by
notaries.)

Dante offers to sit on the wall and converse with the self-identified
Brunetto Latini (1220?–1294?), but the latter says that a hundred years of
increased punishment await him if he stops moving. So they walk together,
Dante bending down respectfully as far as he can.

The teacher inquires, "How did you get here before death, and who
leads you?" In Hell the travelers never identify each other, but Dante does
explain how he had gone astray in the serene life and was being taken
"home" by the shade ahead of him.

Brunetto next speaks two dozen lines of praise for Dante, prophesying
a splendid, virtuous future: "If you follow your star, you cannot fail to
reach a glorious port." His fellow citizens, though, will become his en-
emies because of his good deeds: "See that you cleanse yourself from their
ways." May they not harm any rare plant that happens to grow in their
manure and revive the holy virtues of the pristine Romans who settled
there. (The reader needs to remember that Dante is speaking of himself on
such laudatory occasions.)

Dante returns the praise in heartfelt words: "If my prayers had been
granted, you would still be among the living. For in my mind is fixed and
my heart knows the dear and kindly image of you as a father when, from
hour to hour, you taught how a man makes himself eternal [through fame
from literary excellence]. While I am alive it is fitting that my tongue should
show how grateful I am."

Dante says that he will remember Brunetto's prophecy, add it to

Farinata's, and ask Beatrice to explain both more clearly. In any case, "I am prepared for whatever Fortune intends."

Dante wants to know who are the spirits accompanying his old mentor. "It is well to know of some. Of the others silence is more laudable," Brunetto answers, stating that all were clergy and scholars of great fame. He names three souls, including Dante's former bishop (1287–95). When this prelate's morals became a scandal, Boniface VIII (here sarcastically dubbed "servant of the servants") merely transferred him to another diocese, where he left his "badly stretched muscles." (Such bluntness!)

Recommending his own encyclopedic book *The Treasury* (which he wrote while exiled from Florence), he runs off, "for people are coming with whom I must not associate." Brunetto had actually condemned homosexuality in his writings. Maybe these sinners are after him for false advertising.

Notes

Because of their respective ages, it is unlikely that Brunetto taught Dante other than in the school of life and letters. In a preeminent way this canto refutes the charge that Dante put only his enemies in Hell. But there is a curious irony here. Since Dante is so surprised to meet Brunetto, the latter's sins must not have been generally known. So Dante here permanently glorifies and shames his hero at the same time. From such admirers one might pray, "Deliver me, O Lord!"

After all these years, deliverance of a sort may have come to Brunetto and the other spirits in this circle from Richard Kay. In his *Dante's Swift and Strong* (Regents Press of Kansas, 1978), he has proposed a novel and ingenious theory that the sins against nature punished in this circle include sodomy but might well include sins against natural truth, and against the natural authority of the emperor.

Philosophers of various kinds can commit the one kind of sin, especially when they are chiefly interested in fame. Politicians can do so with respect to sins against the emperor.

Seven of the eight persons Dante meets in this canto and the next had no reputation for sodomy. But even now in the afterlife, they show a keen interest in the personal glory and fame that may have guiltily motivated them on Earth—at the expense of humble service to the truth, and humble subordination to imperial authority.

Canto 16

DANTE AND VIRGIL are now close enough to the inner edge of the seventh circle to hear water falling into the next circle. Just as Brunetto had separated himself from his band of running sinners, three other men break away from their band, yelling for Dante to stop because his garb seems to show them that he is a fellow Florentine. Virgil suggests that Dante oblige them: "To these we must be courteous, though brief."

To avoid being punished for stopping, the trio run in a circle beneath Dante. Speaking for his companions, whom he identifies, Jacopo Rusticucci begs Dante to honor their fame by revealing who he is. All three were eminent Guelphs of the generation before Dante. Jacopo, in fact, and his companion Tegghiaio Aldobrandi are the very ones about which Dante had asked the gluttonous Ciacco, who described them as "among the blackest souls" in Hell.

Dante the Guelph answers by stressing his grief at seeing them thus and his long-standing affection for their deeds and their names. As he didn't tell Brunetto who his guide is, so he doesn't tell these three either. But he describes his situation: "I leave the gall and go for the sweet fruit."

Jacopo inquires whether "courtesy" and valor remain alive in Florence, since they have heard disturbing news lately. Raising his face, as though looking at Florence, Dante replies, "New people and sudden gains have generated pride and excess in you, O Florence!"

Together the three thank him for his "courtesy," begging that he speak of them to others if he escapes this dark place, returns to see the beautiful stars again, and can delight in saying of the underworld, "I was there."

Off go the three as fast as you could say *Amen.* The poets continue toward the waterfall, now so loud that they can scarcely hear each other.

A strange incident occurs next. Virgil asks for the cord around Dante's waist. This is the first we've heard of such a cord or of the fact that Dante tried to use it yesterday to catch the leopard with the painted hide.

Virgil now throws the cord into the central well, and Dante expects some strange response to this strange signal. Sure enough, Dante soon sees an amazing creature swimming up from the deep, stretching forth its arms and drawing up its feet. Again talking directly to the reader, Dante swears that this is true. He swears it "by the strains of this Comedy, hoping that it may long be in favor." This is the first mention of his *Comedy,* and those of us who read it with appreciation are fulfilling his wish.

Notes

The symbolism of the cord is uncertain. There is a tradition that Dante, who is buried in a Franciscan church, was affiliated with the cord-girded Franciscan friars, perhaps even a novice temporarily after Beatrice's death. Often a sign of chastity, the cord may no longer be needed since Dante has descended below the circle of incontinence. Or Dante may be implying that chastity itself can rope you into more subtle evils, for example, hardheartedness. In any case, Virgil was clearly in need of something disposable to use as a signal.

The dignity of the sinners in the "Sodom" circle, and the courteous way in which they are spoken of in those two cantos are remarkable and quite different from the treatment given to other sinners in this circle—the blasphemous Capaneus and the unnamed usurers in the next canto. Did Dante himself experience homoerotic impulses, as Virgil most likely did? Also, as a marginal man himself, Dante the wifeless exile shows unusual regard for other marginal people in his society, like Jews and Muslims.

A puzzlement: When, as in this canto, Dante insists so strongly that some episode is true, does he want us to take him literally, or is he playing a literary game? Critic Charles Singleton has said that "the basic fiction of Dante's poem is that it is not a fiction." But should a deeply religious man like Dante swear that a fiction is true? Or did he really have a mystical experience that he put into fictional form—"a truth that has the face of a lie" (*Inferno* 16:124)? (On this knotty dilemma, see Barolini.)

Canto 17

IN GREEK MYTHOLOGY Geryon was a Spanish king with three heads. He used to entice guests to eat with him and then slay them. Later he himself was slain by Hercules. Looking for an image of fraud, and drawing further from the New Testament book of Revelation (Apocalypse), Dante constructs a Geryon with an honest human face, the paws and hair of an animal, a reptilian body decorated with colorful loops, and a venomous, scorpionlike tail.

(Boccaccio's commentary on the poem ends abruptly in the middle of a sentence dealing with this description. He died [1375] "as though with pen in hand." For her part, translator Dorothy Sayers died in 1957 after completing twenty cantos of the *Paradiso*. She had not yet begun her commentary on it.)

In a canto in which Dante speaks but one croaking sentence, Virgil begins by identifying the beast that has swum upward into view: "Behold the beast...that can cross mountains and break through walls and weapons...the one that infects the whole world." Virgil nevertheless summons this beast, this foul image of fraud, this worst of all wild beasts, to come ashore near himself and Dante.

As they reach the beast, Dante notices some people sitting on the sand close to the edge of the pit of fraud. These are the usurers, who sin against the nature of things and against the Author of nature because they turn something sterile into something fertile by lending money at a price. (The sodomites, by contrast, have rendered sterile their own fertile natures—unless, of course, they are also married.)

Virgil says he will negotiate the use of this beast's strong shoulders while Dante pays a quick visit to these sad, weary souls "...so that you may take with you complete experience of this circle."

Thus alone, Dante approaches these unrecognizable shades whose eyes gush forth grief even as they dote on the purses hanging from their necks. From the family crests on these emblems of greed, Dante can tell that two are fellow Florentines. A third shade asks what Dante is doing in this hole and bids him depart. He identifies himself as a native of Padua waiting for a living compatriot to join him here, while the Florentines yearn loudly for the arrival of an idolized Florentine usurer.

Without speaking a word, Dante hastens back to his master, who is already seated behind the monster's shoulders. Be strong and bold, Virgil urges. The frightened Dante means to say, "See that you keep holding me," but his voice comes out other than he expects. Next, Virgil commands Geryon by name to descend in slow, wide circles.

Dante compares his situation with two disastrous flights recorded by mythology: that of Apollo's son Phaëthon, who borrowed his father's chariot (the Sun) but lost control of it, scorched the sky where the Milky Way now is, and was kept from incinerating the Earth by a thunderbolt from Zeus; and that of Icarus, who ignored the warning of his father, Daedalus, and flew too close to the Sun, which melted his waxen wings and sent him to a sea death.

At first Dante is aware of movement only by the wind on his face coming from below. Hearing the fierce crash of water below him, he looks down and grows even more fearful at the sight of fires and the sound of laments (which must have been very loud). Finally, angry and sullen, Geryon deposits his two passengers in the deeps of fraud at the foot of a jagged rock, then darts off like an arrow from its string.

Note

In line twenty-one Dante takes a generic slap at "the gluttonous Germans." (Incidentally, his poem in German is called *Die Gottliche Komodie*.)

Canto 18

DANTE AND VIRGIL have arrived at the eighth circle at this point on Holy Saturday morning and will remain there through the next fourteen cantos. In this circle are punished ten varieties of "simple" fraud—that is, fraud without the added malice of treachery. These acts of fraud are pandering and seducing, flattery, simony, sorcery, graft, hypocrisy, theft, evil counseling, discord-sowing, and counterfeiting.

Dante calls this circle Malebolge (evil pouches), probably in reference to the money-pocketing greed so often linked with fraud. (Here belong those people who consider everything for sale.) In this instance the pouches are a metaphor for a series of ten concentric ditches or valleys that slope down from the surrounding stone walls to the open well at the center.

Two stone banks edge each ditch. Across each ditch run a number of rough stone bridges connecting bank with bank and forming a kind of spoke, the hub of which is the well.

Shaken from Geryon's back, Dante and Virgil turn left (as they almost always do in Hell), putting the first ditch on their right. Peering into this ditch, Dante sees "new misery, new torments, and new tormentors." There he makes out two lines of naked sinners running in response to whips striking them from behind and wielded by horned demons—the first devils of the *Inferno*. The nearer line, advancing toward the travelers, is composed of panderers—go-betweens in sexual intrigues. The farther line consists of seducers, who are traveling in the same direction as Dante and Virgil. (This traffic pattern reminds Dante of the way crowds approached and left St. Peter's in Rome during the Jubilee Year 1300—the date of the poem.)

Dante sees a face he thinks he recognizes. Retracing his steps, he finds a shade trying to hide his face—the first such instance in the poem. Dante calls out his name and asks to know why he is in such a pickle *("pungenti salse")*. As though unwilling to speak, Venedico Caccianemico admits his identity and the cause of his punishment—he sold his own sister to a marquis. He says this place is full of other avaricious citizens of Bologna. A devil now whips him, calling him "ruffian," which originally meant a pimp.

Dante rejoins Virgil and together they cross an old bridge *("ponte vecchio"*—as in Florence!) that permits them to gaze down at the oncoming seducers. Virgil points out Jason, captain of the Argonauts, who seduced the young Hypsipyle, leaving her pregnant and forlorn:

> Look at that great one coming,
> who for all his pains sheds no tears.
> What a regal bearing he has!

Quickly traversing the second ditch, Dante hears moans from people who are puffing their snouts and hitting themselves with their hands. A noisome mold encrusts the banks on either side, while at the center people are plunged in excrement as from human privies. Dante stares at one figure, who resents the attention. "I saw you once with dry hair," the poet explains with dry wit. This Alessio, otherwise unknown, confesses that he was once an incessant flatterer.

Virgil instructs Dante to look beyond to a filthy and disheveled wench scratching herself with dirty fingernails. He identifies her as a harlot named Thais, whose greatest sin was the prostitution of words, as instanced by her fulsome praise of a lover. "With this let our sight be satisfied."

Note

Dante is rushing Venedico the panderer. He died three years after the time from which the poem is dated.

Canto 19

FROM HIS SUDDEN OUTBURST in the first line to almost the end of this canto, Dante engages in "apostrophes"—addressing as though they were present Simon Magus, all simoniacs, Divine Wisdom, and Constantine the Great. As described in the eighth chapter of the Acts of the Apostles, Simon Magus (magician) sought to buy spiritual power from the apostles. Simoniacs likewise prostitute the sacred for cash. Seeing how simoniacs who perversely stuffed their purses with sacrilegious gain are here stuffed upside down into the holes that pock this ditch, the poet lauds the artistry of divine retribution. (It's really his own artistry, of course.) The feet of the sinners are afire and twitch like the wicks of votive lights at a shrine.

One shade twitches more than the rest. Virgil carries Dante down to the bottom of the ditch so that he can question this one who was "lamenting with his legs." This sinner proves to be Pope Nicholas III (1277–80). He has been expecting Pope Boniface VIII (1294–1303) to be pushed in above him and thus mistakes Dante for one of Dante's favorite enemies, mentioned uniquely here by name. Nicholas is therefore surprised that his near successor has come so soon after seizing and outraging "la bella Donna" (the papacy). Put straight by Dante, the pope reveals that Boniface will in turn be pushed in by Pope Clement V (1305–14), the creature of France's Philip the Fair, the king who helped him gain the papacy and then pressured him to move the Holy See to Avignon.

For only the second time so far, Dante lambastes a sinner, asking scornfully whether Christ demanded any treasure from the apostle Peter, and pointing out that idolaters worship one golden thing, whereas Nicholas the money-lover has adored a hundred. Dante tells us that only reverence for the papacy keeps him from using heavier words than he does. The poet concludes his blast by addressing Emperor Constantine (280?–337), whose supposed vast gift of land to the papacy created "the first rich father" and was the mother of so many evil consequences.

In this upside-down episode, Dante the layman takes the posture of a father confessor at the execution of an "assassin" and gives the pope a sermon that is likened to a holy chant. Virgil is so pleased with his indignant pupil that he embraces him tightly as he did in the Filippo Argenti episode, then carries him back up the bank and places him down softly on the rough and steep rocks.

Notes

Dante is becoming bolder: here he assigns to Hell several contemporary popes, including one who was reigning while he wrote.

A Catholic scholar, Lorenzo Valla, proved in the fifteenth century that the "Donation of Constantine," with its gift to the papacy of vast lands in Italy and the West, was an eighth-century forgery.

There is an intriguing autobiographical reference. Dante says the holes in this circle are about the width of the several stone tubs in which priests stood during mass baptisms in his beautiful St. John's in Florence. On one occasion, a child got dangerously stuck in one of these, and Dante broke it to free the child. In view of the rumors of sacrilege, Dante wants to clear the record here. What is now the Baptistery with Ghiberti's famous bronze panels was the cathedral before the present Duomo was completed in the fifteenth century.

Canto 20

WITH UNIQUE EXPLICITNESS, this canto opens by naming itself the twentieth canto of the first book *("canzon")*. Other unusual aspects are that Virgil does most of the talking, Dante talks little, and the sinners in the circle speak not at all. Nor is there any demon punishing them.

Virgil—who himself had a medieval reputation as a magician—identifies these sinners in the fourth pouch as people who tried to make the mind of God subject to their will as augurs, diviners, and fortunetellers. Having said too much, they say nothing here. Because they tried to see ahead too far, they now have their heads twisted toward their posteriors. They must, therefore, walk backward slowly, and in a "debasement of sorrow" their tears flow down degradingly between their buttocks.

Virgil points out four soothsayers of ancient literature, one each from the four long Latin poems known to Dante: the *Metamorphoses* of Ovid, the *Pharsalia* of Lucan (we met these last two poets in the first circle), the *Thebaid* of Statius (whom we shall meet in Purgatory), and Virgil's own *Aeneid* (here called "my high tragedy," which, he says, Dante knows thoroughly).

The sage seizes the occasion to give the correct, entirely natural link between the female soothsayer Manto and his own native city of Mantua, built in northern Italy over her cruel bones. He is thereby correcting his own earlier version of that city's founding, as given in the *Aeneid* (X:200). This older and wiser Virgil now denies any magical aspect to that founding. (Sketching the neighborhood, Virgil mentions Trent, site of the future council, and Bergamo, the native diocese of Pope John XXIII, who summoned another council [Vatican II]).

Virgil points out some more modern diviners, including a group of nameless, wretched women who should have stuck to their sewing. Apart from the mythical Myrrha in canto 30, these are the last women sinners mentioned in Hell.

Revealing that the Moon has now set—which he now mentions as having been round the night before—Virgil hurries on with his protégé.

At the start of this canto, Dante weeps to see the human bodies of these sinners so contorted. In a famous rebuke, Virgil implies that Dante is witless, since in this underworld pity is alive (correct) when it is quite dead. The ironic point is made by the double meaning of the Italian word *pieta:* "pity" and "piety."

Notes

This canto tells in brief the story of Manto's father, the Greek soothsayer Tiresias, who was turned into a woman for seven years when he touched two mating snakes. Upon encountering and touching such snakes a second time, he became a male again. Jupiter and his wife were later arguing about which gender got more out of sex. They consulted Tiresias, who agreed with Jupiter that women did. Juno then blinded him. Jupiter feared to undo his wife's revenge, so he granted Tiresias the gift of prophetic seeing.

In the Middle Ages, "St. Thomas and Dante, almost alone, lift their voices against the superstitious practices of astrology" (E. G. Parodi). Like Aquinas, Dante regarded as secondary any influence of cosmic forces on human tempers and dispositions.

It is perhaps hard for us moderns to realize how much Dante's contemporaries believed in the astrology that he so strongly repudiates in this canto. Of course, we have our daily newspaper horoscopes. A recent first lady had her trusty stargazer, who supposedly influenced presidential decisions. Hitler had his astrologers, and Churchill his (to guess what Hitler's were telling him).

Canto 21

DANTE WILL DEVOTE more words to this fifth pouch than to any other place in Hell. Here those "sticky-fingered" souls who committed sins of barratry (graft) are submerged in boiling pitch. This pitch reminds our poet of Venetian shipyards, where sailors caulk their damaged ships. Fierce, winged demons called Malebranche (evil claws) puncture with forks anyone who tries to rise out of the pitch. "Just so do cooks make their helpers push the meat down into the cauldron with their forks, so it doesn't float." Since Dante was accused of barratry, that is, political corruption as expressed in the barter of official positions, and since he spent the latter part of his life in exile and under pain of death because of that charge, it makes sense that he should devote so much time to this place and should show himself to have been in unusual peril while there. Only in this canto does Virgil tell him to hide. This he does after a devil runs onto the bridge they are traversing and tosses a freshly arrived sinner into the pitch. This wretch is from Lucca, where, says the devil, everyone is a barrator and where, for money, a "no" becomes a "yes."

Warning him, "Beware! beware!" Virgil first tells Dante to crouch behind a stone. Virgil advances alone and is assailed by a rush of demons. Unflinching, he demands to speak to one of them. Malacoda (Evil Tail) steps forward. "Do you think I got this far without divine aid?" the guide asks. "It is willed in Heaven that I show another this savage way." Malacoda's insolence melts. He drops his fork and commands, "He must not be touched."

Virgil then summons the hiding Dante, who goes quickly to his master, worrying that the demons might not obey Malacoda. "Shall I nick him on the rump?" whispers one devil. "Yes. Let him have it!" replies another. "Stop it!" Malacoda orders. Then he advises Virgil that the bridge just ahead was broken exactly 1,266 years ago yesterday, though five hours later in the day. (That would have been the time of the crucifixion, then commonly dated as happening in the year A.D. 34; thus is the year 1300 indicated for the date of the journey.)

Malacoda orders ten demons under the lead of Barbariccia to escort Virgil and his charge. Alarmed by the looks and the grinding teeth of these demons, Dante urges Virgil to proceed without escort. Virgil is convinced that the threatening behavior of the demons is meant for the sinners in the pitch.

Pressing their tongues between their teeth, the nine devils look to their leader for a signal. He gives it by using his rump for a trumpet!

Notes

Dorothy Sayers translates the names of these escorts as Grizzly, Hellkin, Deaddog, Pigtusk, Dragontooth, Catclaw, Cramper, and Crazyred.

In this canto and the next, sometimes called "gargoyle cantos," Dante employs his coarsest language. In depicting various grotesqueries, he shows himself "the Master of the Disgusting" and gives literature "the most perfect portraiture of fiendish nature" (John Ruskin).

In the second line, Dante refers for the second time to his *Comedy*. Just nineteen lines earlier, Virgil had referred to his own tragedy. Both words are from the Greek, and the root from which we get *ode* (song) can be detected at the end of each word. *Comedy* means "reveler's-song" or "merry-making song." *Tragedy* means "goat-song" and refers to the goat prize once given in Athens to the winner of a drama contest in honor of Dionysius/Bacchus. He was the wine god of poetry and music, to whom vine-eating goats were sacrificed. Quaintly, Dante thought that the typical tragedy was goatish because the ending stank horribly. (A play by the early tragedian Phrynichus moved the Athenians so painfully that he was fined.) Though Virgil's *Aeneid* doesn't end tragically for its hero, its lofty diction and action led Dante to have Virgil call it a tragedy.

Canto 22

RECALLING VARIOUS MILITARY and sports maneuvers, Dante declares with a straight face that never has he encountered so strange a bugle as the one that ends the previous canto. He and Virgil now follow along after the ten demons—odd company, yes, but "with saints in church; with guzzlers in taverns." Dante keeps his eye on the bubbling pitch, curious about the people within it.

One of the demons forks a sinner who is trying to sneak a moment's relief out of the pitch. Dante wants to know who this hapless wretch is, so Virgil goes up close to question him as a demon prepares to skin him. The sinner identifies himself as a Spaniard who betrayed a king with his barratry. The leader of the demons tells Virgil to be quick about any further questions since the other demons are eager to attack this catch.

"Do you know of any Italian *(latino)* in the pitch?"

"I just left one," answers this man, whom tradition identifies as Ciampolo of Navarre. A frantic demon rips off an arm muscle; another tries to seize his leg before the captain stays him with ugly looks.

Granted further brief reprieve, Ciampolo mentions two Sardinians he knows in the pitch. He says he could summon up some Lombards and Tuscans if the Malebranche would stand back a little so as not to be visible when he whistles the usual all-clear signal. One demon suspects a trick, but as the group argues about taking the risk of losing Ciampolo, the sinner frees himself and leaps into the pitch.

The demon who recommended taking the gamble dives after Ciampolo, "but wings could not outrace fear." Enraged at this ill-advising demon, another attacks him in midair, and they both fall into the pitch. As four demons extend their staffs to pull out the other two, cooked and crusted, Virgil and Dante slip nervously away.

Canto 23

THINKING OF THE STORY of the frog who tricks a mouse only to be caught himself by a hawk, Dante suddenly realizes that the demons were tricked because of himself and Virgil. Surely these hellish creatures will soon come after them with savage intent. Virgil says he has been thinking the same thing and begins to tell Dante his plan of escape.

Then Dante sees the demons racing after them with outstretched wings. Virgil grabs Dante instantly. Then, lying on his back with Dante at his breast, the sage slides down the bank leading into the next ditch. Here occurs a most tender image of Virgil: he's like

> a mother who is awakened by a noise
> and seeing burning flames close to her
> grabs her son and flees and doesn't stop,
> caring more for him than for the fact
> that she is dressed only in her chemise.

As the two reach the bottom, the demons have reached the height just above them. No need to fear, though. Providence deprives the guardians of the fifth ditch of the power to leave it.

In this sixth ditch appears a crowd of souls walking very slowly, weeping and looking weary and overwhelmed. They wear cloaks gilded to a dazzle but lined with the heaviest of lead. Dante asks Virgil to locate someone known by name or deed.

One of the crowd, recognizing Dante's accent, cries out: "Stay your steps; maybe I can fulfill your wish." Virgil gives Dante permission to wait. The slow-moving shade catches up, and with his partner gazes awhile sideways at Dante.

Amazed at the way Dante's throat moves, they implore, "Tell us who you are who have come to this assembly of sorrowful hypocrites." Without divulging his name, Dante describes himself as a Florentine still in his living body.

> And who are you two,
> down whose cheeks such pain distills?
> And why this glittering punishment?

Catalano answers that he and his partner, Loderingo, belonged to the religious order popularly known as Jovial Monks. (One contemporary historian wrote, "They were more intent upon enjoying themselves than upon anything else.") When Dante was a year old they came from their native Bologna at the request of Florence to help keep the peace. But they took sides and fomented destruction, as is still evident in the ruin of the estate of the Farinata we met in canto 12.

Dante starts to reply when his eye is caught by the sight of someone on the ground, crucified by three stakes. Writhing all over and blowing sighs through his beard, this is the Jewish high priest Caiaphas, who persuaded his fellow members of the Council of the Pharisees to condemn Christ to death. All the weighted hypocrites of Hell walk eternally over his naked body, over that of his father-in-law, Annas, and over those of all the members of the Sanhedrin of their time. (Usually Hell's sinners are described as naked; by way of exception the hypocrites are clothed, apart from the last-mentioned.)

At this point the pre-Christian Virgil, who has been marveling at this sight (which was not here when he went to Hell's depths the first time), asks Catalano where he and Dante can find an unbroken bridge across this ditch. When the monk reveals that all the bridges are broken, Virgil realizes that the demon Malacoda lied to him. The monk cites the devil's reputation as a liar and the father of lies. An angry Virgil heads with great strides for the pile of stones over which the friar said they could make their way to the seventh pouch.

Note

For a medieval Christian, Dante was remarkably free of anti-Semitism, though of course he accepted the New Testament view of individual Jewish sinners. According to the *Encyclopedia Judaica,* "The *Comedy* contains no insulting or pejorative references to Jews....There are no Jews among heretics, usurers and counterfeiters, whose sinful ranks Jews during the Middle Ages were commonly alleged to swell" (p. 1,296). At Dante's death the Christian poet Bosone d'Agubbio wrote in verse to the eminent Jewish poet Immanuel ben Solomon of Rome: "Weep, then, weep, Jewish Immanuel, for your own sore loss." Immanuel replied, "Well may Christian and Jew weep together, each sitting on the bench of mourning."

Canto 24

USING ONE OF the loveliest comparisons in the entire poem—involving a frustrated peasant who upon rising mistakes frost for snow, but later discovers that the warming Sun now allows him to take his sheep out to pasture—Dante tells how Virgil's angry countenance shortly changed to a pleasant one again. Coming to the ruins of a shattered bridge, Virgil opens his arms, takes hold of Dante, and begins helping him up from rock to jagged rock. The ascent is tiring, and Dante sits at the top, out of breath.

Appealing to Dante's desire for fame, Virgil urges him to throw off all sloth. At this, Dante responds with more energy than he thought he had left. "Proceed," he replies, "for I am strong and fearless."

Traversing an unbroken bridge over this seventh ditch, the Florentine hears what seems an angry mumbling, but the darkness of the pouch below prevents all recognition. So he asks Virgil to descend the far slope into the ditch. To this fair request Virgil accedes.

There Dante sees a fearful throng of strange serpents. Among them run thieves, naked and terrified, without hope of a hiding place. Their hands are tied behind their backs by serpents who thrust their heads and tails through the guts of the sinners.

Nearby, a serpent springs on a sinner and pierces him at the base of the neck. He instantly ignites, burns, and sinks into his own ashes. Just as instantly, the ashes take on the sinner's old form again. The restored shade rises, stares about him all bewildered from the anguish he has suffered, and sighs as he looks.

Virgil asks him who he is. "I am Vanni Fucci, the Beast, from Pistoia."

"Tell him not to run off," Dante begs. "Ask him why he is here," since his reputation was that of a man of blood and rage rather than a thief. Fucci stares at Dante and blushes with shame. This contemporary of Dante feels compelled to admit that he committed a theft of sacred objects for which an innocent person was blamed. But lest Dante, a "White" Guelph, take undiluted satisfaction in this punishment of a "Black" Guelph, Fucci predicts that civil war in Pistoia will soon spill over into Florence and bring disaster to Dante's political party: "I have told you this so that it may grieve you."

Fucci is referring to the split in a family of Pistoia, the Guelph Cancellieris, into murderous "Black" and "White" factions—so-called because one faction called itself "White" after Cancellieri's wife, "Bianca." When Pistoian ringleaders were jailed in Florence to restore peace, Florentines soon divided into "Blacks" and "Whites" themselves. Dante, a "White," ended up on the wrong side when the pro–Pope Boniface "Blacks" took over. The "Blacks" were led by the wealthy Donati family, to which Dante's wife, Gemma, belonged.

Canto 25

WITH EACH HAND, Vanni Fucci makes the "fig," an obscene gesture in which the thumb is projected through the two nearest fingers. "Take them, God, for I am aiming them at You." One serpent instantly wraps itself around the neck of this thief; another binds his arms. "From then on, the serpents were my friends," says Dante, who nowhere in Hell has seen a spirit so bold against God. Fucci flees as the centaur Cacus, bearing on his back snakes and a fire-breathing dragon, races by in search of him.

Three unnoticed spirits suddenly ask, "Who are you two?" These are the Florentines Agnello, Buoso, and Puccio the Cripple. Agnello will soon be attacked by a fourth Florentine (Cianfa), and Buoso by a fifth (Francesco de' Cavalcanti). When they attack, Cianfa and Cavalcanti are serpents; by attacking they regain the human form their victims lose. In the presence of such thieves on Earth, nothing was safe. Now in Hell they find that not even their human shapes are safe.

As a serpent, the six-legged Cianfa now leaps on Agnello. The two begin to merge, producing temporarily "such members as were never seen." Each changes color and semblance, "just as a dark hue moves ahead of the flame over a sheet of paper, the whiteness dying away before it becomes black." The perverse hybrid, seeming both double and neither, slinks away.

In a flash the small fiery serpent that is Cavalcanti leaps toward the remaining two. It manages to pierce the belly of Buoso, then falls at his feet. The serpent and the stricken shade (who is now yawning) eye each other. Smoke rolling from the mouth of the one and the wound of the other joins together. Part for part, each form begins to change into the other. When the metamorphosis is complete, the smoke stops, and the newly made brute flees hissing. Talking and sputtering, the rehumanized Cavalcanti pursues it—"I want Buoso to run, belly-to-ground, as I have had to run."

Puccio, the remaining Florentine, slips away, but not before being recognized by Dante. The poet concludes this canto by identifying the second attacking serpent (Cavalcanti) as the man whose avenged death brought grief to his murderers in Gaville, a town near Florence.

Notes

Some commentators say that Puccio, already lame, was not transformed in this scene because he was a "mannerly" thief who performed "beautiful and graceful" thefts. Moreover, he worked by day and seemed to care little whether he was seen or not.

Depicting the detailed bodily transformation, Dante modestly refers to "the member that a man conceals."

Francesco de' Cavalcanti was kin to Guido, Dante's poet friend.

The first edition of *American Heritage Dictionary* (1969) defined the "fig" gesture. Curiously, the latest edition doesn't. The fig has long been a female sexual symbol, so the gesture mimics intercourse.

Canto 26

DANTE BEGINS THIS CANTO, a favorite of many, by addressing once again his native Florence, five of whose citizens he is ashamed to have encountered in the hell of thieves. Recently, he has been having early-morning dreams about grievous evils soon to befall his native city. Because he thinks the souls of the sleeping are farthest from their bodies just before dawn, and therefore closer to pure truth, Dante believes such dreams to be prophetic. He knows that the disasters of Florence will weigh more heavily on him as he grows older.

He and Virgil climb back to the bridge over the eighth ditch. Like a hillside peasant spying fireflies in a summertime valley at the hour when flies give way to gnats, Dante looks down on the new ditch and finds it all resplendent with flames, each concealing a sinner. Dante sees one flame approaching that is divided at the top and asks his guide who lies within.

Virgil explains that the flame contains the Greeks Ulysses (alias Odysseus) and his war companion Diomedes, both punished for various trickeries and evil advising connected with the Trojan War. When the flame is near enough, Virgil appeals to the worthiness of his *Aeneid* as a reason why either Ulysses or Diomedes should tell where he met his death. The greater section of the flame shakes, murmurs, and then begins to speak.

In the next fifty-two lines of this canto, detailing a sequence of events invented perhaps by Dante and later influencing the poet Tennyson, Ulysses tells how, after leaving the enchantress Circe, he became restless to undertake new adventures:

> Neither fondness for my son, nor duty toward an old father, nor love for [my wife,] Penelope...could master in me my desire to gain experience of the world, and of the vices and worth of men.

Sailing with a small group of his old companions, he comes to the pillars of Hercules (Gibraltar), beyond which men were not to venture. He then exhorts his comrades:

> O brothers, you who through a hundred thousand perils have come to the West, to the brief vigil of our senses that yet remains, do not refuse experience of the unpeopled world....Consider what

origin you had: you were not created to live like brutes, but to seek virtue and knowledge.

After five months of what turns out to be an insane pursuit, they joyfully sight the highest mountain Ulysses has ever seen. Suddenly, though, a wind arises from that land and whirls the ship three times before it raises the stern and submerges the prow "until at last the sea closed over us."

Notes

Dorothy Sayers has called this canto "the noblest in *Inferno*." Still, Dante seems to have ambivalent feelings about the unbridled adventuresomeness of Ulysses, who seems rather impressed with his own oratorical skills.

Dante doesn't talk to Ulysses (or Diomedes) because his language would reveal him as a Latin, and hence as a descendant of their enemy, the Trojans.

As for the evils portended by Dante's dream: In 1304 the Florentine factions refused to reconcile, so a papal legate excommunicated the citizens and invoked a curse on the city. Not long afterward a large crowd gathered on a bridge to watch a water show about the torments of Hell. The bridge collapsed, and many were drowned, otherwise killed, or maimed. Shortly thereafter, a great fire destroyed 1,700 palaces, towers, and houses. A grateful letter survives that Dante wrote to the legate who tried to help the exiles (see the appendix).

Canto 27

A SECOND CANTO detains us in this eighth ditch. As the Ulysses/Diomedes flame departs with Virgil's permission, another approaches. From its tip emerge confused and doleful sounds. Eventually, words come forth, addressed to Virgil, whose Lombardy accent the flame has heard. Politely it begs to know if its native Romagna is at war or peace. "You answer," says Virgil to Dante; "this is an Italian *(latino)*."

Dante responds that Romagna has always had strife but suffers no open warfare at the moment. "Tell us who you are," Dante presses, "so may your name stay proudly in the world."

Fearing infamy, the flame asserts that it would not reply if it thought the listener would ever return to the world. (These lines are the epigraph of T. S. Eliot's poem "The Love Song of J. Alfred Prufrock.") The sinner confides that after a military career he became a monk eager to make amends for his sinful past. Promising him forgiveness in advance, however, Pope Boniface VIII persuaded him to give advice on how to trick his enemies, the Colonna family, who were holed up in the impregnable town of Palestrina.

"Promise, and then renege" was his not very subtle counsel. In effect, that is what the pope also did to his adviser. Betraying his word, the pope had the town destroyed and salted when the Colonnas left it trustingly.

Wearing the monk's cord "that once made men thin," this Guido da Montefeltro (1223–98) finally died. As Saint Francis came to claim his soul, a black cherub intervened, pointing out that no one can merit absolution while intending to sin. "You didn't think I was a logician," said the witty devil to Guido. "Therefore I am lost here," laments this evil counselor. "I grieve while moving, clothed in fire."

The sorrowing spirit passes on, while Dante and Virgil advance without comment to the ninth ditch.

Note

A contemporary historian, Giovanni Villani, called the eminent Ghibelline leader Guido "the wisest and subtlest man of war of his time in all Italy." In his earlier *Banquet,* Dante called Guido "our most noble Italian."

Canto 28

AWFUL SIGHTS AWAIT in this ninth pouch, full as it is of wounds and blood, worse than a collage of the goriest battlefields. Here sowers of scandal and discord are punished. By the time each sinner completes the circuit, his or her wounds are healed. But then a devil with a cruel sword reopens them.

Dante sees a figure split from the chin "down to where wind is broken." Hanging between his legs are the intestines in which excrement is made. Tearing at his open chest, this sinner identifies himself as Muhammad/Mahomet (A.D. 570–632). In front of him his son-in-law Ali goes weeping, cleft from chin to brow—as indeed he was when he was slain. (Recall those flaming mosques just inside the City of Dis, and Dante's view of Islam as a split-off from Christianity.)

"Who are you?" Muhammad asks Dante.

Virgil does the answering: "Guilt does not bring this man to torment. Rather it behooves me who am dead to lead him from circle to circle so that I may give him full experience." (Virgil's repeated reference to giving Dante *"esperienza piena"* makes of our poet a kind of post-Ulyssean Ulysses and a pre-Faustian Faust.)

Hearing these words, more than a hundred shades in the ditch stop to stare at Dante, "forgetting their pain in their marveling." Preparing to move on, Muhammad raises one foot, gives Dante a satirical message for a schismatic friar who still lives, and only then brings down his foot.

A shade who claims to recognize Dante and calls himself Pier da Medicina gives the poet a warning for the two best men of the town of Fano. A base tyrant plans treachery against them. The shade then points out the tongueless head of Curio, who near Rimini advised Caesar to cross the river Rubicon and precipitate a civil war. (Caesar himself, though, is among the good pagans!)

A handless shade calling himself Mosca confesses that his advice triggered the first polarizing clash in Florence between the Guelph and Ghibelline factions (1215). He advised an Easter Sunday ambush of the family of a man who had jilted a relative of his. When Dante recalls that this advice brought death to Mosca's own relatives, the bleeding sinner goes off like one maddened with sorrow. (Dante asked Ciacco the Pig about this Mosca in canto 6.)

Now for one of the supremely indelible scenes in the whole poem: Dante looks incredulously at a shade carrying his own head like a lantern. At the foot of the bridge, he stretches out his arm, lifts his severed head close to Dante's ear, and reveals that he is the Cistercian monk Bertran de Born (1140–1215). This French lord and knight was one of the earliest and most famous troubadours. Dante believed him guilty of urging Prince Henry of England (1155–83) to rebel against his father, Henry II. "Thus," concludes the shade, "is retribution observed in me."

Notes

Dante's word here for retribution is *contrapasso*. It is his only use of it in the poem. The word can be traced to Aristotle's *Nichomachean Ethics* (named after his son), where it means a return punishment. It doesn't necessarily mean a poetic reflection of the offense, though—as we have seen—Dante tries to make the punishment fit the crime.

In another book Dante praised Bertran as an example of generosity and a supreme poet of arms. As for young Henry, he was the son of Eleanor of Aquitaine and brother of Kings Richard the Lion-Hearted and John Lackland. (See the 1968 movie *The Lion in Winter,* with Katharine Hepburn [Eleanor] and Peter O'Toole [Henry II].)

Elaborating on a brief passage in the *Koran,* early Islamic tradition held that in a dream vision in A.D. 620 Muhammad was transported by the angel Gabriel to Jerusalem during a night journey from Mecca. From there they ascended through seven heavens to the divine throne—a journey with remarkable similarities to Dante's journey. (See Miguel Asin Palacios's *Islam and the Divine Comedy* [E.P. Dutton, 1926]. Once controversial, the argument of this book is now generally credited.) It should come as no surprise that *The Comedy* wasn't translated into Arabic until this century, and then only incompletely. The standard translations omit the reference to Muhammad.

Canto 29

STILL GAZING ON the sowers of division with eyes that want to remain and weep, Dante is reproached by Virgil, who notes that this valley is twenty-two miles around, the hour is late, and much more remains to be seen in the time allotted. Here the sage gives us our first specific mileage in Hell and the first indication that he and Dante are on a schedule. Defensively, Dante says he thought he saw the shade of a relative whose death has not yet been avenged. Virgil says that the relative had indeed been there, making threatening gestures at Dante, but had then departed. This Geri del Bello degli Alighieri was a first cousin of Dante's father and a troublemaker. After thirty years he was finally avenged by some nephews. In the poet's time, the law sanctioned private vendettas.

Arriving at the center of the last bridge, Dante is assailed by a fierce stench and hears diverse laments that make him hold his ears. The two travelers descend to the last bank and see a kind of giant hospital. In this dark ditch, spirits languish in diverse heaps and positions, unable to lift their bodies. This final pouch punishes falsifiers of various sorts.

Dante sees two scab-covered shades leaning on each other, scratching themselves furiously with their nails. "Are there any Latins among you?" Virgil asks.

"We are both Latins," answers one, weeping, "but who are you two?"

"I am showing Hell to this living man."

They and others within earshot turn to Dante, who, in the name of their lengthy remembrance on Earth, asks them who they are.

One says he was from Arezzo but was burned at the stake in Siena after he jestingly told the bishop's son (who was called "wealthy at the expense of the Crucifix") that he could teach him how to fly. "Then if there is any woman in Siena you like, you could fly into her house through the window." But this sinner is in Hell for the fraud of alchemy. Dante asks Virgil whether there was ever a people as vain as the Sienese, who are far worse than the French. (The French were famous for their vanity. One commentator, noting that Julius Caesar himself often remarked on this fact, itemized, "They wear a chain around their necks, a bracelet on the arm, pointed footwear and short clothes.")

The other sinner is the alchemist Capocchio, a Florentine also burned alive in Siena. He was a fellow student of Dante's and asks the poet to look closely at his scabby face and recall what an excellent ape of nature he was. He endorses Dante's comment on the Sienese, sarcastically exempting some of the worst of them, including members of the Spendthrift Club *("Brigata Spendericcia")*. These were a group of wealthy young men eager to get themselves talked about. They rented palaces and put on sumptuous banquets. Afterward, they chucked their gold and silver utensils out the window. Some of them ended up living on charity. One of them is in the gluttons' circle with Ciacco the Pig.

Canto 30

DANTE CITES TWO classical examples of madness but says that their insanity was less severe than what affected two pale and naked souls that now ran into view. Both were impersonators: one, Gianni Schicchi, sinks his teeth into the alchemist Capocchio and drags him away with his belly scraping the ground. The other is identified as the wicked Myrrha, who used impersonation to commit incest with her father. She was turned into a myrtle (myrrh) tree, from which was born Adonis, the beloved of Venus and male health clubs.

Looking about, Dante sees a shade swollen with dropsy and looking like a lute with legs. He names himself Master Adam, a counterfeiter who worked in Romena and was burned alive there. Though exceedingly parched, he would exchange a spring of water for the sight of his two former employers' being punished. Indeed, though this valley circles for eleven miles (another rare statistic), he would be willing to move an inch every century if he could see these disgusting people in pain. (That trip could take seventy million years, give or take a leap year here and there.)

Who, inquires Dante of Master Adam, are the two wretches lying close to your "frontier," steaming like wet hands in winter?

"They were lying here feverish when I arrived," explains Master Adam, "and haven't moved since." They are Potiphar's seductive and deceitful wife from the biblical story of Joseph in Egypt; and Sinon, the lying Greek (who tricked the Trojans into taking the wooden horse inside their city gates).

Displeased with how vaguely he has just been described, Sinon hits Adam in his drum of a belly. Adam responds with an arm in Sinon's face. Dante stands engrossed by the series of barbed insults the two shades exchange—until Virgil chastises him for the low desire to hear such a wrangle. After this rare burst of anger that leaves Dante speechless, Virgil finds in Dante's crimson embarrassment more than sufficient apology.

Note

In 1918 Giacomo Puccini produced an opera titled *Gianni Schicchi* that retells the traditional story. When a wealthy Florentine dies and is feared to have left his goods to outsiders, his frantic relatives hide his corpse under the bed and get Schicchi to impersonate the "dying" relative. Schicchi dictates a new will to an unsuspecting notary. But the greedy relatives must stand by helplessly as the wily Schicchi leaves some of the best things to himself.

Canto 31

FIRST WOUNDED AND THEN healed by Virgil's tongue, Dante follows him silently out of the tenth and final ditch of Hell's eighth circle. Next Dante hears a deafening horn and peers through the dimness to find its source. He thinks he sees many high towers in the distance and asks Virgil what city this is.

Taking him lovingly by the hand, Virgil explains that these are giants whose upper bodies rise above the part of the well in which they stand. Nearing the giants, Dante feels his misapprehension disappear as his apprehension grows. He sees horrible giants, indeed, still being threatened by Jove when thunder roars. Though nature does not repent of elephants and whales, she did well when she stopped producing the like! "For where the force of intellect is added to ill will and power, mankind can have no defense."

The nearest giant turns out to be Nimrod, the would-be builder of the Tower of Babel, who caused the breakdown of human language from one into many. Fittingly, he shouts incomprehensible words. Virgil calls him stupid and advises him to stick to his horn when he wants to express himself. Using several comparisons given by Dante, we can calculate that Nimrod was some seventy feet tall. The Vatican Gardens still contain the ancient, twelve-foot-high bronze pine cone to which our poet compares Nimrod's face.

Proceeding around the well, the two travelers encounter a larger, fiercer giant, Ephialtes, who is bound in chains for once having fought the gods. When the giant suddenly shakes himself, "I feared death more than ever." Dante voices the unmet wish to see Briareus the Hundred-Handed. Virgil says Briareus is bound and built like Ephialtes, though his look is even more ferocious. (Dante will, however, get to see a depiction of him in Purgatory's terrace of pride. You'd think such a giant would have been hard to miss from our poet's vantage point.)

The poets come at length to the giant Antaeus, who is unbound because he was born after the war that frightened the gods. He is induced to set them down in the pit of the well by Virgil's statement that his companion is alive and can give the giant what he longs for—the revival of his fame in the world. Antaeus hurriedly takes hold of Virgil, Virgil takes hold of Dante, and down they go—though, confesses our author, he would have preferred to descend by some alternate route.

Note

Antaeus was the son of the Earth, Gaea (or Ge, as in geography). In a famous fight, whenever Hercules threw him to the Earth, he rose stronger from his contact with his mother. Catching on, Hercules finally lifted him skyward and crushed him to death.

Canto 32

SET DOWN NOW in the very pit of Hell, and using a language that says *mamma* and *babbo* (mommy and daddy), Dante admits that he lacks the sour and hoarse rhymes needed to describe this dismal hole at the center of the physical universe. So, as he did at the top of Hell, he invokes the Muses who once made the lyre of Amphion so magnetic that stones left a nearby mountain and formed the Greek city of Thebes. Dante then addresses the misbegotten rabble he is about to depict, telling them they would have done better had they been sheep or goats.

The river that has been flowing downward through Hell is here called Cocytus (lamentation) and is now a frozen lake, thicker than Danube or Don ever was. Indeed, not even a mountain falling on this ice would crack it. The lake is composed of four concentric rings. The poets were deposited on the outmost ring, known as Caina. Here, traitors to kin are buried in ice up to their necks, which they can still bend. This ring is aptly named after the Cain who slew his brother, Abel.

A voice warns Dante to watch his step. Looking down, he sees shades holding their faces down and hears their teeth chattering. Near his feet are two sinners standing chest to chest, the hair of their heads intertwined. Tears rush from their faces and lock the two in a grotesque, icy kiss.

As these two butt heads against each other, a third (who has lost both ears from the cold) asks Dante why he studies them so. This third soul identifies his neighbors as two brothers, then mentions three other nearby traitors before giving his own name, Camicion de' Pazzi. The sinners here are worse than the Mordred who slew his uncle King Arthur (but not before the king had fatally pierced his nephew's chest so that a ray of sunshine pierced his shadow). De' Pazzi himself awaits another traitor who will make him seem innocent by comparison. Before moving on toward the center, Dante sees a thousand faces made doglike by the cold. Ever since then he shudders at the sight of frozen pools.

In the second ring he finds traitors to party or country, who are frozen up to their stiff necks. This place is called Antenora, after the Antenora who, according to medieval legend, betrayed his fellow Trojans to the Greeks. Homer merely says that Antenora thought Helen should be returned to the Greeks since she was seized by treachery. Walking here, Dante accidentally kicks a shade.

"If you want fame, tell me who you are," bids the poet, who adds that he will add his name to his notebook.

Since, like few others in Hell, the shade wants his fate kept secret, he refuses to identify himself—even after Dante seizes him by the scalp and yanks out several tufts of hair. Ratting on his confrere, a nearby traitor gives his name as Bocca. In revenge, this Bocca then reveals the name of the man who has just betrayed him, and those of four other neighbors as well.

One of these is the Tuscan Sassol, who murdered a relative for his inheritance. Found out, he was rolled through the streets of Florence in a cask of nails and then beheaded. A second is the Abbot Beccheria, papal legate to Florence, who was beheaded by Florentine Guelphs for supposedly conspiring with Ghibellines there. Another is Ganelon, who betrayed to the Saracens (or Basques) his stepson Roland, Charlemagne's nephew.

In this ring Dante finally sees two shades frozen in one hole, the teeth of the one gnawing on the neck of the other. Promising that he will report his grievance if it appears just, Dante asks the shade who gnaws to tell him why he bears such hatred against the other.

Note

Composed around 1100, *La Chanson de Roland (The Song of Roland/ Orlando)* is the oldest, best, and most famous of the medieval chansons, epic poems celebrating heroes and heroic deeds. It tells how Charlemagne was returning from a 778 invasion of Spain with his nephew Roland in command of the rear guard. The traitor Ganelon advised the enemy to attack. Roland was too proud to summon help with his horn until it was too late. He died, the last of all, as he learned that his uncle was on his way. In the previous canto, Dante compares Nimrod's horn with Roland's.

Canto 33

THE ENRAGED SINNER identifies himself as Count Ugolino of Pisa. Both he and his hated partner were guilty of political betrayals. In the longest single speech in the *Inferno,* the count spends seventy-two lines telling how Archbishop Ruggieri, on whom he gnaws, locked him and his four children in a tower (this time the infamous Tower of Pisa) and after six months let them starve to death over an eight-day period. (Actually, they were two sons and two grandsons and older than the story suggests.) Wiping his feasting mouth on the archiepiscopal head, Ugolino begins:

> I was seized, trusting in him....I heard my children weeping in their sleep and asking for bread....I heard the door of the horrible tower being nailed shut....I bit my hands from grief; but, thinking I did so from hunger, one of my children said: "Father, it will be much less painful if you eat of us. You clothed us with this poor flesh; may you now take it from us."...After the fourth day, Gaddo fell at my feet: "Father, why don't you help me?"...I saw them fall, one by one...already blind, I began to crawl over each of them...for two days after they were all dead, I kept calling for them...finally, fasting did more than grief had done.

(The idea that this last phrase implies cannibalism is "hardly worth a serious rebuttal," according to scholar Charles Singleton. For a rebuttal of *that* view, see John Freccero's *Dante: The Poetics of Conversion.*)

As the count returns to his gnawing, Dante calls down a curse on the shameful Pisans, harshly wishing for each a death by drowning.

The travelers move on to the third ring of ice, Tolomea, where those who betrayed guests are punished. (As the story is told in the first book of Maccabees [16:11–17], Tolomy/Ptolemy was a captain of Jericho who slew the Jewish high priest and his sons while they were attending a banquet he gave.) These sinners are frozen in ice, with their faces thrown back. "Weeping there prevents them from weeping" since their tears freeze. At this point, Dante feels a blast of wind, which Virgil says will soon explain itself.

Meantime, one of the damned begs that the frozen tears be removed from his eyes. "Tell me who you are," Dante replies, "and may I go to the bottom of the ice if I don't oblige you!" The pleader says he is Friar Alberigo (a Jovial Friar), who had arranged that a close relative and his son be murdered at a reconciliation banquet when he called for the fruit. The senior relative had slapped the friar during an argument. The assassins had hidden behind a tapestry with their knives.

This shade reveals a unique aspect of this part of Hell: souls often fall here before the death of their bodies, which a demon then takes over. Such was the case with this very friar and with Branca d'Oria, who is "wintering" just behind him. Branca treacherously murdered his father-in-law, Michel Zanche, whom we learned was among the grafters in canto 22. Since to be rude to such a friar is fitting, Dante does not relieve the sinner's eyes. He concludes the canto with an attack on d'Oria's fellow citizens of Genoa, who are estranged from all good behavior and full of every corruption. They should be driven from the Earth.

Notes

Dante deems it just that traitors be betrayed. At the same time, he technically keeps his word to the friar, since he is indeed going to the bottom of the ice in the next canto.

We have met three notable "doublets" in Hell: Francesca and Paolo, Ulysses and Diomedes, Ugolino and Ruggieri. In each case only one partner speaks. But the deeper Dante descends into Hell, the worse he finds the relationships: Francesca lovingly speaks for her partner; Ulysses ignores his; Ugolino gnaws on his.

Canto 34

THIS FINAL INFERNAL CANTO starts as though with a trumpet blast. Unexpectedly, the pagan Virgil quotes the opening of a Latin processional hymn, "*Vexilla Regis.*" It dates to A.D. 569, when it was composed to celebrate the arrival in Poitiers, France, of a supposed fragment of the true cross. With its triumphant opening, "The banners of the king come forth; the mystery of the cross shines out," it later became a hymn for Passiontide. Mockingly, Virgil changes the words to "The banners come forth of the king of Hell." In this immobilizing tundra, of course, nothing can come forth.

The first half of this canto brings the two poets to Judecca, the fourth and innermost ring of the frozen lake Cocytus, and to the full vision of Satan himself. Thus will end their twenty-four-hour journey through Hell—Friday night to Saturday night. Then Virgil will declare: "Now it is time to go, for we have seen everything." (Another Faustian touch, this time in the very presence of Mephistopheles.)

In the second half, as the travelers climb down Satan's shaggy shank (we must assume a little space between the tufts and the imprisoning ice) and pass the center of gravity, they will begin their twenty-four-hour journey to the other side of the Earth. Thanks to a twelve-hour time lag, they will actually exit from the underworld at sunrise on Easter Sunday. This last canto thus covers more time than any other of its predecessors.

The innermost ring punishes souls who have treacherously betrayed their rightful lords and benefactors, both temporal or spiritual. Dante sees these traitors lying in various postures beneath the ice. None of them are named—as was the case with the morally neutral at the very top of Hell, the abusers of wealth, and the usurers. Dante, who, of course, cannot converse with them, remains totally silent during this last scene in Hell itself. He will be similarly wordless when he glimpses Absolute Goodness in the very last canto of the poem.

When he first entered this ninth circle, he saw some giant and distant figure resembling a windmill covered with mist. To protect himself from the blasts of frigid wind proceeding from that figure, he has been walking behind Virgil.

Now, Virgil stops and steps aside: "Behold Dis! Here you must arm yourself with courage." Frozen (appropriately) with dread, Dante feels neither dead nor alive as he sees at the very core of the Earth Satan/Lucifer/Beelzebub, this "emperor of the dolorous realm." Rejecting the true God, Satan wanted to be a god, a center of attention. Now all the weight of the sin-ridden world arrows down on him at the physical center of the universe.

From midbreast down, this giant is fixed in ice. He stands some 1,250 feet tall—about the height of the Empire State Building.

> If he were once as fair *(bel)* as he now is foul *(bruto)*,
>   and still raised his brow against His maker,
>   well indeed must every sorrow flow from him!

Like a perversion of the Holy Trinity, this unholy monster has three faces: one fiery red, one yellow-white, one black. Thus are God's qualities of love, power, and wisdom negatively aped by hatred, impotence, and madness.

In each mouth Satan, the supreme betrayer, chomps on one of his three most loyal servants. In the center is Judas Iscariot, who betrayed Christ for money. His head is inside Satan's mouth, and his legs kick—a posture recalling that of the simoniacs in the eighth circle. It is Judas for whom this final ring is named (Judecca).

Heads hanging down, Brutus and Cassius dangle from the other mouths, left and right. In Dante's view these two Romans betrayed the divinely willed Roman Empire by murdering its founder, Julius Caesar.

Under each of Satan's heads flap two enormous wings, batlike and featherless. From their flapping comes the blasts that keep Cocytus frozen and lock Satan in more tightly the more furiously he tries to escape. From his six eyes he weeps in frustration, while tears and bloody foam drip over his chins. (Unlike Milton's, Dante's Satan has no grandeur and speaks no words.)

Virgil now carries Dante down Satan's side and gives him his first physical contact with a minister of Hell. Having passed the center of gravity, Virgil reverses his direction—to Dante's confusion, and perhaps the reader's.

Thereafter, they follow a cavern stream that will lead them once again to the sight of the heavens. En route, Virgil explains that when Satan fell from Heaven he hit the Earth exactly opposite Jerusalem, whence salvation would come.

As though the land there recoiled from the approach of Satan, this "southern hemisphere" is now almost entirely water. The one exception is a high mountain that was "perhaps" formed from the land within the bowels of the Earth, which also recoiled from the fallen angel and thereby provided him with his tomb.

For all eternity that sunless tomb will remain at the farthest remove from the stars of Heaven—those blazing emblems of divinity with whose name, "*stelle*," Dante ends his *Inferno* and the other two sections of *The Divine Comedy*. Thus the famous concluding line of the *Inferno* reads:

> ...and thence we came forth, gaining again the sight of the stars.
> (*...e quindi uscimmo a riveder le stelle.*)

Notes

The twentieth volume of *The New Grove Dictionary of Music and Musicians* (1980) ends wittily with this final line of the *Inferno*.

In opposition to the cliché that for the medieval soul the physical universe was man-centered, Dante shows it as Satan-centered. In any case, the medieval world was spiritually God-centered.

Unfortunately, Judecca was also a common name in Dante's time for Jewish ghettos (*borghetto*—"little city"?). The words *Jew, Judas,* and *Judea* derive from the name *Judah,* the "praised" son of Jacob and the father of the most dominant and enduring of the twelve tribes of Israel. Ironically, Muhammad (the world's most popular name) also means "praised," just as the Jewish menorah and the Islamic minaret both pertain to light.

You have to wonder about the diameter of Dante's earth if, with two assists, he could walk to its center in 24 hours, and then climb up to the other side in another 24 hours.

The *Inferno* ends on Easter Sunday morning as Dante arrives at the base of the mount of purgatory. You might have expected him to arrive in Paradise on Easter, the feast of Christ's Resurrection. But once a departed soul reaches purgatory, it has already been securely saved by the redeeming events of Good Friday and Easter Sunday.

Part 2

Purgatorio

It is therefore a holy and wholesome thought to
pray for the dead, that they may be loosed from sins.

—2 Machabees 12:46

PURGATORY IS A PLACE for purging—a word derived from the Latin words *purus* and *agere:* "to make pure." In Catholic and some Orthodox thinking, Purgatory provides a merciful chance for a deceased person to become cleansed from serious sins that have been repented of but not atoned for. Thus purged, the soul can enter pure into God's pure presence.

A detailed spelling-out of this concept was slow to develop in Christian thought. From the earliest times Christians prayed for their dead, a practice that would have been pointless if the dead were considered to be beyond the need for or possibility of earthly help.

According to the second book of Maccabees (which contains the first known use of the word "Judaism" and which the early Christians revered as biblical but Jewish and Protestant tradition does not), the pre-Christian Jewish hero Judas Maccabaeus "made atonement for the dead that they might be freed from their sins" (12:43). Jesus himself spoke of a kind of sin that would not be forgiven "either in this world or in the world to come" (Matthew 12:3)—as though forgiveness of some sort was possible in the afterworld.

In Dante's "high fantasy," Purgatory is a towering mountain-island in the Earth's otherwise landless southern hemisphere. "Perhaps" the land mass rose to pull away from Lucifer as he fell from Heaven to the core of the Earth. The "little" island has a threefold division. On its summit is the Forest of Eden. Below it, in Purgatory proper, there are seven circling terraces (ledges/cornices/stories) where the seven capital sins are purged away.

Even lower is Prepurgatory. Here, repentant sinners are made to wait for the start of their purgation because they were excommunicated by the Church, or were lazy about their spiritual health, or died suddenly and had not enough time to do penance for their sins, or were so busy ruling earthly kingdoms that they neglected the kingdom of God that was within them.

In every case, a soul is in Purgatory because it died in God's forgiving grace, no matter how heinous were its sins. Whereas in Hell the focus of punishment is the fruits of sin (evil acts), in Purgatory the focus is the inborn roots of sin (evil tendencies). Christian tradition, especially through the writings of Pope Saint Gregory the Great (590–604), had itemized these roots as the seven capital ("headwater") sins, also called deadly or cardinal sins. Dante and these sins were featured in the 1995 movie *Seven*.

After concluding the *Inferno,* Dante had an artistic problem: he would risk boredom if he followed the same classification of sins he used in Hell. That classification—reducing all sins to varieties of incontinence, violence, and fraud—was pre-Christian in origin. He solved the problem by using a Christian catalog.

In Hell there is no sin of pride as such; in Purgatory it is punished as such and can be seen as the prime root of all sins and sinful tendencies. But avarice and anger and gluttony are punished as such in both places. So too is lust, though its punishing location is interestingly at the top of Hell and at the top of Purgatory. Perhaps because that sin is often entwined with love, it is farthest from Satan in Hell proper and closest to God in Purgatory. In this second canticle Dante seems most personally involved with the sins of pride, anger, and lust—as we might have guessed about a lofty, indignant, and passionate poet.

Although its punishments can seem fearsome, the feel of this second canticle is notably different from that of the first. Hell is always night. Purgatory is night and day, though normally purification requires the presence of the energizing Sun. (The slothful, working a double shift, are an exception.) Moreover, "time is precious in this realm *(il tempo è caro in questo regno)*" (24:91), whereas time is pointless and discontinuous in Hell, and activities there are mindlessly repetitive.

Penitents in Purgatory proper are generally courteous though positively eager to get on with their work. Replacing Hell's staff of monsters and demons are Purgatory's friendly but businesslike angels. Like the entrance gate to Purgatory proper, every terrace has its guardian angel, who shows Dante and Virgil the stairway to the level above and erases one of the scars of sin from Dante's brow. These have taken the form of the letter *P* (*peccatum:* "sin") marked seven times across his forehead.

The symmetry in Purgatory proper is elaborate: each of the seven terraces is linked with one of Christ's beatitudes (Matthew 5:3–11/Luke 3:20–23). Each category of penitents is provided with inspiring examples of the virtue they neglected, and horrible examples of the vice they indulged. Christ's mother is always the first example of virtue. But pre-Christian examples, both biblical and otherwise, are always included.

There is plenty of Latin hymn-singing in Purgatory, and the penitents often seem like monks in a monastery chanting the daily round of the Church's official prayer life.

Dante devotes nine cantos to Prepurgatory; twice nine to Purgatory proper; and six to the Forest of Eden at the summit. This second canticle of *The Comedy* runs to 4,755 lines—35 more than its predecessor.

In his book *The Birth of Purgatory* (University of Chicago Press, 1984), Jacques Le Goff wrote, "*Il Purgatorio* is the sublime product of a lengthy gestation. It is also the noblest representation of Purgatory ever conceived by the mind of man, an enduring selection from among the possible and at times competing images whose choice the Church...left to the sensibility and imagination of individual Christians" (p. 334).

Outline of the *Purgatorio*

EASTER SUNDAY, April 10, to Easter Wednesday, April 13, A.D. 1300

Three Divisions:
- Cantos 1 through 9: Prepurgatory (waiting)
- Cantos 10 through 27: Seven-Story Mountain (purgation)
- Cantos 28 through 33: Forest of Eden (final grooming)

Canto

1. Easter Morning: arrival at island of Purgatory; Cato the guardian
2. Angel boatman brings the elect ashore
3. To foot of the mountain—Prepurgatory: the first group of late repentants: the excommunicated
4. First lower ledge: the second group of late repentants: the spiritually lazy
5. Second lower ledge: the third group of late repentants: those who met sudden, violent deaths
6. Second lower ledge *(continued)*: meeting with Sordello
7. With Sordello to the Valley of the Negligent Princes: the fourth group of late repentants
8. Nightfall Easter Sunday; the serpent repelled by two angels of hope; Nino
9. First prophetic dream; Easter Monday; to Saint Peter's Gate; three steps; guarding angel; seven *P*s on Dante's brow
10. *First (upper) Ledge* (story/terrace): Pride

11. *First Ledge (continued):* Aldobrandesco, Oderisi, Provenzan
12. *First Ledge (continued)*
13. *Second Ledge:* Envy: Sapia
14. *Second Ledge (continued):* Guido del Duca; Rinier da Calboli
15. *Third Ledge:* Anger
16. *Third Ledge (continued):* Marco the Lombard
17. *Fourth Ledge:* Sloth: outline of Purgatory
18. *Fourth Ledge (continued):* Abbot of San Zeno
19. *Fifth Ledge:* Avarice and Wastefulness: second prophetic dream; Easter Tuesday; Pope Adrian V
20. *Fifth Ledge (continued):* Hugh Capet
21. *Fifth Ledge (continued):* the poet Statius
22. *Sixth Ledge:* Gluttony: Statius
23. *Sixth Ledge (continued):* poet friend Forese Donati
24. *Sixth Ledge (continued):* poet Bonagiunta da Lucca
25. *Seventh Ledge:* Lust: Statius on body-soul relationship
26. *Seventh Ledge (continued):* poet Guido Guinizelli; poet Arnaut Daniel
27. *Seventh Ledge (continued):* Dante goes through fire; third prophetic dream
28. Easter Wednesday: *Forest of Eden:* Matilda
29. *Forest of Eden (continued):* Pageant of Revelation: the central chariot; the griffin
30. *Forest of Eden (continued):* goodbye to Virgil; hello to Beatrice (veiled)
31. *Forest of Eden (continued):* Dante is washed in Lethe; he approaches Beatrice (unveiled)
32. *Forest of Eden (continued):* Pageant of Church History: Jesus speaks as griffin; Church as a harlot
33. *Forest of Eden (continued):* Dante and Statius washed in Eunoe—their purgation is complete

Canto I

AT THE VERY START Dante tells us he will now sing of a second realm, where the human spirit is cleansed and grows fit to rise to Heaven. As he did at the top and bottom of Hell, the poet invokes the Muses, but this time he especially calls on Calliope, the Muse of epic poetry. The mythical King Pierus named his nine daughters after the Muses, whom they challenged to a musical contest. The daughters lost and were changed into magpies. Dante seeks a happier transformation.

Fresh from the Stygian darkness, Dante rejoices in the color of the dawning sky. The day is Easter Sunday, April 10, 1300. The love planet Venus glows in the east, along with four bright stars once seen by Adam and Eve but now unknown to the human race exiled in the northern hemisphere. These four may represent the cardinal virtues: prudence, justice, fortitude, and temperance—qualities opposed to the cardinal sins, which will be rooted out in this realm.

Suddenly, Dante notices a solitary old man standing near him. His long beard is streaked with white, his face bright from the four stars. "Who are you who have fled from the eternal prison—are the laws of the abyss thus broken?" Both Virgil and Dante bend their knees and their heads. Virgil explains that a heavenly lady begged him to help this man, whose folly had led him close to ultimate disaster. "I have shown him all the wicked people and now propose to reveal those spirits who are purging themselves under your charge. For he is seeking freedom, which is precious—as you well know."

Virgil knows that this is the Roman philosopher Cato the Younger (95–46 B.C.), who took his own life rather than survive the end of civil freedom that presumably was going to occur under a victorious Caesar. Virgil says he is from the circle of Hell where Cato's wife Marcia seems still to be longing for him—the husband who allowed her to marry his best friend and then forgivingly received her back as wife after the friend's death. She wanted her tombstone to identify her as Cato's wife. "For love of her, let us traverse your seven kingdoms."

Cato (identified here only by inference) replies that Marcia can no longer motivate him since he has left Hell(!)—presumably from Virgil's own first circle. But to honor a celestial lady (Beatrice), he gladly obliges. Take your charge, he says, to the edge of this little island, gird him with a slender reed (Virgil used Dante's belt ["cord"] to summon Geryon in canto 16 of the *Inferno*), and cleanse from his face the tears and other stains of Hell. With these words, Cato disappears.

The travelers walk down to the shore and fulfill Cato's directives. Virgil spreads his hands gently over the dewy grass and then cleans Dante's face.

When Virgil next plucks out a lowly stem, Dante (who is wordless in this canto) is amazed to see it instantly replaced. Thus is portrayed the resurgent strength of humility, a quality requisite in anyone seeking purification.

Notes

Dante sleuths have figured out that on Easter 1300, Venus was an evening star. So, against tradition, they have argued that the date should be 1301, when it was a morning star. Later, some other sleuths discovered that the almanac that Dante was likely to have used mistakenly listed Venus as a morning star on Easter 1300. *Caveat emptor!*

Cato "the glorious" was a great favorite of our poet. Elsewhere he wrote, "O most hallowed breast of Cato, who shall presume to speak of you?...What earthly man is so worthy to signify God as Cato?" *(The Banquet).*

It is downright flabbergasting that Dante seems to find no problem in the fact that the guardian of the gateway to salvation was an enemy of Caesar (like Brutus and Cassius), a suicide, and once a resident of Limbo. ("Are the laws of the abyss thus broken?") Perhaps our poet regarded suicide as a sin only for Christians, since he met only Christians in the circle of the suicides. Will Cato eventually climb this mountain himself and become a pagan in Paradise? (Virgil says that Cato's body will shine bright on the great day.) Cato would not be the first to do so (as Dante will discover, to his happy surprise).

Canto 2

THE SUN IS NOW RISING as Dante and Virgil linger near the seashore. Suddenly, a white light races toward them from across the sea. It is an angel whose gleaming wings speed to the shore a slender vessel bearing "more than a hundred" spirits. They are singing Psalm 113/114 about Israel's escape from Egyptian slavery.

Virgil orders Dante to fold his hands and kneel before this heavenly minister, who makes the sign of the cross and impels his passengers to leap out onto the beach. Then he leaves as rapidly as he has come. The blessed crowd asks the two poets to show them the way up the mountain.

"We are pilgrims just as you are," Virgil responds. By now the amazed group notices that Dante is breathing. One of them steps forward to hug Dante, who keeps trying to return the embrace but finds his arms passing through the spirit. Recognizing his old friend Casella, who set some of Dante's poems to music, our poet begs him to tarry awhile and speak. Saying, "Just as I loved you in my mortal body, so I love you freed from it," Casella consents, but wonders what his living friend is doing here.

"I am making this journey so that I can return here another time," Dante responds. Then he inquires why his friend, who had died three months earlier, is just now arriving here. Casella explains that the answer involves the free but just choice of the angel who brings to this shore all the saved souls who gather after death at the point where Rome's Tiber meets the sea.

"If you can," pleads Dante, "sing me a love song as you did on Earth and console my weary spirit." As all listen attentively, the amiable Casella decides to begin singing one of Dante's own ninety-line poems: "Love that converses with me in my mind"—one of the three canzones he treats at length in *The Banquet*. (Thus, a few centuries later, will Mozart playfully quote in his opera *Don Giovanni* one of his own earlier melodies.) Dante uses autocitation twice more in the poem: see *Purgatorio* 24 and *Paradiso* 8.

In the middle of the song Cato reappears, chastises the dallying spirits, and bids them "run to the mountain and get rid of the slough [dead outer tissue] that keeps you from seeing God." With that the recital abruptly ends. Everybody scatters toward the slopes.

Note

From Psalm 9 through Psalm 147, the numbers of the individual psalms in various translations differ by one, depending on whether the translation derives from the Hebrew original or from the early Greek translation known as the Septuagint—"70" or LXX. This first of all biblical translations, by "70" Jewish scholars, was completed around 250 B.C. for Greek-speaking Jews in Alexandria, Egypt.

The trouble started when this translation made a single psalm out of the Hebrew Psalms 9 and 10. The discrepancy was healed at the last minute when LXX makes two psalms out of the Hebrew Psalm 147. English Protestant translations (like the famous King James Bible) tend to follow the Hebrew numbering; Catholic ones, the LXX. Hence, "The Lord is my shepherd" is Psalm 23 for Protestants, 22 for Catholics, as for Dante, who used the Latin Vulgate translation (390–405) made from the LXX by Saint Jerome. The Catholic number is always the lower one if there are two number cited, as in 50/51. More recent Catholic translations are reverting to the Hebrew/King James numbering.

Canto 3

HEADING TOWARD the mountain with the embarrassed Virgil and trying to ease his master's self-reproach, Dante panics when he sees his own shadow on the ground but not Virgil's. For a moment he thinks he has lost his guide.

Virgil reminds his protégé that a living body follows laws different from those affecting a disembodied spirit. In any case, the ultimate laws of reality are beyond the probing of reason. Otherwise, geniuses such as Plato and Aristotle would not be in Limbo, nor would there have been need for Mary of Nazareth to give birth. This is the first explicit use in the poem of the name of Christ's mother, whose concern for Dante triggered the whole action of the poem.

The travelers finally arrive at the foot of the mount—the world's highest—which they find hopelessly steep. Virgil ponders their problem, while Dante looks off to the left and sees a crowd moving slowly toward them. Virgil asks them where the mountain is sloped enough to permit climbing. The spirits are at first startled to see Dante's shadow but are reassured by Virgil. Then they instruct the poets to walk ahead of them.

One of the shades asks Dante whether he recognizes him. The poet says no. He reveals that he is Manfred (1232?–66), the bastard son of Emperor Frederick II. The year after Dante's birth, in the last great imperial battle against the papacy in thirteenth-century Italy (Benevento, 1266), Manfred was gashed by two mortal blows. He was first buried beneath a pile of stones, but Pope Clement IV ordered the local bishop to disinter him and scatter his bones outside papal territory.

In this ritual punishment of the excommunicated, lighted tapers were turned upside down and quenched. But the ban of the clergy cannot exclude from Heaven a soul that dies repentant. "Horrible were my sins, but infinite Goodness has arms so wide that It embraces all who turn to It....In tears I consigned myself to Him who freely pardons." (Manfred was accused of having murdered his father, his brother Conrad, and two nephews.)

Nevertheless, Manfred must wait below the mountain for a period thirty times the duration of his excommunication. Only the prayers of the living can shorten that delay. Hence Manfred wants Dante to tell his daughter of her father's need.

Notes

Dante's Manfred is unrelated to the subject of Lord Byron's verse play of that name, which inspired Tchaikovsky's *Manfred Symphony.*

Line 132's "with tapers quenched *(a lume spento)*" was the title of the first book of poems (1908) by Ezra Pound, who later wrote cantos of his own. This taper-quenching is part of the phrase "bell, book, and candle." For the excommunicated person the death bell would also be tolled and the book of the Scriptures shut.

Canto 4

TIME PASSES SWIFTLY as Dante walks along listening to Manfred. Suddenly the shades shout, "Here is what you asked for." They point to a steep pathway up the mount. Dante realizes that for this journey a man has to fly with swift wings and the plumes of immense desire. Using hands as well as feet, Dante continues behind Virgil. He grows weary and nearly stops in his tracks before they pause and sit on a ledge. "Then both of us sat down facing the way from which we had climbed, since looking back usually heartens a climber."

While the Florentine catches his breath, Virgil explains the unusual path taken by the Sun in the southern hemisphere. He also consoles Dante by promising that the going gets easier the higher you climb this mountain. "At the end of this road, there expect to rest from your weariness."

At this point a voice suggests, "Perhaps first you will have need of sitting down." Puzzled, the poets walk to a large boulder nearby and discover shades languidly resting behind it. One shade sits with his arms around his knees and his head drooping. He tilts his head and looks at the visitors, casting his glance along his thigh. "Go on ahead, then, if you're so vigorous."

Dante recognizes him as the notoriously lazy Florentine Belacqua. The poet asks why he is seated here. "Brother, what's the use of going up?" He must wait here for as long as he postponed his "good sighs" on Earth. Echoing Manfred, he declares that only the prayers of good souls on Earth can shorten his waiting period.

By now the impatient Virgil has begun his upward trek again. "Come, now," he says, "it's already noon." Six hours have passed since their arrival.

Canto 5

AS DANTE FOLLOWS his maestro, another shade notices the marvel of the Florentine's shadow. Dante slows down to stare at the spirit who is staring at him. Virgil rebukes him for caring too much about what others think and weakening his resolve by too many spin-off considerations. "I'm coming," says Dante, with a blush.

Now they encounter another group coming toward them and singing from Psalm 50/51: "*Miserere* ([God] have mercy [on me...])." These too are amazed by Dante's shadow. Told that Dante is still alive, they press about him, hoping he can recognize some and bring back news about them. They acknowledge that they all met violent deaths and were sinners until their last hour. Before beginning their purification, they must now wait for as long a time as they lived. Dante promises to help them "in the name of that peace that I am made to seek from world to world."

Three shades speak up. The first, Jacopo del Cassero of Fano, tells his story and begs prayers in twenty-one lines. The second, Buonconte da Montefeltro, tells his story in thirty-eight lines. No one on Earth, alas, has a care for him. At the moment of death, however, he tearfully called upon the name of Mary. For that one little tear *("per una lagrimetta")* the devil was deprived of his soul but works to profane his scattered bones. (In Gounod's opera, Faust too was snatched from a devil at the last minute. It was this Buonconte's father, Guido, who had just the opposite deathbed experience! See *Inferno* 27.)

Finally, in a mere six lines a gracious shade named La Pia asks Dante a favor in beguiling words: "When you have returned to Earth and have rested up from your long journey, remember me, La Pia." Murdered by her husband shortly after their marriage, this Sienese woman is one of only two purgatorial women who address Dante before he reaches the top. Only women will speak to him after he arrives at the summit.

Canto 6

ONLY BY PROMISING to solicit prayers for them on Earth can Dante free himself from these shades who died violent deaths. They are like the companions of a winner at dice, who crowd around asking to share in the winnings. Once again alone with his mentor, Dante delicately asks him about words he wrote in his *Aeneid* ("cease hoping to deflect by prayer the fates decreed by the gods" [VI:37]). Did Dante misread this advice against prayer, or are the shades wrong to seek the help of prayer?

Virgil says his meaning was plain, but he was referring to prayers rising from hearts that were not united to God. In any case, Dante should ask such questions of Beatrice, whom he will see smiling and happy at the top of this mountain. At this first mention of his beloved in the *Purgatorio*, Dante's eagerness to journey upward is intensified.

Virgil points out, however, that they are not free to journey entirely as they wish. Then he notices a shade seated all alone and watching them like a lion at rest. (Dante could have seen lions in the zoo of Florence in his day.) Virgil is sure "he will tell us the quickest way up"—goodwill is presumed in this world. When Virgil tells the shade he is from Mantua, he leaps up and identifies himself joyfully as the poet Sordello, another Mantuan. The two then embrace ardently. (Curiously, on this occasion shades are able to hug.)

The sight of two Italians showing affection leads the Florentine to a "digression" filling up the remainder of the canto and attacking three targets: Italy, full of fratricidal warriors; Emperor Albert of Austria, who should have come down to tame Italy, the garden of his empire; and Florence, which he condemns with heavy sarcasm.

In the course of this seventy-five–line apostrophe, the poet mentions the Montecchi and Cappelletti—the feuding Montagues and Capulets of *Romeo and Juliet* fame. He curiously addresses Jesus as "the supreme

Jove," whose eyes seem to overlook Italy's needs. Perhaps such evils will lead to unforeseeable good. Finally, in excoriating Florence's economic decadence, he notes that "the thread you spin in October does not last beyond the middle of November." Thus a medieval example of built-in obsolescence.

Note

Writing in the Provençal language, Sordello (1200?–69?) was the most famous Italian troubadour. Robert Browning composed a poem about him in 1840.

Canto 7

AFTER REPEATED EMBRACES, Sordello asks his fellow Mantuan his name. "I am Virgil," comes the astonishing answer, never given in Hell. Overcome, Sordello falls to his knees and hugs the knees of the great poet: "O glory of the Latins, eternal honor of my native city, what merit or what grace shows you to me?"

Without mentioning Dante, Virgil replies that he is on a divine mission away from the sad circle, shared with unbaptized infants, where he dwells with those who lacked vice but also the virtues of faith, hope, and charity. Tell us, continues the dutiful guide, how can we most quickly gain the true gate of Purgatory? (Line thirty-nine gives us the first of only two appearances of the word *purgatorio* in the poem.)

Sordello offers to be their guide but warns that the power to advance in this realm disappears with the setting of the Sun. In the dark a shade may wander down but not up. Since this Easter day is now declining into night, Sordello suggests that they seek a resting place nearby. He takes them to a hollow filled with gloriously colored flowers and rare fragrances.

Here Dante sees many souls seated on the ground and singing the "*Salve, Regina* (Hail, O Queen)," the traditional sunset hymn of the Church. Through the clear air Sordello points out eight rulers, all of whom died in Dante's youth—as did Sordello himself. Some of these were once mutual enemies. But all of these "negligent" princes neglected their own souls on Earth because they were overly preoccupied with royal cares. Now, along with the excommunicated, the lazy, and the violently killed, they must wait to begin their purification. Almost humorously Dante describes three of the kings in terms of their noses: one small, one virile, and one big. The nose is usually prominent in Dante's portraits and busts; Boccaccio, who talked with people who knew him, claimed that his nose was aquiline.

Canto 8

It was now the hour that turns homeward the longing of those at sea, and melts their hearts on the day when they have bade farewell to sweet friends, the hour that pierces with love the man fresh on a journey if he hears from afar a bell that seems to mourn the dying day.

AS EASTER SUNDAY SUNSET arrives at this resting place near the top of Prepurgatory, one soul rises and devoutly leads the rest in a final Vesper hymn, "*Te lucis ante terminum* (Thee, before the end of the light, [we pray…]." This prayer asks for help against bad dreams and other phantoms of the night—evils of the unconscious to which even shades safely lodged on this mountain are apparently still subject.

In response to this prayer, two angels dressed in the green of hope and bearing blunted swords—full weaponry is not needed on this occasion—descend and station themselves on either side of the valley. Before long a serpent will try to enter the valley, but the sound of the green wings cleaving the air will frighten it away.

Before growing drowsy, our poet gets to converse with two rulers, one a Guelph, the other a Ghibelline. The first is Judge Nino Visconti (died 1296), whom Dante hails as an old friend. Nino has a daughter, Giovanna, whom he asks Dante to tell of her father's need for prayers. Nino's widow has remarried and seems to have forgotten him. "From her it is easy to see how briefly love's fire endures in a woman if sight and touch do not often rekindle it." (Thus an early version of Verdi's "*La donna e mobile* [Women are fickle]").

Called over by Nino to see the living Dante, Currado Malaspina (died *circa* 1294) asks for news of the coast of Tuscany, "for there I once was great." Dante has not yet visited that area, but he says everybody knows that with unique honor the Malaspinas maintain the glory of the purse (generosity) and of the sword. Pleased, Currado predicts that within seven years the poet himself will experience the needed hospitality of his family, so that "this courteous opinion [about my family] shall be fixed within your brain by stronger nails than men's words."

Notes

In 1306 Currado's brother Franceshino hosted the exiled Dante.

Longfellow produced the first complete American translation of *The Comedy* in 1867. The *Inferno* was not translated into English until 1782, nor the whole *Comedy* until 1806—by an Irish Protestant pastor at that! The opening verses of this canto were a favorite of the early English partial translators and influenced poets like Thomas Gray (1716–61) and Lord Byron (1788–1824). Gray's churchyard elegy begins, "The curfew tolls the knell of parting day." In his *Don Juan* (3:108 ff.), Byron wrote:

> Soft hour! which wakes the wish and melts the heart
> Of those who sail the seas, on the first day
> When they from their sweet friends are torn apart;
> Or fills with love the pilgrim on his way
> As the far bell of vespers makes him start,
> Seeming to weep the dying day's decay.
> Is this a fancy which our reason scorns?
> Ah! surely nothing dies but something mourns.

Canto 9

THIS TRANSITIONAL CANTO will take our two poets from the first to the second of the three divisions of this mount "that cures by being climbed."

About 9 P.M. on Easter Sunday, as the Moon is rising against the constellation Scorpio, Dante falls asleep on the grass in the presence of his companions. He concludes each of his three nights of sleep in Purgatory with a dream that he considers prophetic. When he wakes on Easter Monday, he recalls dreaming that a golden eagle seized him and lifted him through the sphere of fire that covers the Earth.

The scorching in the dream felt so real that it awakened Dante. He finds himself alone with Virgil at the top of Prepurgatory. It is already 8 A.M., and Virgil tells him that his patron, Saint Lucy, transported him here while he slept. Sordello stayed behind; we won't hear of him again.

The two proceed to an entrance that Lucy pointed out. Seated on the diamond threshold is a guardian with gleaming face and sword. The angel challenges the two unescorted travelers but yields when Virgil tells of Lucy. Three steps lead up to the gate: the first is of smooth white marble, so clear that Dante can see his face in it; the second, of the darkest purple, is cracked and scorched; the third is red as spurting blood.

Obeying Virgil and thrice striking his breast, Dante throws himself at the angel's feet and begs him to unlock the gate. With the point of his sword, the angel marks the letter *P* seven times on the poet's brow: "See that you wash away these wounds when you are within."

Then, from beneath his ash-colored vesture, the guardian withdraws two keys, one gold, one silver. These "keys to the kingdom," first given by Christ to Saint Peter, are here represented as entrusted by Peter to this angel, with the admonition that the angel err on the side of generosity when souls who truly humble themselves seek admission. Unlocking the door and pushing it open, the angel commands Dante to enter but warns him not to look back (as Lot's wife did).

The gate opens with a loud creaking, as though seldom used. Dante hears sweet voices singing the Church's hymn of jubilation, "*Te Deum laudamus* (We Praise Thee As God)."

Notes

Dante alerts his reader that since his theme now becomes more exalted, he must write with greater art (that is, symbolism). The three steps may represent a repentant sinner who examines his conscience, bruises himself with a sorrowful confession, and is then washed sacramentally in Christ's purifying blood. Or Dante may also be retracing the path of humanity from original innocence through mankind's fall from grace and then to redemption by Christ.

The silver key stands for the wise counseling of a confessor; the golden one, for the mediated act of divine forgiveness. The second key is more precious, but the first requires more human skill.

The Latin word for sin is *peccatum*: it is probably connected with the word *pes*—"foot"—and suggests a misstep. The seven *P*s represent the seven capital sins, one of which is purged at each level of this *Seven Storey [sic] Mountain*, as Trappist monk Thomas Merton titled his 1948 autobiography.

Canto 10

NEARLY A THIRD of the way through the *Purgatorio*, the two wayfarers finally arrive at Purgatory proper. After climbing through the cleft of a rock, the pair come out upon a lonesome ledge less than twenty feet wide. The sheer inner wall of the ledge is made of white marble and adorned with incredibly realistic carvings.

On these Dante recognizes outstanding examples of humility. For the sin of pride is purged at this level, and every ledge provides its penitents with some sort of "spurs" or "goads" to the virtue they neglected, as well as with "checks" or "reins" against the vice being atoned for. At all seven ledges, the first example of the virtue is always associated with the mother of Jesus. There is always an inspirational example from some non-Christian source as well.

At this level of pride, one carving shows Mary, "the handmaiden of the Lord," being greeted by the archangel Gabriel at the pivotal moment of Christ's conception. Another scene depicts King David, "both more and less than a king," dancing devoutly naked before the ark of the covenant when it was being transferred to Jerusalem. His wife Michal looks on in scorn, for which she will be punished by sterility. Finally, the pagan emperor Trajan is virtuously consenting to a poor widow's insistence that he postpone his imperial business and avenge her son's unjust death. These depictions, like a kind of visible speech, are so convincing that Dante's sense of seeing, hearing, and smelling dispute over whether such details as the music and incense portrayed are real or not.

At length the poets see figures moving cumbersomely toward them. Dante is shocked when he realizes that these are human beings loaded down with stones of various weight, the lightest of which seems insupportable. He fears that his readers may find this report of purgatorial penance a discouragement to their plans for reformation. (Why bother, if even the reforming soul faces such penalties?) Don't think of the pain, he advises, but of the gain, and of the limited duration of such penalties. Dante, not notably addicted to humility himself, famously addresses all proud Christians who do not know how to bow to God or to human superiors in this life:

> Do you not see that we are worms,
> born to form the angelic butterfly
> which wings its way without defense to judgment?

Canto II

AS ONCE-PRIDEFUL SOULS draw near beneath their crushing burdens, they recite a paraphrase of the Lord's Prayer emphasizing human limitations and lowly concern for others. Addressing these penitents, Virgil inquires about the easiest path upward, for Dante too is weighed down by the burden of his prideful body—the "heavy bear that goes with me" of poet Delmore Schwartz.

The penitent who replies with helpful advice represents the first of three kinds of pride that this canto will dramatize: pride of blood, pride of talent, and pride of power. Made disdainful toward all by the authority and accomplishments of his Tuscan family, Omberto Aldobrandesco (died 1259) now modestly wonders whether his listeners ever heard of them. His erstwhile cockiness led him to an early death in a battle with the Sienese.

Bent over in a gesture of humility to hear Omberto, Dante is recognized by another penitent, who calls out to him. The poet in turn recognizes him as Oderisi (1240–99), an artist skilled in "illuminating" manuscripts, as they call it in Paris. Though once consumed by the desire for superiority, the painter now courteously sings the praises of a former competitor.

He stresses the vainglory of human talent and notes how fads of popularity send the "in" names into sure eclipse. Someone always comes along who seems better, unless a whole culture falls into decline. For example, the great Florentine painter Cimabue is being overshadowed by Giotto (Dante's intimate friend, who painted a portrait of him from memory). Poet Guido Cavalcanti (Dante's first friend) has replaced Guido Guinizelli as "the glory of our tongue, and perhaps a man has already been born who will drive both of them from the nest." Was Dante referring to himself, despite his newfound humility? In any case, history agrees with that judgment. Still,

> Worldly fame is nothing but a breath of wind
> that blows now here, now there,
> and changes its name when it changes its path.

(Compare Virgil's pagan view of fame in *Inferno* 24:49.)

Ahead of Oderisi staggers a once-powerful politician, Provenzan Salvani (1220?–69), whose name is now scarcely mentioned in the Siena where he once flourished. Dante wonders how the late-repentant Provenzan has gained admission into Purgatory proper so soon. Oderisi explains the preferential treatment: that proud man once humbled himself in public by begging ransom money for an imprisoned friend. The painter concludes with another dark hint about Dante's future: the poet will soon taste the embarrassment of asking for alms.

Canto 12

AT VIRGIL'S DIRECTION, his protégé resumes his upright posture, though his thoughts remain bent over in newfound humility. Already Dante feels lighter. Virgil now calls his attention to carvings beneath his feet; plainly visible to the penitents, these are horrible examples of pride.

Describing these examples, the next four stanzas begin with the letter *V* *(U)*, the next four with *O*, and a final four with *M*. These letters create an acrostic based on the Italian word for "man," *uom(o)*—as though sinful pride were the very definition of human nature. Summing up, the thirteenth stanza spells out the word *uom* all at once.

These stanzas cite biblical and other embodiments of pride, such as Lucifer, Nimrod, King Saul, Rehoboam, Sennacherib, Holofernes, Briareus, Niobe, Arachne, Cyrus the Great, and ancient Troy. Dante finds the portrayals in stone amazing even to a subtle mind (his own?).

At length Virgil again bids Dante lift up his head and speed his pace. For it is now past noon on a unique day. "Consider that this day will never dawn again [re-day itself] *(Pensa che questo di mai non raggiorna)*." They are nearing a stairway guarded by an angel in white with a face like the trembling morning star. The angel brushes a wing over Dante's forehead and enables him to ascend with his newfound humility. Promising him that henceforth the climb will be easy, the angel wonders: "O human race, born to fly, why do you fall so at a little gust of wind?"

As Dante peers up the stairway, he hears in song the words of Christ's first beatitude: "Blessed are the poor in spirit"—that is, happy are those who realize that spiritually they are poor (Matthew 5:3). He wonders why he can now mount these steps so easily. Pride is apparently one of the poet's dominating flaws. Since in some preliminary way he has been purged of it on this level, he is well on the road to a lightness of being. Virgil points out that one of the seven *P*s branded on his forehead is now wholly wiped out and that all the others are fading. When the letters have totally disappeared, rising will be delightful and effortless.

Dante raises his hand to feel his forehead...and Virgil smiles.

Canto 13

WHEN THE POETS CLIMB to the second ledge, where envy is purged, they find an empty road the color of hardhearted stone. Following the path of the Sun, they walk about a mile before three disembodied voices rush past them.

The first repeats the concerned words of Christ's mother at the marriage feast of Cana: "They have no wine" (John 2:3). The second says, "I am Orestes," recalling the self-sacrificing attempt of Pylades to die in the place of his condemned friend. The third, paraphrasing the words of Jesus, urges, "Love those from whom you have suffered wrong" (Matthew 5:43).

Since the envious are made sad by the good fortune of others, the "checks" against this vice are examples of love for one's neighbor. These checks are voices because, as the poets will soon discover, sinners at this level have had their eyes sewn together with iron wire. Thus they make up for a sin that uses the eye to stare hatefully. (*Envy* is from the Latin word *invidia*, which contains the idea of staring or looking into—see the derivation of *invidiously*.)

Seated along the bank, the penitents lean on and pray for one another, renouncing thereby the self-centered quality of their vice. Since the stony quality of envy bruises the envious and often causes bruises in those they envy, the haircloth cloaks worn here partake of the livid color of the road itself.

Dante tearfully feels a kind of delicate shame at looking upon those who cannot see him. "Through my eyes I was milked of a heavy grief." As always, he wonders whether he might know of some of them. With Virgil's permission he asks if there is an Italian among them. Rejecting her old individualism, a voice replies that they are all citizens of Heaven's one true city—though she was once a pilgrim in Italy.

Dante figures out which shade has spoken because she has raised her chin expectantly—like a blind person. The voice belongs to a woman of Siena named Sapia (1210–65?), who wasn't as sapient as her name suggests. "I rejoiced far more at what others lost than at my own good fortune." When Guelph Florence defeated her own Ghibelline Siena, she rejoiced, though her own nephew was killed. (He was the Provenzan we met in the ledge below.) She repented at the end of her life and would still be waiting in Prepurgatory had not a poor comb-seller named Peter prayed for her out of charity. But who is this man looking for a fellow Italian?

Dante replies: "My eyes will someday be taken from me here, but only for a little, since they have offended little with looks of envy. Far greater is my fear of the torment below...already the load down there [pride] is heavy upon me." He feels lighter but knows that he must someday be definitively purged on the level below.

Can Dante do her a favor? "Yes, pray for me," asks Sapia. And tell her kinsfolk where she is. The poet will find them among the foolish Sienese who are putting their hopes in a new seaport. The city has already wasted much money looking for an underground stream.

Notes

As for Dante's pride, an early commentator wrote, "This Dante, because of his learning, was somewhat presumptuous, haughty and disdainful, and being rude, as philosophers are, knew not how to speak with the unlearned." (Yet he wrote this poem in the vernacular for the common man and woman.)

It helps memory to notice that the only two women to address Dante in Purgatory proper are La Pia and Sapia, both from Siena.

Canto 14

TWO PENITENTS FROM the Romagna district north of Tuscany (including Bologna, Ravenna, and Rimini) overhear Dante conversing with Sapia. They wonder who he is and finally ask him his name and origin. Dante says he comes from the bank of a river in mid-Tuscany. As for his name: "To tell you who I am would be to speak uselessly, for my name as yet does not resound much *(il nome mio ancor molto non suona)."*

Guido del Duca (dates uncertain), who asks the questions, guesses that Dante is referring to Florence's Arno river. His partner, Rinier da Calboli *(circa* 1200–65?), wonders why Dante doesn't use the name of the river— as though it were something horrible.

Guido proceeds to explain why the name ought to perish: all along its course, virtue is shunned as though it were a hostile water snake. He likens the riverbank people of Casentino, Arezzo, Florence, and Pisa, respectively, to hogs, curs, wolves, and foxes. Regretfully, he tells Rinier that his grandson will one day (1302) become a cruel hunter of these Florentine wolves; he will deprive them of life, and himself of honor. (You wonder why Rinier couldn't foresee this for himself.)

At this point Dante begs to know the names of the two shades. Guido replies: "You want me to do for you what you wouldn't do for me. But since God wills that His grace should make such a shining in you, I won't be grudging." Giving his name, he confesses that he used to be so inflamed with envy that he would turn livid if he saw another person grow happy.

After introducing Rinier, Guido details how their native Romagna has degenerated since the old days of worthy men. "But now, go on your way. It pleases me far more to weep than to talk, so much has our conversation wrung my heart."

The poets resume their path. Because the courteous shades can hear their footsteps but say nothing, Virgil and Dante are confident they are headed in the right direction—toward the next upward stairway. Once again they hear disembodied voices, this time warning of envy. Cain, who invidiously murdered Abel, cries out: "Everyone who finds me shall slay me" (Genesis 4:14). Aglauros, turned to stone for being jealous of her sister, identifies her petrified self.

Virgil laments the folly of humankind: "The heavens call to you and revolve about you, revealing to you their everlasting beauties. But your eyes stay fixed on the ground." That is why He who sees Heaven and Earth tries to knock some sense into human beings.

Note

Vietnam defoliation and Agent Orange find a fourteenth-century image in this canto's prophecy about Rinier's grandson: "He comes forth bloody from the sad wood; he leaves it such that in a thousand years it will not forest itself as it was before."

Canto 15

IN A RATHER ROUNDABOUT fashion Dante says it is now about 3 P.M. on Easter Monday—or about midnight in Italy. The poets are walking west on the north side of the mountain. Afternoon sunbeams are striking Dante's eyes. Then, to the sunshine a new and advancing brightness seems to be added, and the doubly dazzled poet has to shield his eyes.

Virgil explains that the angel of this level has come to invite them to ascend the nearby stairway. As their journey progresses, these blazing presences will be easier to gaze at and will eventually prove delightful to behold. As the two poets begin their ascent they hear the singing of another of Christ's beatitudes: "Blessed are the merciful"—who wish good to others, unlike the envious.

Dante is still puzzling over something that Guido said in the previous canto: "O human race, why do you set your hearts on things that exclude a common sharing?" As they climb the stairway, Virgil tries to clarify: "Envy pumps the bellows of your sighings because your desires are fixed where the share is lessened by sharing. But if love for the highest sphere bent your longings upward, that fear of losing would not lodge in your breast. In that lofty place the more there are who say 'our,' the more good each one possesses, and the more love there is."

(In other words: material goods are by their nature divisive in a way that spiritual goods are not. If I have a piece of paper on which Robert Frost wrote a poem, you and I cannot possess that paper simultaneously. But if we both memorize the poem, each of us can possess it completely without taking anything away from the other.)

In Dante's Heaven, true wealth is reflected from one soul to another. Everybody shares, and everybody gains. Virgil tells his protégé to ask Beatrice for a further explanation of these matters when he sees her.

By now the poets have reached the third ledge, where sinful wrath is purged. Dante is seized at once by a series of "ecstatic visions" that dramatize the opposite of the vice:

- Mary gently asks the youthful Jesus why he let her think he was lost when he was teaching in the Temple.
- The ruler of Athens, Pisistratus, tries to calm his wife. She wants him to execute a youth who kissed their daughter in public. "What shall we do to those who want to harm us," he asks, "if we condemn those who love us?"
- Saint Stephen, the first Christian martyr, dies praying for the forgiveness of his killers.

Coming out of these "not false hallucinations," the groggy, staggering Dante is sermonized a bit by Virgil. The sage tells his sometimes irascible companion that he was granted these visions so that henceforth "you might not refuse to open your heart to the waters of peace that are poured from the eternal fountain." As they converse, little by little a smoke dark as night rolls toward them. Finally, it robs them of their sight and of the pure air.

Canto 16

NOT EVEN IN HELL was Dante's sight ever so impeded as by the harsh and heavy smoke that punishes, on this third ledge, sinners who once fumed in rage on Earth. Since the poet must close his eyes, the presumably smokeproof Virgil offers his shoulder as an escort. "See that you are not cut off from me" is the voice of reason speaking to a man who undoubtedly succumbed at times to irrational wrath.

Dante hears voices reciting the *Agnus Dei,* a Mass prayer addressed to Christ, the meek Lamb of God. Virgil identifies the voices as belonging to formerly discordant wranglers who now act in unison.

One spirit speaks up, suspecting the presence of a live person. He turns out to be a man named Marco (dates uncertain)—a Lombard like Virgil.

History knows little of him, except that a man of this name served at court and had a quick tongue. There is no record of his having had a violent one.

Marco assures Dante that the stairway up lies straight ahead. Grateful, the Florentine explains his situation: "With those swaddling bands that death unwinds I make my way upward...God has so received me into His grace that He wills me to see His court in a way totally outside modern usage *(tutto fuor del moderno uso)*."

Having asked for and received assurance that Dante will pray for him, Marco reveals that he knew the world and once loved the values at which nobody aims any more. Dante concurs that virtue is dead and wickedness rampant. Marco's words, coupled with those of Guido on the ledge below, are making Dante burst with a basic question: Are human ills caused by nature and fate, or by man's own abuse of free choice? (Dante's eminent commentator, Charles S. Singleton, calls free will "the central subject of the *Purgatorio*.")

Marco heaves a sigh and grieves that human beings blame everything on the influence of the stars, or the material heavens, or inescapable impulses. Outside influences do exist, but not exclusively or irresistibly. The light of conscience shows right from wrong; divine reward and punishment presume free will.

If your will agrees to struggle from the start against the downward tug of nature, it can finally nourish itself into complete victory. In your freedom you are subject to a better nature (God) that creates in you a mind that is not a slave to the undoubted influences of the material heavens. "Therefore, if the present world goes astray, in yourselves lies the cause."

Marco continues with charming imagery: "From the hands of Him Who loves it fondly before it exists comes forth in the guise of a playful child, now weeping, now laughing, a simple little soul knowing nothing except that, proceeding from a happy Maker, it turns eagerly to whatever delights it." But this mindless hunger for pleasure must be bridled. Hence the need for laws and for rulers. "Laws there are, but who enforces them?...You can see that bad leadership has made the world wicked."

A current chief cause of bad leadership is the political power of the papacy. The sword of Caesar was not meant to be joined to the shepherd's crook. (To change the imagery, borrowed from Leviticus 11:3, the pope can chew the cud meditatively, but he has not the cloven foot to take appropriate political steps.) In better times Rome had two suns: emperor and pope. Each is needed to complement the other. Ever since the pope clashed with Emperor Frederick II, affairs have degenerated in northern Italy. In three elderly, virtuous Lombards, old-time values rebuke modern ones: Currado da Palazzo, Gherardo, and Guido da Castel.

Dante doesn't seem to know who Gherardo is, but he sees more clearly why in ancient Israel the priestly class (the Levites) were wisely forbidden to inherit property. Suddenly, through the smoke, Marco sees the gleaming angel of ascent, whom he is not yet prepared to meet. Wishing Dante Godspeed, he turns back and ends the discussion.

Notes

The words of Marco will remind many readers of lines from Shakespeare's *Julius Caesar* (I, ii, 134): "The fault, dear Brutus, is not in our stars / But in ourselves, that we are underlings."

Medieval popes, increasingly asserting the superiority of the Church over the state, claimed that emperors derived their power from the popes, as the Moon borrows light from the Sun. Dante came to believe in two, independent suns. (He developed these points in his *De Monarchia*. See the appendix.) Marco's reference in line 127 to "the Church of Rome" is the only such phrase in the poem.

Canto 17

IN THIS MIDCANTO of the *Purgatorio*, the two poets arrive at the midterrace of Purgatory, where Virgil provides Dante with an outline of the moral layout of the seven terraces. During a similar rest period in the *Inferno*, Virgil similarly sketched a map of Hell (canto 11).

But first: the smoke thins out on the third terrace, and the pair of travelers emerge into the fading sunlight of Easter Monday. Dante's "high fantasy"—a phrase he uses at the very end of *The Comedy* to signify his poem—is promptly seized by a series of visions that exemplify the folly and destructiveness of sinful rage:

- He sees Procne, who murdered her son in rage and was turned into a nightingale, "the bird that most delights to sing" (a strange transformation).

- He sees the Persian Haman, who planned to slaughter many Jews but was himself executed, looking as fierce in the dying as in the living (see the biblical book of Esther 3).
- He sees the enraged Amata, who committed suicide when her daughter Lavinia decided to marry the foreigner Aeneas rather than the local Turnus. (Virgil's *Aeneid* recounts this very story.)

Thus the checks on anger experienced at this level.

Coming out of himself, Dante is blinded by the angel of peace who, without being asked, courteously points out the way upward. Dante feels the fanning of a wing on his face and hears Christ's words "Blessed are the peacemakers." When they reach the top of the stairs, stars are already appearing, and Dante feels his legs weakening. Virgil tells him this is the ledge of the slothful.

Now they must rest for the night, so the maestro explains to his pupil the layout of these levels of purgation. Love motivates the Creator and all creatures. Natural gravitation acts unerringly. As for human beings, "love must be the seed in you of every virtue, as well as of every action deserving punishment."

Purification is called for when the human heart loves the wrong things, loves the right things too little, or loves the right things too much. Punished on the lower levels were sins of the spirit: pride, envy, and anger. In these sins the wrong thing is loved, namely, some kind of evil wished upon one's neighbor. Virgil can't conceive of a rational creature truly hating the Creator or itself (despite suicides and blasphemers).

The slothful love goodness, but not enough, and are purged at this middle level. At the three upper levels, sins of the flesh are atoned for: too much love for material things (greed), for food and drink (gluttony), and for sexual pleasure (lust).

Canto 18

AS IS USUAL WITH DANTE, every explanation leads him to further questions. He fears he may be annoying Virgil with too many questions, but that lofty teacher encourages him. So the pupil asks his sweet and dear father: "Explain to me love *(mi dimostri amore)*, to which you reduce every action, good and bad." A logical inquiry from a poet who even in his youth was a star in a group of love poets.

It is natural, replies Virgil, for the soul to gravitate toward whatever pleases it. Though that necessary gravitation is good, not every object of it is. Even so a wax may be good, but not every seal that is stamped upon it.

But, counters the pupil, if the attraction is necessary, how can a person merit praise or blame? Virgil will clarify what reason can see on its own—actions that manifest hidden nature. (Beatrice will have to illumine the depths of what faith discerns.) Nobody can explain the human grasp of primary ideas and the primary bent of human desiring. These are like the bee's mysterious zeal for making honey.

Human beings, however, also have an inborn faculty that distinguishes between good loves and guilty ones. This faculty, which Beatrice will call free will, should control the threshold of consent. Acknowledging this faculty, philosophers who thought deeply wrote books about morality.

It is nearly midnight now, and the Moon quenches many a star as it rises like a heated cauldron. As Virgil gives Dante clear and explicit answers, the pupil grows drowsy.

His drowsiness is suddenly shattered by a great throng of shades running beneath the moonbeams. (He is reminded of the two rivers in Thebes where devotees of Bacchus once gathered at night to pray for a good vintage.) Two shades in front tearfully shout examples of zeal: the first recalls that Christ's pregnant mother went in haste to visit her cousin Elizabeth, pregnant with John the Baptist; the other reminds his fellows how Caesar sped to Spain for a showdown with Pompey. All the rest cry out: "Hurry, hurry, lest time be lost for lack of love, while zeal for well-doing waters the greening of grace again."

Virgil begs these shades to tell him where the upward stairway begins. "Come behind us and you will find the gap. We are so filled with the desire to keep moving that we cannot rest. Pardon us, then, if you take our penitential zeal for discourtesy." Virgil will follow, but not until dawn.

The reply comes from a man who was once the abbot of San Zeno in Verona—in the days when the "good" Emperor Frederick Barbarossa destroyed nearby Milan (1162). Someone who already has one foot in the grave will soon lament that he forced his unworthy son on that monastery as abbot (1292). (Dante is referring to Alberto della Scala, who died in 1301 and was the father of his hero Can Grande. The imposed abbot was Can Grande's bastard brother.)

Dante continues: "I don't know whether he said more or was silent—he had run on so far beyond us." Bringing up the rear are two shades who recall instances of laziness: the followers of Moses who grumbled and never saw the Promised Land; and the weary, lotus-eating Trojans whom Aeneas abandoned in Sicily to a life without glory. Dante's weary mind begins to wander from thought to thought, and then falls to dreaming.

Notes

Shiftless on Earth, the penitents of this level are the only ones who work a double shift of reparation, night as well as day. They make the briefest impact of any group in Purgatory. On Earth they probably neglected their prayers. This is the only level where Dante hears neither praying nor hymns. Nor does he receive any requests for prayers.

Though Virgil describes himself as a Mantuan, he was actually born in a town three miles south named Pietola (modern Pietole and ancient Andes), to which Dante refers in line eighty-three.

Dante's 675-year-old words, "Tell me what love is" (line fourteen) is echoed in a modern song by Foreigner: "I want to know what love is; I want you to tell me."

Canto 19

THE HOUR IS THE CHILLY one just before dawn. Now Easter Tuesday, this will be Dante's third day on the mountain, his last day before reaching Paradise Lost on its summit. Today he will traverse the last three ledges of purification, where the sins of the flesh are purged: avarice, gluttony, and lust.

First, he has a second prophetic dream. He sees an ugly woman—stammering, cross-eyed, with crooked feet, maimed hands, and sickly complexion. As he stares at her she becomes transformed: she straightens up and gains both a ready tongue and a charming color. "I am the sweet siren," she begins to sing, "and he who dwells with me rarely departs." (Dante here seems to think that the siren turned Odysseus/Ulysses aside from his journey, whereas Homer has his hero strap himself to a mast in order to resist her.)

Another woman, holy and alert, appears and calls angrily to the negligent Virgil. (Against some entanglements reason is not defense enough; grace is needed.) Virgil now seizes the siren, rips her garments, and reveals a stinking belly. Dante is startled awake; Virgil says he has repeatedly tried to rouse him.

The pair walk with the Sun at their back till they meet a gracious angel of ascent who aims them up a stairway, fans Dante with swanlike wings, and declares that those who mourn are blessed. Those who truly lament their own needs and others' will vanquish various kinds of laziness.

Still puzzling over his dream, Dante walks bent over like the arch of a bridge. Virgil gives him an explanation and bids him look upward like an eager falcon. They next arrive at the fifth level, where avarice is purged, and find souls stretched out on the ground, face down and bound hand and foot. Weeping, they recite words from Psalm 118/119:25: "My soul hath cleaved to the pavement."

As usual, Virgil asks where the next upward stairway is. A voice advises: keep your right hand always on the outside. Dante asks the respondent who he is, why he is positioned as he is, and whether he needs a favor done for him on Earth.

Using Latin to reveal he was a successor of Saint Peter, the speaker turns out to be Adrian V (1276), who ruled for a mere thirty-eight days when Dante was eleven: "I discovered how heavily the great mantle [the papacy] weighs on him who keeps it from the mire....My conversion was late, but when I was made Roman shepherd I learned what a lie life is. I found that not even in that role was my heart at rest. No loftier attainment existed in that world, so a love for this one was enkindled within me. Till that moment I was a soul wretched and separated from God, and wholly avaricious."

Out of reverence, Dante kneels and starts to speak. The erstwhile pope calls him "brother" and bids him stand up—"I am a fellow servant of yours." When Jesus said that in Heaven there is neither marrying nor giving in marriage, he was declaring that earthly relationships do not count in the next world (as Cato already pointed out).

Asking Dante to move on because "your staying hinders my weeping," he implies that the only living soul who might care to pray for him is a niece named Alagia.

Notes

Elected as a deacon, Adrian died before he could be ordained a priest, consecrated a bishop, and crowned as pope. There is no evidence of his having been especially avaricious or of his having undergone a late conversion.

Dante's dream about the witch *(strega)* recalls these lines from Alexander Pope's *Essay on Man:*

> Vice is a monster of so frightful mien,
> As to be hated needs but to be seen;
> Yet seen too oft, familiar with her face,
> We first endure, then pity, then embrace. (217 ff.)

Canto 20

DANTE OBLIGES THE once avaricious pope. So he omits further questioning and "draws the sponge unfilled from the water." Seeing all the other penitents, he laments the evil greed that fills the world, thanks to the accursed and ancient wolf who has more prey than all the other beasts. These words recall the she-wolf Dante encountered in the opening canto of the poem.

As he walks with slow, careful steps over a road strewn with spirits, he hears a voice crying out tearfully in praise of examples of detachment from riches: Mary, who was so poor that she gave birth to Christ in a stable; the Roman Fabricius, who refused to betray his country for money; Saint Nicholas (Santa Claus), who saved three destitute girls from prostitution by providing them with dowries.

Dante asks this speaker who he is and why he alone speaks these praises. If he answers, Dante will as usual be glad to ask the penitent's kinsfolk on Earth to pray for him. The penitent doubts that his living descendants are the type who pray. But he responds because God's grace shines so brightly in his questioner.

He identifies himself as Hugh Capet, first of the Capetian kings who ruled directly in France from 987 until seven years after Dante's own death in 1321. Thereafter, the collateral Valois and later the Bourbon kings perpetuated the Capetian bloodline on the throne until the French Revolution in 1789. (Note the mnemonic reverse of 987.) In the next eighty-three lines Capet recalls or predicts various low points in the history of his royal family.

In this summary there are several inaccuracies that need not detain us. Our poet may at times be confusing Hugh with his father, Hugh the Great. Suffice it to say that Dante had a dim view of these French rulers. As he saw it, their sins were many, and their expanding power weakened the Holy Roman Empire, which the poet supported. Also their mounting influence on the papacy, especially during its "Babylonian Captivity" (1309–77), wreaked serious damage on its spiritual independence. (As much as Dante detested Pope Boniface VIII, he shared Europe's outrage at the violence visited on him in 1303 by creatures of France's Philip the Fair.)

Philip's brother, Charles of Valois, helped the "Black" Guelphs take over Florence in 1301 and exile our poet. (This Charles was the son of a king, the brother of a king, the uncle of three kings, and the father of a king, but never a king himself.) Another Capetian, Charles of Anjou, king of Naples, was groundlessly rumored to have poisoned Thomas Aquinas (here simply *Tommaso*) lest the saint bring a bad report about him to the Ecumenical Council of Lyons (1274). ("What will you tell the bishops of me?" "Only the truth," supposedly replied the saint.) Where Capet says repeatedly that his various descendants made amends for wicked deeds, he is being ironic.

Hugh Capet concludes by explaining that by day all the penitents on this level cite examples of generosity; by night, examples of avarice. But not everyone speaks up with the same force at all times. The evil examples are Pygmalion, Carthaginian Dido's brother, who killed her husband for his wealth; Midas, who was granted his wish that everything he touch turn to gold, so even his food did; Achan, who stole booty after the biblical battle of Jericho; Sapphira (and her husband, Ananias), who lied to the apostles about the profits they made; Heliodorus, who was kicked by a mysterious horse as he attempted to steal the Temple treasures in Jerusalem; Polymnestor, who killed his ward, a son of Troy's King Priam, for his money; and money-loving Crassus, partner of Caesar and Pompey, the mouth of whose decapitated head was mockingly filled with molten gold by an enemy king.

His sponge more than filled this time, Dante travels on until the mountain shakes in a way that produces a deathly chill in him. A great shout goes up from all the penitents, who begin singing the hymn *"Gloria in excelsis Deo.*" Virgil pulls his pupil close, advising him not to be afraid. While the trembling and the shouting persist, they stand motionless. Then they move on swiftly. Timid and pensive, Dante amazingly asks no questions about what is going on.

Note

When Hugh Capet speaks of Philip the Fair setting his sails against the Temple, Dante is referring to Philip's savage persecution and destruction of the Knights Templar, a wealthy military order that grew out of the Crusades and was originally quartered near Solomon's Temple in Jerusalem. (See the notes for *Paradiso,* canto 30.) Dante says nothing about why Hugh Capet is being purged at this level.

Canto 21

CONTINUING ON THE LEVEL of avarice, this canto records a meeting and a conversation involving three poets: Virgil of the century before Christ; Statius of the century of Jesus' birth; and Dante of the second millennium after Christ. (In line eight, the word "Christ" appears for the first time in the poem.)

Publius Papinius Statius (*circa* A.D. 45–96) was an ardent admirer of Virgil and his *Aeneid.* The author of one epic about ancient Thebes and an uncompleted one about Achilles, Statius was known as a preeminent poet of Rome's Silver Age, which followed the death of Caesar Augustus in A.D. 37. Dante here gives his biography an element that history does not validate, conversion to Christianity. Perhaps Statius was meant to represent the Christian humanism of the new Rome, as Virgil embodied the best naturalism of the old Rome. As a freshly purified soul, Statius will accompany Dante to the very end of the *Purgatorio*—even after Virgil disappears.

Statius has come up behind Virgil and Dante just as the risen Christ approached two disciples on their way to Emmaus. Anonymously explaining himself to the stranger, Virgil gives another indication of Dante's ultimate salvation: "if you look at the marks this man bears [on his forehead]...you will plainly see that he must reign with the righteous." But can the stranger explain the recent earthquake and shouting?

Statius points out that Purgatory proper lies beyond the climatic changes within the Earth that were thought to produce quakes. Here the mountain trembles only when some soul feels itself pure enough to rise upward. Salvation being a family affair, a general cheering ensues. In his own case, Statius had already possessed the ultimate "will" to ascend, but his "desire," formerly fixed on sin, was divinely inspired to fix itself first on purgation. (The whole poem's final sentence, which distinguishes between will and desire, should be read with this remark in mind.)

The stranger says he has waited to feel that quake for more than five centuries. Virgil asks who he is and why he has had to wait so long. Revealing his name, Statius gives his city of birth as Toulouse. (Actually, it was Naples, where Virgil lies buried, according to his request. Dante is confusing him with another Statius.) He adds that he lived in the time of the Emperor Titus, who destroyed Jerusalem in A.D. 70. Gaining "the name that lasts the longest and honors the most," he was a poet deeply inspired by Virgil. To have been a contemporary of that divine poet, Statius avers, he would have been glad to spend another year in purgatorial pain.

Now for the closest thing to comedy in *The Comedy*. The silent Virgil glances at Dante to command him to be silent. "But laughter and tears follow so closely the emotions from which they spring, that they are least subject to control in the most truthful people." So Dante smiles, and Statius too is suddenly silent. Then he asks, "Why did your face just now show me a gleam of mirth?"

Dante, now betwixt and between, heaves a sigh. Virgil signals a change of mind, so Dante tells the newcomer the happy truth. Statius starts to embrace the feet of the Sage, but Virgil calls him "brother" and begs, "Don't do that. You are a shade, and so am I."

"Now," replies Statius, "you can grasp the degree of love for you that burns in me, since I forgot our emptiness and treated a shade as something solid." (Yet shade Sordello embraced shade Virgil fifteen cantos ago, and Dante pulled some tufts of hair from the head of a hellion. It's a puzzlement!)

Notes

In the *Odyssey*, Odysseus thrice tried in vain to embrace his dead mother in the otherworld. The identical thing happened with Aeneas and his father in Virgil's *Aeneid* and with Dante and his friend Casella in the second canto of the *Purgatorio*.

When Virgil wants to tell Statius that Dante is still alive, he uses the imagery of the three Fates who determine life span: Clotho, who puts a measure of wool on the distaff; Lachesis, who then spins it; and Atropos, who snips it off at a certain point.

Explaining the local weather, Statius uses familiar words: "neither rain nor hail nor snow nor frost...."

Statius says that "poet" is the "name that lasts the longest and honors the most *(nome que piu dura et piu honora)*" (line 85). Virgil says of the great pagan poets that their fame wins grace in heaven, which grants them special advantage in limbo (*Inferno* 4:78). Dante certainly grants poetry and poets a special place in his *Comedy*. The word *poet* is thrice mentioned in the very first canto. Dante and Virgil are, of course, themselves poets. In limbo Dante converses with Homer, Horace, Lucan, and Ovid. Later in Hell he listens to the disconnected troubadour Bertran de Born (but discreetly omits the poetry connection). In Purgatory he talks with Sordello, Statius, Forese Donati, Bonagiunta da Lucca, Guido Guinizelli, and Arnaut Daniel, and reference is made to poet Guittone d'Arezzo. In the *Paradiso* he talks with Folquet, another troubadour. He talks with Aquinas, who wrote hymns that are still used; and references are made to the psalmist David and to Francis Assisi ("Canticle of the Sun").

Canto 22

THE POETIC TRIO now arrives at the sixth level, where gluttony is purged, but in this canto they meet no penitents. In an unusual flashback, Dante tells us how the angel at the avarice-atoning level below had erased another scar from his brow and proclaimed part of another beatitude with the words "Blessed are they that thirst [for holiness in the use of things, and therefore don't hoard or squander]".

As the three were mounting the stairway, Virgil told Statius how the poet Juvenal (60?–140?), when he arrived in Purgatory, reported the love that Statius bore him. Relying on the reciprocal affection this news begot in Virgil, he now dares to ask Statius how a man so wise could have succumbed to the vice of avarice.

Statius smiles a little, as Dante did before. He was purged on the level below for the opposite excess in the use of wealth—wastefulness. For this vice he might have ended in Hell, had not a statement in Virgil's own *Aeneid* caused him to reform: "O sacred hunger for gold, why do you not control human appetite?"

A famous puzzle: what Virgil had actually written in Latin was "O cursed hunger for gold, to what [extremes] do you not drive the appetite of mortals" (3:53–57). The poem's Italian version of what Virgil said, as quoted by Statius, implies that a moderate love for gold is possible, and thereby constitutes a clear wrenching of Virgil's meaning in Latin.

Apparently, there is a library in Limbo. For Virgil says he didn't get the impression from Statius's writings that he was a Christian. "What sun or candles dispelled your darkness, so that you decided to sail after Peter the fisherman?"

Here again our poet seems to be inventing, but beautifully. Statius replies that after reading Virgil's *Fourth Eclogue* and its prophecy of a fresh age about to dawn with the birth of an offspring from Heaven (5:7), he became aware of the teachings of the Christians and their exemplary lives. When they were persecuted, he wept with them and befriended them.

Finally, he was secretly baptized, but as a closet Christian still pretended to be a pagan. For this spiritual tepidity he had to spend four centuries on the fourth level. (He must have been kept waiting in Prepurgatory for four centuries too.)

So, declares Statius to the pagan Virgil, "Through you I was a poet, and through you a Christian. You were like a man who walks by night and carries behind him a light that doesn't help him, but illumines those who follow him." Statius now asks the whereabouts of a number of ancient poets.

Virgil says they are in Limbo with him, along with Homer, whom the Muses nursed the most. There they often talk of Mount Parnassus, where the Muses dwell. Also there are famous people Statius wrote about, including Antigone and Tiresias's daughter Manto. (Another slip: Dante already told us he saw Manto among the soothsayers in Hell's eighth circle.)

It is now about 10:30 A.M. The poets have finished their climb and, as we were already told, are traversing the ledge of the gluttons. Shortly, they encounter a curious tree in the middle of the walkway. Laden with sweet-smelling fruit, the rising tree expands in such a way as to make climbing it difficult. Clear water falls from above into its branches but is quickly absorbed (lest any penitent drink of it).

A voice among the branches insists that no one may eat of this tree. It also praises four examples of self-control in eating and drinking: Christ's mother at the wedding feast of Cana, who was interested in the spouses and not in the wine shortage as such; ancient Roman women who were pleased enough with a drink called water; Daniel, who could fast when principle required; and John the Baptist, who survived on locusts and wild honey.

Notes

Early in his career Virgil published ten short poems called *Eclogues* (eclectic selections) or *Bucolics* (herdsmen, or countryside pieces). Because of Virgil's *Fourth Eclogue,* many Christians regarded him as a herald of Christ. (For many years during the Middle Ages, Virgil was commemorated as "The Gentile Prophet" during Christmas Mass at the Cathedral of Rouen and elsewhere.) This poem, written around 40 B.C., probably referred to the expected birth of a son to the Roman consul Pollio (to whom it is addressed) or even to Antony or the future Caesar Augustus. But Christians naturally thought of someone else when among its sixty-three lines they read such phrases as "The Virgin has returned…a new offspring is sent down from high heaven…a new order of the ages begins…whatever traces of our guilt remain shall vanish and free the Earth forever from fear…begin, then, little boy to recognize your mother with a smile."

Reverence for Virgil even among pagans like the Emperor Hadrian led to the practice of *Sortes Virgilianae* (Virgilian lots), in which (like the Bible) a book by Virgil would be opened at random and a haphazardly chosen passage regarded as prophetic.

A verse once sung at a medieval Mass referred to the legend that Saint Paul visited Virgil's tomb at Naples—"Led to the mausoleum of Maro, he shed over it the dew of reverent weeping: 'What I could have made of you,' he said, 'had I found you alive, O greatest of poets!'"

On the Great Seal on the back of the U.S. dollar bill, the words "*NOVUS ORDO SECLORUM* (A New Order of the Ages)" are from this passage in the *Eclogues* to which Statius referred. The additional words "*ANNUIT COEPTIS* (He has blessed our beginnings)" are adapted from lines in Virgil's *Aeneid.* Thus, most Americans carry around with them two quotations from Dante's guide.

Canto 23

VIRGIL HAS BEEN CONVERSING with a literary friend he never met before. In this canto Dante will converse with a personal literary friend whose death he mourned a few years earlier. But first his "more than father" prompts him to quit looking at the strange tree and continue walking energetically.

Soon the poets hear behind them words from Psalm 50/51:17: "O Lord, [Thou wilt open] my lips [to Thy praise]" (and not just to food and drink). The words are both sung and wept in a manner both sad and lovely. Then a crowd of devout shades hastens by them and gazes in wordless wonder at the poets. Each soul has sunken eyes, pallid hues, and wasted frames. Dante thinks of the legendary Erysicthon, whose doom of endless hunger led him to consume himself. He thinks of the woman who reportedly devoured her own child during the siege of Jerusalem in A.D. 70.

The eye sockets of these shades seem like rings without gems. The skull around the eyes clearly suggests the letter *M*. Dante recalls what an imaginative Franciscan friar had once pointed out in a sermon: the Latin word for man—*(h)omo*—could be read in the eyes and in the bone structure surrounding them; *Dei* (of God) could be seen in the *d* of the ear, the *e* of the nostrils, and the sideways *i* of the mouth. Our poet now clearly sees the point with respect to the *omo*. He wonders what could cause such hunger. He will learn that it is the fragrance of fruit that can't be eaten, of water than can't be drunk.

One of the shades staring at Dante suddenly blurts out, "What a grace I've been granted!" Though Dante could never have recognized the face, he recognizes the voice of his old friend and rhyming partner, Forese Donati, who had died nearly four years earlier. Forese belonged to one of the leading Florentine families, as did Dante's own wife, Gemma.

Friend speaks to friend: "Your face, which once I wept for dead, now gives me no less cause for tears." Though eager to hear Dante's story, Forese first obliges him and explains how the fragrance of the tree famishes him and his fellow penitents, all of whom indulged beyond reason their appetites for food and drink. Dante could scarcely have been surprised to meet his friend on this level, for he once wrote sonnets mocking Forese for his gluttony and for pilfering in order to indulge it. He consoled Forese's coughing wife for what was lacking in her bed—probably the warmth of her carousing spouse.

But something else surprises Dante. Forese came quite late in life to penitence, that "good grief that remarries us to God." Why, then, has he not been made to wait in Prepurgatory? His friend gives credit to his loving and devout wife, Nella, to whom Dante may here be apologizing for some discourteous things he once said about her in verse. She has prayed her lost husband through Prepurgatory and any appropriate circles below this one.

Nella is a rare and decent woman among the brazen hussies of Florence. The women of Sardinia's barbarous Barbagia region were more modest than these, who expose breast and nipple and provoke rebukes from the pulpit. Before long, impudent Florence will be punished by a series of disasters (including the one that led to Dante's exile).

Dante finally satisfies his friend's earlier inquiry. "If you bring back to mind how I was with you, and you with me, the memory will be grievous even now." From that low life, Virgil (whom by way of exception Dante names and points to) has led him through the profound night of the truly dead, up the mountain that straightens those whom the world has made crooked, and now onward to Beatrice. (Only to his friend does our poet ever name Beatrice thus, without further explanation.)

The journey began when the Moon—the sister of that Sun to which he now points in a unique series of pointings—was round, as it would be at Eastertide. Of his second companion Dante merely says that it was for him that the mountain shook a short while ago.

In his Rime #72 Dante wrote to the late-carousing Forese about his wife, Nella:

> Her cough, her cold, her other maladies
> Were not incurred because she's getting grey
> But from a lack she suffers in her nest.

In #74 he added, using Forese's nickname,

> Bicci, my boy, you son of God-knows-who
> (Though I could ask your mother—if she knows),
> Your goods diminish as your belly grows
> And stealing now must keep it full for you.

Forese gave as good as he got—"scurrilously," as the critics say. Replying that, given Dante's character flaws, there can be no doubt that he is Alighieri's son, he mentions Dante's response to a recent quarrel:

> Fear has filled your trousers up so well
> Two pack-mules couldn't carry them away.

Canto 24

WITH THIS CANTO Dante will end his Easter Tuesday visit to the terrace of the overindulgent. But first he concludes his conversation with his poet-friend Forese and has a brief but celebrated discussion about poetry with a kind of poet-enemy.

Treating family affairs first, Forese says that his sister Piccarda is in Heaven (Dante will meet her there tomorrow). He can't decide whether her beauty or goodness was greater. But his brutal, Hell-bent brother Corso will come to a violent end (1308) after bringing ruin on Florence. (Corso was a chief cause of Dante's exile.) What divergent fates for one family! Stressing that "time is precious in this realm," Forese dashes off to continue his purification. Souls who once lingered too long over food and drink now seem eager for speed.

Earlier, Forese had identified many fellow penitents, including Pope Martin IV (1281–85), who had reigned in Dante's youth. Martin and his near predecessor Adrian are the only popes we encounter or hear of on the mount.

The first penitent pointed to here, however, is another Florentine poet, Bonagiunta da Lucca, who had died three years earlier. "Good at finding rhymes, but better at finding wine," according to a commentator, he was an acquaintance of our poet. He seems most eager to talk to Dante. Invited to do so, the shade foretells, rather murkily, that a woman of Lucca named Gentucca will one day befriend Dante. Some say Dante fell in love with her. Maybe he is apologizing here for having had a devil say that everybody in Lucca is a crook.

Now follows a famous passage. Bonagiunta, whose poetic style Dante criticized in his *Eloquence in the Vernacular,* now asks whether he is looking at the very Dante who produced a new kind of poem, starting with the one that begins, "You Ladies who have an understanding of love." This poem appeared as the first canzone (eighty-nine lines) in Dante's earlier mix of prose and poetry, *La Vita Nuova*. (Such a mix is technically called a prosimetrum.)

Acknowledging his identity, Dante famously replies, "I am one who, when love inspires me, take note, and then proceed to speak of love in the manner that love dictates within me." Calling him "brother," the shade says he now understands why other poets, including himself, were hindered from practicing Dante's "*dolce stil n(u)ovo* (sweet, new style)." (Here is the origin of the celebrated phrase. Whether or not there actually was a poetic school of *Dolcestilnovisti*, these remarks seem to be contrasting a traditional, artificial, and abstract way of versifying with the more spontaneous and natural way heralded by Dante.)

Having finished talking with two fellow poets who are penitents, Dante continues walking with his two companion poets until they detect a second tree in the roadway. Beneath its branches, shades beg for fruit, then turn away unfulfilled. As before, a voice speaks from within the foliage and, ordering the penitents away, declares that this tree sprang from the Bible's fatal Tree of Forbidden Fruit—which Dante will see tomorrow.

Whereas the previous tree-voice cited examples of self-control, this tree's does the opposite. Recalled are the centaurs whose drunkenness led them to attempt rape at a wedding and to suffer defeat from Theseus; also, Gideon's impatient soldiers, who leaned over to drink directly from a river and thus lowered their guard. By contrast, his disciplined soldiers drank from their cupped hands.

At this point a blinding angel appears and points out the upward stairs. Self-controlled people actually experience pleasure more sharply than others. Describing the angel's motion, Dante stresses his own purified, heightened sensitivity by ending this canto with four uses of the word "feel," two of them quite unusual:

> As a May breeze announcing the dawn stirs and smells sweet, perfumed as it is with grass and flowers, such a wind I *felt* strike full on my brow, and I plainly *felt* the moving of his wings, which made me *feel* the odor of ambrosia, and I *felt* the words, "Blessed are they...who hunger always so far as is just." [Emphasis added.]

Canto 25

AT THE END OF THIS canto Dante and his two escorts will have mounted to the seventh and final level, where the soul is purified of the vice of lust. There they will spend the rest of Easter Tuesday.

First, at Virgil's request, Statius will deliver for our poet a highly technical lecture on the relationship between the human soul and the human body. The lecture is triggered by Dante's puzzlement that the penitent "souls" he has just seen could hunger and look as gaunt as starving human "bodies."

Superficially, this lecture will give a rationale for Dante's poetic invention of gaunt shades. More deeply, it will permit Dante to assert three basic Christian beliefs:

1. The human soul is not produced by the body but directly created by God.
2. Body and soul become one unified person.
3. The soul continues to exist and be matter-oriented even after death.

The arguments employed by Statius are based on the reasoning of theologians like Thomas Aquinas. These men, whose faith in revelation caused them to search for an underpinning of rational understanding—*fides quaerens intellectum*—did the best they could with the tools of science at their disposal. Their searching was rooted in the optimistic conviction that the world of grace builds on the world of nature, and that a correlation exists between the two, however mysterious and ultimately beyond total human grasp.

Virgil briefly tries to find a parallel for the correlation between body and spirit in the way a mirror reflects an object facing it, and in the way that, according to legend, Meleager's life was dependent on the persistence of an unburned log.

In his lecture, Statius distinguishes between the heart's production of ordinary blood and of another, "perfect blood." The first creates its good effects throughout the body in general. The latter, in males, becomes semen and descends to the genitals ("of which silence is fitter than speech"— a paraphrase of Aristotle's own comment; see also *Paradiso* 16:45).

Through sexual intercourse, this active semen flows onto the passive blood of the female, and an embryo may be generated.

At first this embryo is only vegetative in nature. The soul of a plant has already arrived; the human soul of an embryo is still on its way. At the point of quickening, however, God the prime mover, "delighted with such a masterpiece of nature," breathes into the now animal soul a spiritual soul, which takes up into itself the lower functions of the body and becomes one person.

This soul is individual—and not just a temporary and generic borrowing from some supersoul, as the Muslim philosopher Averroës taught. This soul also survives death and preserves its matter-oriented abilities. These (according to Dante's ingenuity) it projects onto the surrounding atmosphere in Purgatory and gives souls fasting from sin the appearance of starved bodies.

Dante makes no comment on this explanation. The group has arrived at the top of the stairway, from which they behold a roadway engulfed with flames. A blast of air from the ledge side of the road forces the flames back a bit and provides a narrow pathway. Virgil, indulging in a double meaning at this level of lust, warns, "Along this pathway the eyes must be tightly controlled, for it would be easy to take a false step."

Dante hears a hymn being sung within the flames—"*Summae Deus clementiae* (O God of Mercy Supreme)." He turns his head cautiously and sees spirits inside the burning. Each time they end the hymn, which begs for the power to overcome lust through refining fires, the shades invoke some model of chastity: the Virgin Mary, declaring, "I know not man"; the chaste moon-goddess, Diana, dismissing her seduced attendant; and faithful husbands and wives practicing chastity. (Dante rejects the heresy that in itself sex is sinful and that only celibacy can be virtuous.)

Note

Some critics say that Dante would have been an even greater poet had he been less of a philosopher. They probably have a canto such as this one in mind.

Canto 26

IT IS NOW LATE in the afternoon of Easter Tuesday as Dante strains to
avoid the flames on his left and the precipice on his right. Walking behind
the poets Virgil and Statius, he will soon converse with two more poets,
these being purged of lust—as his two previous discussants had been po-
ets guilty of overindulgence in food and drink.

Noticing the darkening effect of Dante's presence on the flames purify-
ing them, a group of shades approaches him. One of them requests an
explanation of his "nonfictitious" body. Our poet starts to reply, but he is
distracted by a phenomenon within the flames.

He has already seen shades advancing in the same direction he is tak-
ing. But he now sees other shades passing in the contrary direction. As the
two files of shades pass each other, they don't stop, but do slow down to
exchange brief, chaste kisses—the kind that the apostle Saint Paul recom-
mended in Romans 16:16 and elsewhere. (For Dante, lust is always asso-
ciated with restlessness.)

Then each group tries to outshout the other. One, with unnamed shades,
cries out the names of Sodom and Gomorrah—biblical cities traditionally
linked with homosexual rape. The other yells a reference to the legendary
Pasiphaë, who lusted for a bull and gave birth to the Minotaur. As already
mentioned, she hid herself inside an artificial cow to achieve conception.

Obliging his questioner at last, Dante concedes that his body is real.
Thanks to a heavenly woman, he is taking this journey to rid himself of
his blindness. But who are the shades gazing at him in wonder, and why
was the other group heading in the opposite direction? (One suspects that
Dante could have easily figured the latter question out for himself. In any
case, he wants this information so he can "line pages" and write it down.)

Explaining that he hasn't time to name other names, the original ques-
tioner identifies himself as Guido Guinizelli, a poet of Bologna who died
when Dante was eleven. (He was lauded in canto 11 of this canticle as a
dominant poet who has lately been overshadowed by Dante's friend Guido
Cavalcanti.) Now he praises Dante in memorable words:

> Blessed are you, who in order to die better,
> burden yourself with experience of our confines!

(The philosopher Boethius wrote that the purpose of philosophy is "to teach a person how to die.")

Then Guido explains the unbridled lusts burned away here: the unnatural kind that once caused Caesar to be called a "queen"—it was joked that Caesar was the husband of every wife, and the wife of every husband—and the natural kind ("hermaphrodite": Hermes/Aphrodite [Mercury/Venus], male/female), which the penitents failed to keep within the bounds of reason.

Like a child joyously finding a lost parent, Dante stands in silent amazement when he realizes who the shade is. Before him stands "the father of me and of others my betters [unnamed], whoever have used sweet and graceful rhymes of love." Dante places himself totally at the service of this influential poet who anticipated some of the natural and spontaneous qualities of Dante's own poetry. (Guido's concept of true love was not quite so spiritual as Dante's, however; and that may help explain why Guido is where he is.) No other thirteenth-century poet was more often quoted and praised in Dante's writings.

Guido asks why this stranger is being so courteous. It is because of "those sweet lines of yours, which as long as the modern use [of vernacular verse] endures, will ever make their very ink precious." Calling him "brother," but without asking his name, Guido modestly points to another poet nearby as "a better craftsman" of the vernacular. This unnamed poet is clearly the superior of poets like Guittone and Giraud of Limoges, whom the foolish overrate. Guido finally asks Dante to say in Heaven an Our Father on his behalf and then disappears back into the flames, like a fish into water.

The unnamed poet ("the better craftsman") gladly identifies himself as Arnaut Daniel (flourished 1180–*circa* 1210), "the great master of love," an eminent troubadour of a century earlier, possibly the originator of the poetic form called the sestina. (Dante wrote at least four of them.) Speaking his eight lines in the Provençal tongue, which was a cousin of Dante's Tuscan dialect, he says,

> I weep and sing as I go. Grieving, I recognize my past follies; but rejoicing, I anticipate the day I hope for. By the goodness that guides you, take thought of my pain in due time.

Speaking thus the final words we'll hear from a purgatorian, he too vanishes into the fire.

Notes

Poet T. S. Eliot was quoting from this canto when, in dedicating *The Waste Land* to poet Ezra Pound, he calls him, in Italian, "the better craftsman."

In her English translation, Dorothy Sayers cleverly translated Arnaut's Provençal words into Border Scots: for example, "Waefu' I mind my fulish deeds lang syne." An early critic, Benvenuto da Imola, said Dante used these Provençal words "to show that he knew something about everything: *'aliquid de omnibus.'*"

We have already met a troubadour in Hell (Bertran de Born, canto 28); we've met two in Purgatory (Sordello and Daniel); and we'll meet one in Heaven (Folquet, canto 9). In the two centuries before 1300, more than four hundred known poets labored to become "finders" of new ways to sing of a new subject—courtly ladies to whom the poet was like a vassal pledged to utter faithfulness. (The Provençal word *troubadour*—like Verdi's Italian *Il Trovatore*—is linked to the French *trouver,* "to find," and to our word *trove*—as in treasure trove.)

Centered in southern France (Provence, the first Roman *province* beyond the Alps), northern Italy, and northern Spain, these revolutionary poets idealized the aristocratic ladies whose marriages were often loveless, having been arranged by others for political or other nonromantic reasons. Their castle homes typically contained few women and many men. Outwitting husbands was often the name of the troubadour game, with adultery as a common result. With the figure of Beatrice, Dante spiritualized the whole dynamic. With other, later poets, the pursuit of courtly love turned into a courtship stage leading to virtuous marriage.

Provence was also the center of the Albigensian (Catharist/Manichean) heresy, and the troubadour movement suffered from the fact that some of the poets and their lords were, or were suspected of being, Albigensian or at least sympathizers. The eminent troubadour Folquet became a bishop and, foreshadowing the Inquisition, violently persecuted the Albigensians (named after the city of Albi, one of their centers in southern France).

A fine study of courtly love may be found in C. S. Lewis's *The Allegory of Love.*

Canto 27

THE SUN IS NEAR setting on Easter Tuesday as Dante and his two companions encounter on the outside of the flames a joyful angel who sings Christ's words "Blessed are the clean of heart [for they shall see God]." The angel's next words are terrifying to Dante, who had seen burned bodies and was condemned by Florence to be burned alive if captured.

> There is no going farther unless first the fire bites. Enter into it, and be not deaf to the singing beyond.

Virgil reassures Dante: "Trust me. There is torment here, but not death…not even a hair of your head will be destroyed…test the flames with the hem of your garment." Dante still doesn't budge. Irritated, Virgil adds, "Now look, son: between Beatrice and you stands this wall [of flame]." When Virgil stations Dante between himself and Statius, our poet relents.

"As soon as I was in the fire, I would have leaped into boiling glass to cool off." Indulging in poetic license, Virgil encourages: "I seem to see her eyes already." The three are guided by "a voice that sang beyond." (Lust is cured not by cold reason, but by a higher love—"Only the passionate heart is pure" [Saint Augustine].)

They issue from the flames and see before them a stairway and a blinding presence reminiscent of the cherubim with flaming swords who guarded the paradisiacal garden whence Adam and Eve were expelled. This unique, second angel of a terrace cites the words of Christ "Come, ye blessed of my Father" (Matthew 25:34), then urges the trio to start climbing at once.

Before long the Sun sets, and the travelers make beds of the steps. Dante gazes at the stars, bigger and brighter than usual, and drifts into sleep, sleep "that often brings news before the event." Thus, before dawn on Easter Wednesday he will have his third and final prophetic dream on the mount:

A beautiful young woman named Leah is walking through a meadow, singing, and gathering a garland with which to adorn herself. Her sister Rachel, satisfied with seeing rather than doing, gazes at her own eyes all day in a mirror. According to the Bible, both these women were wives of the patriarch Jacob/Israel. On this day Dante will encounter in the lost Eden a flower-gathering woman named Matilda, emblem of the active life. Soon thereafter he will be reunited with his lost love, the contemplative Beatrice.

Earlier than usual, Dante wakes and rises. Already risen is Virgil, who makes a triumphant promise: "This day that sweet fruit for which driven mortals keep looking on so many branches will bring peace to your hungering." Without delay the three travelers continue their climb out of Purgatory proper.

When they reach the top step, Virgil fixes his eye on our poet—the Virgil who has been his dear and safeguarding leader, master, sage, father, and more than father, during the sixty-seven cantos covering somewhat more than a hundred hours. Now this lofty poet, author of the "divine" *Aeneid,* speaks sublime final words to his "dear son":

> You have seen the fires, both eternal and temporal, and have arrived at a place where I have no further discernment. I have brought you here with understanding and with skill. Henceforth, let what delights you be your guide....No longer expect word or sign from me. Your will is free, upright, and healed. It would be wrong not to do its bidding. Therefore, I crown and miter you to rule over yourself.

Note

Restored to innocence, at least temporarily, Dante no longer needs the guidance and restraint of Church or state. He has become his own king and bishop, indeed his own emperor and pope.

Canto 28

IT IS EARLY MORNING now on Easter Wednesday, April 13, 1300, the start of Dante's fourth and final day in Purgatory. According to the general reckoning, it will also be the last day of his entire journey.

Our poet spent nine cantos in Prepurgatory and then eighteen in Purgatory proper. These last six cantos he will spend in the earthly Paradise Regained. Here he will lose Virgil and gain Beatrice. After a final purification in the two rivers of Eden (Lethe and Eunoe), he will begin his ascent through the spheres, in the company of Beatrice, to the true, heavenly Paradise.

Dante never calls this Paradise Lost a garden but rather a divine forest, in dramatic contrast with the dark, wild, and fearful forest in which his journey began, and the dismal wood of the suicides. Though Virgil and Statius are still with him, Dante now feels free to seize the initiative and move slowly (at last!) but eagerly into this forest of gentle light and breezes, fragrant air, happy birds, and perpetual shade (the quest of those familiar with the hot Mediterranean sun.) He comes at length to a narrow stream of purest water and senses that he should not cross it yet.

On the other side of the stream (which he will later learn is called Lethe) he spies among fresh-flowering boughs a *"bella donna,"* a smiling, song-ful woman who matches his dream of a few hours earlier. He will learn only in canto 33:121, some 830 lines later, that her name is Matilda (Matelda/Maud), the caretaker of humankind's first nest.

(Since her movements remind Dante of a dancer's, she can be more easily remembered as waltzing Matilda, though in the song the phrase means a shifting knapsack [swag] on the back of an itinerant laborer [swagman]. Her name, rather inappropriately, means "mighty in battle.")

Dante begs her to come closer so that he can understand her song, which he doesn't share with us. The lady graciously but modestly obliges, not "be-stowing on me the gift of lifting her eyes" until she stands just across the stream, a few paces away. Seeing her beauty, Dante thinks of three women of legendary loveliness: Proserpina, snatched away by the god of the under-world; Venus, wounded by Cupid's accidental arrow and now enthralled with the handsome Adonis; and the priestess Hero, whose lover Leander was willing to risk drowning in his nightly swim across the Hellespont to visit her.

"You are newcomers," she declares, "so perhaps my smile makes you wonder. You will find the answer in the psalm [91/92:5] that says, 'Thou hast given me, O Lord, a delight in Thy doings.'" She invites Dante to ask any questions he may have. Well, Statius (standing nearby) had told him in canto 21 that Earth's atmosphere has no impact above Purgatory's gate. Yet our poet feels breezes and sees water that must require rain or snow. Was he misinformed? (It is Dante the observant meteorologist who makes a weather report his first concern in Eden.)

Matilda explains that the air here is stirred by the circling of the heav-enly spheres. That air is impregnated with seeds of every fruit, some of which are wafted to the inhabited world. From an unfailing fountain willed by God derive two streams: Lethe ("oblivion"), whose waters remove the memory of sin and evil; and Eunoe ("well-minded"—a Dantean coinage), whose waters restore the memory of every good deed.

The lady adds a grace note: perhaps the ancient poets who sang of a golden age of happiness were dreaming of this place. Dante looks at his two poet companions and finds them smiling at her words.

Notes

Commentator Sayers finds the identity of Matilda "perhaps the most tantalizing problem" of *The Comedy*. The earliest commentators identified her with Matilda, La Gran Contessa of Tuscany, at whose castle in Canossa the dramatic confrontation occurred between Pope Gregory VII and the Emperor Henry IV in 1077. She was the first woman to be buried in the new St. Peter's Basilica.

For those who think the guardian of Eden's forest is based on a real person, other candidates are two German visionary nuns named Mechthild. They were older contemporaries of the poet and described scenes from the world beyond.

Sayers forcefully argues that Matilda was the young-dying friend for whom Beatrice wept, on whose corpse Dante gazed, and about whom he wrote the sonnet *"Morte villana,"* which concludes, "Let him who does not merit salvation never hope to have her companionship." (See *La Vita Nuova*, chapter 8.) There is no proof, however, that her name was Matilda.

The name, incidentally, was introduced into England by the wife of William the Conqueror (alias William the Bastard). William also had a daughter-in-law, a grand-daughter-in-law, and a granddaughter of that name. The last-named became empress by marrying Henry V, to whom Countess Matilda of Tuscany troublesomely bequeathed property she had already given to the papacy. A son by a second marriage became King Henry II of England and was called Henry Fitzenpress.

Canto 29

HAVING ENDED HER WORDS, Matilda starts walking along the stream, singing from Psalm 31/32:1 the words "Blessed are they...whose sins are covered." (For one reason, they will be readied thereby to uncover divine showings such as those that are about to take place.) Dante has been following Matilda from the other side of the twisting riverbank, and when they are finally facing east—the rising place of revealing dawn—the lady says, "My brother [singular!], look and listen!"

In gradual steps, an astonishing pageant is about to advance toward Dante through the Forest. (Oh, if only Eve's apple had not so long deprived the Florentine of this place!) Leading the procession are seven blazing candles representing the gifts of God's Spirit: wisdom, understanding, counsel, knowledge, fortitude, piety, and reverence for the Lord (Isaiah 11:2). Flames from these unheld candles are varied in color like a rainbow and trail like a canopy over the whole procession.

As viewed by Dante, God's gift of revelation had three biblical stages: the Hebrew Scriptures, the four Gospels, and the later books of the Christian testament. So the pageant too has three sections.

First, twenty-four elders dressed in white and crowned with lilies walk two by two behind the candles—more slowly than freshly married brides. White is a sign of illuminating faith, and these elders stand for the books of the Hebrew bible. (See Revelation 4:4.) They are singing to a woman, telling her she is blessed among Adam's daughters; blessed too be her everlasting beauties. Dante must wait a little to learn who she is. The *"Hosanna"* that has just been sung has already alerted us that someone special is in the wings.

Second, a chariot appears that represents the ideal Church. This symbol of both war and victory is being pulled by a legendary creature, the winged griffin, half golden eagle of the heavens, half lion of the Earth—an emblem of a Christ both divine and human.

The chariot has two "living creatures" in front of it and two behind: these are a man, an ox, a lion, and an eagle—ancient representations of the four Gospel writers, Matthew, Mark, Luke, and John. Each of these, crowned with the green of hope, has six wings, as Revelation 4:6–8 says, not four as Ezekiel thought (Ezekiel 1:4–14). John the Divine agrees with Dante! The poet tells the reader he can't spare more rhymes to describe these creatures; other needs prevent him from being lavish here.

On the right side of the chariot walk or dance three ladies signifying the theological virtues of faith (white), hope (green), and charity (red). Symbolizing the supremacy of charity, the first two dance to the music of the third. On the left side are four women dressed in imperial purple who stand for the cardinal virtues that "rule" a good person's actions: justice, fortitude, temperance, and dominant prudence, which sees past, present, and future. For her triple vision, Dante gives prudence a third eye. Some find this feature "grotesque," or "a lapse of taste," but many depictions of the Buddha give him some sort of third eye symbolizing inward vision. In yoga tradition, the sixth chakra (center of psychic energy) radiates through the imagined third eye, located in the center of the forehead.

Third, seven white-robed men, balancing the seven candles in front and the seven ladies around the chariot, represent the follow-up books of the New Testament: side by side, the healing physician Luke (author of the Acts of the Apostles) and Paul (author of the major epistles) with his frightening, sin-wounding sword; then two more sets of men representing other epistle writers: Peter, James, John, and Jude. Last of all is an old man who sleeps but sees keenly as he walks—John the Divine (supposed author of the book of Revelation). Though dressed in the same white robes of faith as the twenty-four elders, these final seven are crowned with roses and other red flowers emblematic of the charity energized into the world by Christ's coming.

When the chariot has advanced to the point where it is opposite Dante, the whole procession comes to a halt. A canto that began with lightning ends with thunder. Earlier, the poet had turned in amazement to look at "good" Virgil, who can only respond with such a look himself. Dante doesn't realize it, but he has just exchanged goodbye glances with his sweet father.

Notes

The Muses, who were invoked at the top and bottom of Hell and at the bottom of Purgatory, are once again invoked at its top. Now Dante begs help in view of the hunger, cold, and vigils he has endured in their name, and because he is trying to put into verse things difficult to conceive. A final invocation will occur in mid-*Paradiso*.

Usually, Dante represents ideas through people: for example, Hell's real Farinata stands for lofty pride. In this allegorical pageant, the poet represents people through symbols: for example, the mythical griffin stands for the real Christ.

This particular pageant would have reminded Dante's contemporaries of a procession honoring the Sacrament of the Body of Christ *(Corpus Christi)*—a subject that is curiously scanted in this great Catholic poem.

(Nor does the word "sacrament" even appear.) The reason for the scanting may be that, for Dante, the beauty and holiness of Beatrice make her so much a "sacrament" of God's presence that she herself is a Christ-figure and a Eucharist-figure. In the pageant, Christ is not present as a human being, but the human Beatrice upon the chariot is its focus, just as the consecrated Eucharistic bread would be in a *Corpus Christi* procession.

The allegorical style strikes many moderns as artificial and, in this case, requires the Apostle John to be represented three times: as an eagle, as a humble man, and as an old man. Dante is not at his most attractive when allegorizing, but of this particular pageant one critic has insisted, "here beats the heart of the great work." (See Sinclair, *Purgatorio,* p. 387.) French poet Paul Claudel wrote, "The part of the great *Commedia* that impresses me most, both for workmanship and sheer delight of the spirit, is the last six cantos of the *Purgatorio.*"

Canto 30

COMMENTATOR DOROTHY SAYERS has called this canto "the great focal point" of the poem. As John D. Sinclair has noted, "Revelation is not revelation until it reveals a man to himself." Hence the impersonal pageantry of revelation presented in canto 29 finds a vivid counterpoint in the intimately personal drama now unfolding.

Upon the halting of the seven candles, the twenty-four elders had turned around to face the chariot. One of them, probably King Solomon, calls out words from his Song of Songs (4:8): "Come from Libanus [Lebanon], my spouse." All his companions take up the cry.

Suddenly, a hundred angels appear above the chariot, showering flowers and singing words from Psalm 117/118:26 that are used to introduce the most solemn part of the Mass: "Blessed is He who cometh." Quoting with gracious aptness from Virgil's *Aeneid* (6:883), the heavenly messengers continue, "Throw forth lilies from crowded hands." (Visited in the world beyond, the father of Aeneas used these words to refer to a noble descendant, Caesar Augustus's nephew, who would die young, as Beatrice did.)

It is at this point, in the midst of the angels, that there appears a lady in red with a green mantle and a white veil, crowned with the olive leaves of wisdom. Thus she summarizes the crowning colors of all the devotees who surround her. (The Italian flag has three vertical bands bearing these same colors.)

Dante feels the mighty power of an erstwhile love. He turns to Virgil, preparing to quote from him: "There's not a drop of blood in me that doesn't tremble. I know the telltale flickerings of an old-time flame." (When Dido, the widowed queen, starts falling in love with Aeneas, she thus tells her sister that she is feeling what she hasn't felt since her husband's death. See *Aeneid* 4:23.)

Turning as a frightened child to its "mother," Dante discovers that his "sweetest father" has vanished. Not even in these joyful woods of "mother" Eve can he resist tears "again." In the first canto of the *Purgatorio*, this very Virgil had washed away from his son the stains of tears shed in Hell.

A stern voice commands, "Dante, do not weep because Virgil leaves, do not weep yet, for you must weep because of [the wound from] another sword." (Dante apologizes for the necessity of this unique mentioning of his own name, which is the first word Beatrice speaks—perhaps the first she ever spoke to him. Her third word is "Virgil," and her own name is the seventh word of her second sentence.)

He turns back and sees again the reprimanding lady, her face still covered with the white veil. "Look at me closely," she demands from the near side of the chariot. "I am, I am indeed Beatrice. How did you [being a wretched man] dare to come to this mount where men are happy?"

In canto 6 above, Virgil had told Dante to expect a smiling Beatrice. Now he is jolted by this unexpected "tough love *(pietade acerba)*." (The male Virgil could be motherly; here the female Beatrice will show herself a severe father.) Dante's eyes fall to the stream, but he sees reflected there his unhappy self and stares instead at the grass. As though pleading with the stern lady for the shamed poet, the angels sing words from Psalm 30/31:1: "In Thee, O Lord, have I hoped." Their compassion melts his heart into tearful sobs.

Beatrice replies that the angels know the full story, but she will speak explicitly for Dante's sake, since his sorrow must match his sin. She recalls how favored he was by nature and grace (but "Lilies that fester smell far worse than weeds"). How promising he was in his youth! (She calls it his *vita n[u]ova!*) Her spiritual beauty drew him to virtue, but after she died he forgot her for another and followed false and lying paths. She sent him dreams and other inspirations, but to no avail. His only hope was to be shown the damned, so she visited Hell and tearfully won the help of Virgil.

Notes

In line thirty-two Dante says that upon the chariot "a woman appeared to me." There are those who say it is no coincidence that it is in the sixty-fourth line (thirty-two times two) of this sixty-fourth canto of the whole poem that, ten years after her death, the poet finally sees Beatrice directing her eyes at him: "*Vidi la donna...drizzar li occhi ver' me.*" Six plus four equals ten—a "perfect" number for a number of reasons. (For one, it is a Trinity times a Trinity, plus a Unity.)

In the poem, Dante never addresses Beatrice by her own name, though he uses it sixty-three times: twice in Hell, seventeen times in Purgatory, and forty-four times in the *Paradiso*.

Canto 31

IN THIS CANTO Dante will make his confession, faint briefly, be pulled across the river Lethe by Matilda, drink of its obliterating waters, and then be brought close to Beatrice and the griffin.

Earlier, after addressing the angels, Beatrice had again addressed Dante directly. She wants him to admit that he had gone astray. At first Dante can't speak; then he utters a scarcely audible "Yes" to her charges, and dissolves again into tearful sighs. Finally, he acknowledges the roots of his guilt: "Things at hand *(le presenti cosi)* with their false pleasures turned my steps aside as soon as your face was absent."

To make him stronger the next time he is tempted by siren voices, Beatrice underscores his folly. If her supreme earthly beauty had failed him by proving to be mortal, he should have learned to pursue thereafter undying spiritual beauties. No sweet young thing or other vanity should have tripped him up thereafter. (Her "sweet young thing" is *pargoletta* [that is, *parvoletta*]—"a little baby." In this context the word suggests our slangy "babe" or "baby doll.")

At this point she bids Dante, who has been staring at the ground, to lift up his "beard *(barba)*" so he can see by her heavenly beauty how much he lost by forgetting her. Though a grown and bearded man, he has acted like a child. With great effort he raises his eyes and now finds Beatrice's eyes gazing at the half-eagle, half-lion griffin that represents Christ. Though still veiled, her beauty overwhelms him with remorse, and this is when he faints.

When he comes to, Matilda (who walks on water) is pulling him across the sacred stream. Reaching the other side, she directs him to drink of the waters of forgetfulness while words of purification are sung: "*Asperges me* (Thou shalt sprinkle me)" (Psalm 50/51:9).

Rising from the water, he is surrounded by one set of maidens (prudence, justice, fortitude, and temperance), who crown him with their hands and then lead him to the griffin. They bid him look into the eyes of Beatrice, still fixed on the griffin. In her reflecting eyes Dante sees now the human nature of Christ, and now the divine. (Only in the final lines of the whole poem will he somehow glimpse both natures simultaneously.)

At this point the three other maidens (faith, hope, and charity) plead with Beatrice on behalf of a man who has now returned to his first love: "Turn, Beatrice, turn your holy eyes on your devotee who, for sight of you, has made so great a journey." They also beg that she show Dante her "second beauty," her smile. Beatrice obliges completely. Dante gains what he has been looking for. Trying to describe her, even the greatest poet would be doomed to fail.

Notes

In *The Banquet* Dante wrote that the soul operates chiefly in the eyes and in the smiling mouth. On these two "balconies" the soul often reveals itself, "though as it were under a veil."

For her part, Beatrice here mocks Dante's beard. In *Paradiso* 25:7 he will imagine himself returning to Florence with voice and "fleece" altered since the lamb time of his christening. Some see the later fleece as referring to his beard. His early biographer Boccaccio reported that Dante's beard was thick, black, and crisp. Yet countless drawings and busts of him show no beard! Maybe he got rid of it, though in *The Banquet* he found being full-bearded an amiable male quality.

Canto 32

WITH ITS 160 LINES, this is the longest canto in the whole poem. Longing to gaze at the now fully visible Beatrice after a ten-year thirst,

Dante stares too intently. Reminded not to neglect the general for the particular, he turns away and finds himself briefly blinded.

Regaining his vision, he discovers that the pageant has now reversed itself and is heading east, back toward the Sun. Dante employs a number of military words (army, squadron, soldiery) to indicate that the pageant now signifies the Church Militant as it struggles on Earth with the bruising realities of history. Dante, Statius, and Matilda follow the procession deeper into the woods.

As they approach a blasted, leafless tree, Beatrice descends from the chariot. All murmur, "Adam"—the name of him who ate the forbidden fruit from the Tree of the Knowledge of Good and Evil. They praise the griffin (Christ, the new Adam), who was obedient to God's will and did not abuse the tree.

Paraphrasing his own words from the Gospel, and speaking through the mouth of the griffin, Jesus makes his only direct utterance in *The Comedy:* "So is preserved the seed of all righteousness" (cf. Matthew 3:15). He then binds the chariot's shaft and its probable crossbar(!) to the ruined Tree of Righteousness, which thereupon blossoms into a springtide apple-blossom color—"less than rose and more than violet"—perhaps the hue of Christ's blood. (A legend claimed that the wood of Christ's cross came from the tree of Adam's sin.)

Overcome by the song now being sung by the heavenly spirits, Dante falls into a stupor. Bright light and a summons, "Arise, what are you doing?" call him back to himself. The poet wonders where Beatrice is. Matilda points to her, surrounded by the seven virtuous maidens and seated humbly on the ground beneath the tree as if guarding the earthly Church. The griffin and all the rest of the pageant have departed. Probably referring to his life on Earth, and maybe his approaching death followed by a brief stay in Purgatory, Beatrice says to Dante: "Here [on the battlefield of the earthly Church] you shall be for a little while a forester, but then you shall be with me forever, a citizen where Christ is a Roman [in the heavenly Rome, Saint Augustine's City of God]." After this firm assurance of his final salvation, Beatrice continues, giving Dante his poetic mission to the world: "For the good of that world that lives badly, fix your eyes on the chariot, and when you have returned to the world, write what you see."

What he sees is a series of devastations that have afflicted the Church throughout history and culminate in current Church troubles:

1. The fierce persecution of the early Church—signified by attacks from the imperial eagle (Jove's bird).

2. Early heresies such as Gnosticism, represented by a ravenous fox, which actually gets inside the chariot before Beatrice chases its fleshless bones away.

3. Ruinous favors of power and property bestowed on the Church by the emperor Constantine (a friendly eagle); a heavenly voice, perhaps Saint Peter's, cries out, "O humble barque of mine, you have taken on an evil burden!" As mentioned earlier, this "Donation of Constantine" was proven an eighth-century forgery in the fifteenth century.

4. Loss of part of the chariot to a dragon—perhaps a reference to Islam, which Dante regarded as a Christian schism.

5. More well-meant but corrupting land grants from various earthly ruler (like Pepin, Charlemagne, Otto the Great, and Countess Matilda of Tuscany).

6. Contemporary afflictions of the Church. Invoking imagery from the book of Revelation (especially chapter 13), Dante sees the chariot sprouting the seven horned heads of the seven deadly sins. Seated upon it as on a mountain fortress is a brazen harlot representing the corrupt papacy. (She is loosely clad, as loose women often are.) She kisses repeatedly the kissing giant standing beside her. When he finds her looking at Dante (an advocate of reform and suddenly a participating spectator), he beats her savagely and drags her and her chariot into the woods beyond.

The giant probably stands for France's King Philip IV (the Fair) in his growing abuse of the Church. His minions attacked Boniface VIII in 1303. He pressured his creature, Clement V, to move the papacy in 1309 from Rome to Rhône, the river of Avignon. In this city was built a Gothic papal palace, a fortress on a hill.

Dante represents those fourteenth-century Catholics who pleaded that the papacy return to its true mission and traditional location. (Riotous Rome and its many factions had undeniably made it at times almost an ungovernable site for the papacy. The uproar in Rome at the conclave that precipitated the Great Schism of 1378–1417 proved this most disastrously.)

Canto 33

THE VISION OF the woeful state of the Church causes the seven maidens to weep as they sing the biblical words "O God, the heathens are come into Thy inheritance, they have defiled Thy holy temple" (Psalm 78/79:1). Beatrice looks stricken, almost like Christ's mother at her son's crucifixion. But then she rises and, glowing like fire, invokes Christ's own hopeful words: "A little while and you shall not see me; and again a little while and you will see me" (John 16:16).

The group now heads for Eunoe (well-minded), the second stream of the Forest, most likely a Dantean invention. En route, Beatrice discusses the vision just seen. She calls Dante "brother," but he calls her "madonna" and continues to use the respectful you *(voi)*.

The shattered chariot stands for the Church, "which was and is not"—at least not as God meant it to be. But He prepares retribution. A deliverer will soon come to slay the harlot and the giant. In a "hard enigma," she calls this savior "a five hundred (D), a ten (X), and a five (V)."

After the destruction of Solomon's Temple, his descendant Zerubbabel set about building a second one, which was dedicated in 515 B.C. Does this enigma pertain to a sacred renewal of some sort? In Roman numerals, rearranged, this enigmatic number becomes a *DVX* or *DUX (Duce)*—a leader, perhaps the emperor Henry VII, in whom Dante placed so much hope, but who died in 1313. Of course, such an interpretation would mean that these words were written before that disastrous year. Can Grande, the emperor's vicar in Italy, was, however, still alive at Dante's death. In any case, the meaning of the *DVX* is one of the most argued in Dantean studies.

Beatrice tells Dante to memorize her prophecy, even if obscure, and to report her message to those who are still living "the life that is a race to death." (Saint Augustine used this image.) Like a pilgrim returning from the Holy Land with a palm-wreathed staff that shows he had been there, Dante should tell what he has heard, at least in symbolic pictures. But why is she being so enigmatic? To show how deficient are his usual ideas and the school of human knowledge from which he derived them. Feeling rebuked, Dante says he can't remember having sinfully failed her. That, she replies, is proof that you have drunk the waters of Lethe.

By now it is noon (the supposed time of Christ's Ascension), and they have come to another stream at the edge of the Forest. Here the stream is at its source and flows away from its companion stream (Lethe)—"separating slowly, like friends (*quasi amici* [a sudden, rich phrase!])."

Our poet asks what water this is. Beatrice replies, "Ask Matilda"—thus finally giving us the name of the *bella donna* who tends this Forest and ministers to all the souls who have been freed from Purgatory. Matilda says she has already told Dante. How timely it is then, replies Beatrice, to revive the weakened memory of his good deeds with the water of Eunoe. Matilda takes Dante by the hand and bids the recently purged Statius to come with them. (This is the last we'll see of Statius.)

> If, reader, I had more space for writing I would sing of some of the sweetness of that drink, which would never have sated me. But since all the pages set aside for this second canticle are full, the curb of art prevents my saying more. From the most holy waters I came forth remade, like a fresh plant renewed with fresh leaves. I was pure and disposed to leap to the stars (*puro e disposto a salire a le stelle).*

Notes

Like Dante himself in his prose works, medieval writers could be quite verbose. For Dante the poet to impose on himself "the curb of art" (as he will do again through Saint Bernard just before the final canto of the poem) was remarkable.

The image of a fresh plant with which the *Purgatorio* ends echoes the renewed reed with which its first canto concludes.

In Genesis 2:14, the Tigris and Euphrates are the last two mentioned of the four rivers watering the Garden of Eden and arising from one source. Dante ignores the Pishon and Gihon, which are unidentifiable. His favorite, Boethius, mentions the Tigris and Euphrates in his *Consolation of Philosophy* (V, i) but has them separating soon *("mox")*. By having them separating lazily *("pigri"),* our poet gains a rhyme for *Tigri* and then beautifully compares them with separating friends.

As with the other two, this second canticle ends with the word "stars."

Part 3

Paradiso

Blessed are the clean of heart:
for they shall see God.
                    —Matthew 5:8

THE THIRD AND FINAL PART of *The Divine Comedy* is entitled *Paradiso* (Paradise). The root of the word is Old Iranian (Persian) and means a place that is "around-walled" *(pairi [peri]-daeza)*. In Dante's usage, it is a divine or heavenly place that is fortified on all sides against the invasion of evil or unhappiness. This section runs to 4,758 lines—a trinity of lines longer than the *Purgatorio*, 38 lines longer than the *Inferno*.

Dante presented this climactic part of his masterpiece, written between 1313 and 1321, as a journey from the Forest of Eden atop the seven-story mountain of Purgatory to the very presence of God Himself. Clearly at work again is Dante's basic dynamic of "correspondence with contrast." For instance, the final and successful Godward action at the very end of the final canto echoes the opening scene of the poem, when Dante unsuccessfully expended himself struggling to ascend a sun-topped mountain.

Then he descended into Hell by traversing a shrinking spiral and had a climactic vision of absolute Evil. Next he ascended the mount of Purgatory by climbing a shrinking spiral and encountered Goodness incarnate in Beatrice. Now he will cut across an expanding spiral to a vision of absolute Good as three interlocked circles.

In Hell, where it is always night, time is discontinuous and pointless. In Purgatory, where day alternates with night, time is continuous and purposeful. In Heaven, where it is always an April spring day, time is simultaneous and totally blissful.

This final journey, made almost entirely in the immediate company of Dante's beloved Beatrice, involves his rising with speed swifter than lightning through the various spheres of planets and stars to the outermost circle of the heavens, the Empyrean. (As the kindred word *Pyrex* suggests, the ancients thought of the Empyrean as a flaming sphere distantly encircling the Earth.) There he attains God's own special dwelling place. In some cases we are to think of Dante and Beatrice as actually passing into these heavenly bodies and revolving with them awhile.

En route, Dante will encounter various groups of saints in the vicinity of the different planets and stars. These encounters are just one-time heavenly courtesies intended to help Dante see the link between some quality of a given sphere and the character of the particular saints temporarily seen there for his private benefit. Thus saints who are intellectually bright are visualized in the sphere of the Sun. But the true and normal abode of all these souls is God's Empyrean.

The purpose of this final stage of Dante's journey is to accustom his eyes to ever-increasing brightness, so that he will be as prepared as possible for the transcendent vision of God's own glory. The reader should not forget the darkness of Dante's world—a world without electricity. Seeing was a great preoccupation with him. He used some form of the verb "to see" on an average of eight times per canto in the poem. He employs few other word roots that often.

His mind's eye too is being readied for the moment of Beatific Vision by the advances in wisdom and understanding that he gains on the way. His soul will then be ready for a final healing: the split between his blind passions and his spiritual vision will disappear. Spun by love, they will circle smoothly, like a single wheel, in the fully converted sinner, Dante.

Commentators argue about the relative merits of the three canticles of *The Comedy*. The poet Shelley deemed this canticle "the most glorious imagination of modern poetry...a perpetual hymn of everlasting love." He deemed many of Dante's words "pregnant with a lightning that has as yet found no conductor." John Ruskin wrote, "Every line of the *Paradiso* is full of the most exquisite and spiritual expressions of Christian truth, and this part of the poem is less read than the *Inferno* only because it requires far greater attention, and, perhaps, for its full enjoyment, a holier heart." (These words recall the challenging remark You don't judge Dante; Dante judges you.)

Outline of the *Paradiso*

NOON OF WEDNESDAY, April 13, A.D. 1300

Canto

1. Beatrice and Dante rise from Eden through the spheres of air and fire
2. They enter the sphere of the *Moon:* Beatrice explains its dark spots
3. *Moon (continued):* inconstancy of vows; Piccarda and the Empress Constance
4. *Moon (continued):* the location of souls; the absolute versus the conditional will

5. *Moon (continued):* compensation for broken vows. Arrival in *Mercury*

6. *Mercury (continued):* excessive thirst for fame; Justinian's song of the Roman Empire

7. *Mercury (continued):* Beatrice discusses the Mystery of Redemption

8. *Venus:* excessive love; Charles Martel

9. *Venus (continued):* three more excessive lovers—Cunizza, Folquet, Rahab

10. *Sun:* wisdom; Saint Thomas Aquinas

11. *Sun (continued):* Aquinas lauds Saint Francis of Assisi

12. *Sun (continued):* Saint Bonaventure lauds Saint Dominic

13. *Sun (continued):* Aquinas discusses Solomon and warns of hasty judgments

14. *Sun (continued):* Solomon talks. Arrival in *Mars:* warriors for faith; symbolic cross

15. *Mars (continued):* Dante's great-great-grandfather Cacciaguida

16. *Mars (continued):* Cacciaguida's Florence

17. *Mars (continued):* Cacciaguida's prophecy about Dante's future

18. *Mars (continued):* goodbye to Cacciaguida. Arrival in *Jupiter:* lovers of justice

19. *Jupiter (continued):* the symbolic eagle speaks of the justice of "who gets saved"

20. *Jupiter (continued):* two pagans in Paradise, Trojan Ripheus and Trajan! the mysteries of grace

21. *Saturn:* symbolic ladder; contemplation, monasticism; Saint Peter Damian

22. *Saturn (continued):* Saint Benedict. Arrival in *Gemini/Fixed Stars*

23. *Gemini (continued):* preliminary triumph of Christ, Mary, and the saints

24. *Gemini (continued):* Saint Peter examines Dante's faith after Christ and Mary leave

25. *Gemini (continued):* Saint James examines Dante's hope

26. *Gemini (continued):* Saint John examines Dante's charity; Adam speaks

27. *Gemini (continued):* Heaven's wrath at the sinful Church. Arrival in the *Primum Mobile*

28. *Primum Mobile (continued):* the hierarchy of angels; their relation to God
29. *Primum Mobile (continued):* the creation and fall of angels
30. *Empyrean:* the river of light; the city of God; the mystical rose
31. *Empyrean (continued):* farewell to Beatrice; Saint Bernard takes over
32. *Empyrean (continued):* Bernard gives Dante a visual tour of all the saints
33. *Empyrean (continued):* Bernard prays to Mary; Dante gains glimpse of the Trinity and Christ's dual nature

Canto I

IN THE OPENING STANZA of the two previous sections, Dante had referred to himself. Growing less self-centered, he begins the *Paradiso* by speaking of that divine glory that moves all things, the glory that will now move the poet himself through the spheres of Heaven to a vision of Itself, the glory that will be shown in the very last line of the poem to be a "love that moves the sun and the other stars."

Striking a central theme that will often recur in this third and final canticle, Dante asserts that God's glory is reflected in varying degrees throughout the universe (even among angels and saints) and that he has visited the Empyrean, the heaven that receives most of God's light.

Four times previously the poet has invoked the aid of the Muses. Aiming to speak next of an experience that overwhelmed his memory and beggars vocabulary and imagination, he must now invoke the master of the Muses, Apollo himself, the god of light and song. He also invokes the influence of both peaks of that Mount Parnassus where Apollo had his chief shrine, Delphi. A little inspiration will do: a great flame can follow a small spark.

Thus inspired, the poet hopes to become worthy of the laurel leaf, alias the Peneian leaf. (The river god Peneus changed his daughter Daphne into a laurel as she was trying to escape from Apollo.) To achieve his final task, Dante prays to his "father" Apollo that he may play the lyre of his poem as winningly as Apollo played his on that famous occasion when the Muses judged his music better than that produced by the magic flute of the satyr

Marsyas. The goddess Minerva had thrown that flute away when she realized that playing it distorted her face. The satyr found it and discovered that it played itself gloriously. That's why he dared to challenge the god of music himself. For his fraudulent audacity he was flayed alive by Apollo. (Dante also wants the god to pull him out of himself, according to the root meaning of the word *ecstasy*.)

The *Inferno* began with sunset, the *Purgatorio* with dawn. Dante finds a good omen in the fact that he begins his heavenly journey at noon—the traditional hour of Christ's return to his Father on Ascension Thursday. Moreover, the Sun is in the constellation of the Ram (Aries), as it was believed to have been at the dawn of creation. Nor have many days elapsed since the start of spring, when the celestial equator, the circle of the zodiac, and the so-called colure of the equinoxes crossed the circle of the horizon and created the propitious effect of four circles intersecting to form three crosses. Dante knew his astronomy and how to use it poetically.

Seeing his beloved Beatrice gaze at the Sun as only the eagle was thought able to do, the poet imitates her and finds that he can now do the same. Soon he experiences a great sparkling, as though daylight were being added to daylight. Puzzled, he looks at Beatrice and feels himself being "transhumanized *(trasumanar)*": that is, rising above his human condition. He recalls the legendary fisherman Glaucus who, after eating an herb that had sent his fish leaping back into the sea, plunged into the sea himself and became a sea god.

Like Saint Paul when he was lifted to the third heaven (2 Corinthians 12:3), the poet doesn't know whether he is making his journey in his body or only in his soul (the part of his nature created last). Only that divine lover knows who lifted him with His light. Dante next becomes aware of the heavenly spheres revolving and creating music in their desire for God. With "brief, smiled words," Beatrice explains that he and she have left the Earth and are now rising faster than lightning.

In the remaining lines Beatrice gives the first of several overviews of the working of the whole cosmos. (She has been compared to an older sister with a Ph.D.) All things have order among themselves ("Order is Heaven's first law.") and thereby reflect God, who wishes intelligent creatures to rejoice in that reflection. A natural instinct moves all creatures toward their proper goal:

they move to diverse ports over the great sea of being
(si muovono a diversi porti per lo gran mar de l'essere).

This is true of intelligent creatures too. In creating them, God shoots them toward himself, like an archer (with a boomerang for arrow). Only in the Empyrean will they find their joyful target and their ultimate repose. By seeking false pleasures, however, intelligent creatures can be diverted to unnatural targets. With sinful hindrances now removed, Dante should no more wonder that he rises than that a stream would flow down a mountainside, or that a flame would strive upward.

Having said these words, Beatrice once again turns her eyes upward, toward the distant goal of their cosmic journey.

In his *History of Animals* (9:45), Aristotle cited the legend that the eagle forces its young to gaze at the sun, beats any that seem unwilling, and kills the first to weep from the glare.

Canto 2

DANTE STARTS THE SECOND CANTO by giving his readers second thoughts. If you are following his singing vessel in too small a boat, you had better turn back to shore lest you get lost. (This must surely be one of the earliest examples of a writer's deliberately discouraging potential readers; Isaac Newton and Immanuel Kant supposedly used a difficult style to discourage half-hearted readers—though it is not Dante's style as such that is difficult.) He is undertaking a journey never before attempted in poetry; therefore, he himself needs special help from various divinities of inspiration.

Dante allows that at least a few of his readers may have searched for wisdom over the years. These may safely follow in his furrow. They will discover things more amazing than did Jason and his Argonauts, those legendary pioneers of perilous sea voyages.

But back to his journey. Dante gazes at Beatrice and suddenly finds himself in a wondrous place. In a curious reversal of sequence he says he traveled as fast as a crossbow hits, flies, and is loosened from its notch. He uses this backward technique twice again in the *Paradiso*, perhaps to emphasize the nearly simultaneous stages of the action.

Referring to the Moon, which the poet believed to be a star possessing light of its own as well as reflected light, he declares that "within itself the everlasting pearl *(l'etterna margarita)* received us." If he is still in his body, he wonders how he could have penetrated the substance of the Moon. He is now all the more eager to see how the human and divine natures of Christ could penetrate each other. He will glimpse this mystery at the very end of the poem.

After voicing his gratitude for arriving at the Moon, Dante asks Beatrice to explain its dark spots, which popular legend ascribed to the presence there of Cain, the first murderer, and to the bundle of thorns he was doomed always to carry with him.

This may seem an odd first question from one on such a journey. (Remember, though, his first question in the Forest of Eden.) But it gives his guide a chance to sketch the dynamics of the cosmos through which they are now traveling. In brief: the activities of the physical world are a mirror of the spiritual world. That latter world derives from the Divine Energy centered in the Empyrean and radiating down to the Earth through interlocking spheres. This is the great chain of being that begins with the farther and swiftest heaven, known as the Primum Mobile—"the first movable"— and also as the Crystalline, transparent and invisible.

This heaven, the ninth from the Earth, is the same in all its parts, so the energy it receives from God is undifferentiated. Only when the energy is transmitted to the eighth heaven (the fixed stars/constellations) does it take on a qualitative difference depending on the star with which it merges. This process of differentiation continues down through the other seven heavens (the five planets, plus the Sun and the Moon). All these differences exert their influence on the living creatures of Earth, the stationary body at the physical center of the universe.

Like a body animated by many souls, each of these nine physical heavens (the organs of the universe) is under the influence of varying spiritual intelligences (angels) who help to determine the qualitative differences to be found in each heavenly sphere. Apparently, many angelic natures are acting upon the Moon, and angelic variations account for the varying degrees of lunar brightness. (The traditional nine choirs of angels thus differ not only between themselves, but even within their own group.)

In his earlier *Banquet*, Dante had ascribed the Moon spots to mere differences of quantity in the Moon's makeup. Through the mouth of Beatrice, he now refutes that error and opens his mind to a more unified, spiritual, and qualitative view of the variations in the Moon and everywhere else in the cosmos. Thus does all creation reflect variously the unvarying nature of God. (In the words of the Jesuit poet Gerard Manley Hopkins, with this pied beauty "he fathers-forth whose beauty is past change.")

At the end of the first canto Beatrice had explained the ascent of nature toward God. At the end of this one she explains the descent of God through nature. John Sinclair has pointed out that "a great part of Dante's spiritual recovery is to think spiritually of the whole of things and to know creation as the seamless garment of God...the spots on the moon are, for Dante, Tennyson's 'flower in the crannied wall,' to understand which is 'to know what God and man is.'"

Note

In line ninety-five, Beatrice is echoing Aristotle when she says that experience (experiment) is the fountain of human arts (sciences). Hence, she suggests that Dante sometime make an experiment with three mirrors. In 1921 the Russian mathematician Florenskij theorized that Dante's geometry and physics surpassed Euclid's and anticipated modern theories on mass, matter, and light.

Canto 3

DANTE IS ABOUT TO TELL Beatrice that he now sees his error, but he is distracted by the sight of many faces that seem eager to speak. These faces appear so vague, like pearls on a white forehead, that the poet turns around, presuming he has seen reflections. The mythical Narcissus, by contrast, mistook an image for a reality when he saw his face in water.

Amused, Beatrice assures him that he is looking at true substances, "relegated" to this sphere for some failure to keep a vow—and for his private tutoring. They have been inconstant, like the light of the Moon. Asking her name and condition, Dante addresses the face that seems most desirous of speaking. She says she is Piccarda and that Dante should recognize her. She is here because she left a vow unfulfilled.

Dante now apologetically realizes that she is the sister of his friend, Forese Donati, whom he met in Purgatory (23:48), and of Corso Donati, who is destined for Hell (same: 24:82). The poet was related to all three by his marriage to Gemma Donati.

The competitive Dante asks Piccarda whether she and her companions yearn for a higher place in Heaven so that they can see more and make themselves more dear. She replies that all heavenly souls desire only what God desires, for "*E 'n la sua volontade e nostra pace* (And in His will is our peace)." ("That is the sea toward which everything moves.") Thus to his fellow Florentine Dante gives what is perhaps the most beloved line from the poem. Incidentally, he meets only two other Florentines in Paradise.

Piccarda explains how as a Franciscan in the order of Saint Clare she was forced from the convent and into marriage by her brother Corso (though—like her brother in Purgatory—she avoids using his name). The waters of Lethe, however, have made her forget the evils that followed. (So it is apparently not just the memory of sins that these waters obliterate.)

Piccarda, who took the name Costanza as a nun, points out that the soul near her is the Empress Constance (1154–98), the mother of Frederick II, the daughter-in-law of Frederick Barbarossa, and the grand-mother of the illegitimate Manfred. She was also the aunt of Sicily's William the Good, son of William the Bad. She married into the Swabian line of the Holy Roman emperors, whose brief and violent reigns were like blasts. She too was forced out of the convent (so Dante believed), "though the veil was never loosened from her heart."

Piccarda ends her words, begins to sing the first song Dante hears in Paradise *("Ave Maria"),* and sinks away into invisibility. Dante glances again at Beatrice, who blinds him momentarily with her heightened beauty.

Notes

In line eighty-nine, Dante uses the word *paradiso* for the first time in this canticle.

It is curious that in this realm of the inconstant the two nuns mentioned bore the name Constance. Like Piccarda, the empress had one family member in Hell (her son Frederick II in *Inferno* 10) and one in Purgatory (her grandson Manfred in *Purgatorio* 3).

Of this canto's beloved words about peace and God's will, writer Maurice Baring declared, "This line seems to me to hold the glory and the secret of Dante's music and inspiration, as a drop of dew holds all the glory of the sun." Saint Gregory of Nazianzus (329–89) had written, "*Voluntas Dei, pax nostra"*; in his *Confessions* Saint Augustine had declared to God, *"In bona voluntate tua pax nostra est."*

Canto 4

PICCARDA'S WORDS HAVE RAISED two problems in Dante's mind, though he remains silent because he can't decide which one he wants to ask first. Like the biblical prophet Daniel, who told King Nebuchadnezzar not only his forgotten dream but the meaning of it, Beatrice reads her charge's mind and answers his questions.

In his dialogue *Timaeus* (which Dante would have known only through a Latin paraphrase), Plato seemed to teach that each soul has preexisted on some heavenly body and, if worthy, will return there after death for a greater or lesser period of bliss. Catholic doctrine taught otherwise: the soul was created after the body, and God's face is our goal.

But Dante has just seen souls on the Moon. Was Plato then correct? Beatrice asserts that all blessed souls, from the highest to the lowest, are in God's presence forever in the Empyrean. Though each is fully happy, not all have the same measure of sweet life *("dolce vita")*. Dante will be seeing souls in the various spheres as a concession to his human understanding. The Bible and the Church make the same concession when they speak, for instance, of the "hand" of God.

Beatrice is still respectful of Plato and suggests that his words may have an acceptable meaning: for example, that the various stars and planets exert influence on human affairs, though the pagan world erringly made gods of them. (The illness known as influenza was once thought to have been caused by such planetary influences. And consider what a few days of sunless skies can do to your disposition.)

Dante's second question is how Piccarda and Constance could lose merit if they were forced from the convent. Wouldn't that be unjust? First, Beatrice replies encouragingly, if heavenly justice seems unjust to mortal eyes, "that is an argument of faith and not of heretical wickedness." (Our poet was said to have been denounced to an inquisitor for heresy.)

As for Piccarda and Constance, they could have fled back to the convent if their wills had remained unbroken. As examples of such determination she cites Saint Lawrence, who was roasted to death on a gridiron, and the pagan Mucius Scaevola (left-handed; died 82 B.C.), who held his right hand unflinchingly in a fire because it had failed to kill an enemy of Rome. Such a will (rare indeed) is like a flame that may bend in the wind but will always straighten up when force desists.

Beatrice's answer raises a third problem: didn't Piccarda say that Constance persisted in her love for the nun's life? Beatrice agrees that a saint cannot lie. Piccarda referred to what the empress would have done if the doing were absolved from further consideration. But that will, in practice, was conditioned by Constance's desire to avoid the further trouble that would have resulted from her attempt to return to the convent. So did the ancient Alcmaeon do what he should not have done, lest he incur some evil. In his case he slew his own mother (who was responsible for his father's death) lest he fail to honor a promise made to his dying father.

Dante thanks his beloved ardently for her enlightenment and affirms his faith in ultimate answers—which must be attainable, since nature keeps us restless until we find them. "Thus, at the foothills of truth, questioning grows and pushes us on from peak to peak toward the summit." (Dante himself is now going "from peak to peak.")

But a further question arises: can a person substitute some other good work for an unfulfilled vow? As she prepares to answer, Beatrice shines so brightly at him that Dante has to look away.

Notes

The *Paradiso*'s device of gradual ascent and multiple interviews has the crucial dramatic advantage of creating diversity and suspense before Dante arrives in the "real" Heaven. Even he would have found it hard to sustain interest throughout thirty-three cantos in one location!

In line twenty-eight, speaking of the Seraph that is closest to God, the poet uses the word *s'india,* which literally means "in-God's itself." He probably coined it, as he is credited with coining ninety-two other words.

This canto, which has one word with six syllables *("differentemente"),* has one line with eight monosyllables: *"si fe di quel che far non si convenne* (that was done which ought not to have been done)" (102). It is out-monosyllabized only by *"Di qua, di la, di giu, di su li mena* (From here, from there, from below, from above, it drives them)" *(Inferno* 5:43) and *"e al si e al no che tu non vide* (either to the 'yes' or to the 'no' that you do not see)" *(Paradiso* 13:114).

Canto 5

BEATRICE EXPLAINS HER GLANCE of unearthly love directed at Dante: she who already sees and loves the eternal light sees in Dante a reflection of that light and a love for it. Indeed, if anything but goodness seduces human affections, it is only because some misunderstood or inordinately desired vestige of divine light shines in it.

Answering Dante's question about unfulfilled vows, Beatrice proceeds to cite free will as God's greatest gift to intelligent creatures. Whence the sublime value of any vow by which a person freely sacrifices that freedom to God. To take back such a gift would be to possess ill-gotten goods.

Yet the Church grants dispensations from vows. Is there a contradiction here? Beatrice says that it will behoove Dante "to sit awhile longer at the table, for the tough food that you have taken still requires some aid for your digestion." Then she distinguishes between the fact that a vow has been made and the substance of that vow. Only performance can acquit anyone from a vow.

But the substance can be changed if a greater sacrifice replaces it. Such substituting, though, requires the silver key of priestly wisdom and the golden key of priestly authority. (Shades of the gate of Purgatory!) But if a person has already vowed the highest gift of free will (as in monastic vows), what can outdo or even match it?

Therefore, let not mortals take vows lightly. Be faithful to them, unless the vow was a sinful one—as when the biblical judge Jephthah and the Greek Agamemnon made sacred promises that turned out to require the deaths of their own children. (Some promises shouldn't be honored.)

Actually, Dante seems to be discouraging vows when Beatrice pleads, "Be more serious, Christians, in your undertakings...you have the Old and New Testaments and the Shepherd of the Church to guide you. Let these suffice for your salvation." Certainly Christians should reject money-making "pardoners" who presume to dispense from vows. "Be human beings, not senseless sheep, lest the Jew in your midst laugh at you." (Some contemporary Jews considered this remark a compliment. After all, their reactions are taken seriously.)

Her speech ended, Beatrice glows even more brightly as she and Dante speedily mount to the sphere of Mercury. Her beauty makes even the planet brighter, and it seems to smile. Imagine, then, her impact on Dante, "who by nature am in every way impressionable *(trasmutabile)*!"

Like fish in a pond rising to food, "more than a thousand" splendors draw near to Dante, each exclaiming memorably:

> Behold! Here is one who will increase our loves.
> *(Ecco chi crescera li nostri amori.)*

(As Virgil said in Purgatory, "The more souls there are above...the more love there is" [15:74].) One such splendor, flashing joy like the others, addresses Dante the stranger and amiably offers to answer any questions he may have. Beatrice urges her charge to speak with confidence as he would to divine beings.

Dante replies, "I see that you nest in your own light and display it through your eyes, which shine as you smile. Who are you, then, and why are you precisely here in this planet that is so often veiled to human view by the beams of the Sun?"

The addressed spirit glows even more radiantly from fresh happiness and becomes invisible in its own gleaming as it makes its answer in the entire next canto.

Note

When the Greek fleet was becalmed on its way to Troy because its leader Agamemnon had killed a stag sacred to Diana, he promised the goddess the death of the most beautiful thing to be born in his realm that year. It turned out to be his own daughter, Iphigenia. The biblical judge Jephthah made a vow to Yahweh that if He granted him victory in battle, he would upon his return sacrifice the first person to exit his house to meet him. It turned out to be his daughter, his only child (see Judges 11:30–40).

Canto 6

THIS CANTO IS unique in the whole poem: it is entirely a quote from one person. Replying to Dante's two questions—"Who are you? Why are you here?"—the soul reveals itself to be Justinian, the great lawgiver and Roman emperor (483–565). He lived two centuries after Constantine moved his capital from Rome to what is modern Turkey and thus reversed the westward direction taken by the Trojan Aeneas, legendary ancestor of the Romans.

Born a peasant in what was recently Yugoslavia and named Petrus Sabbatius, Justinian was adopted when he was eight and taken to Constantinople by his uncle Justin, who renamed him Justinian. As commander of the imperial guard, the uncle was proclaimed emperor in 518. Justinian succeeded him in 527.

At first believing that Christ had only a divine nature, Justinian says he was converted to the true doctrine of two natures by Pope Agapetus (535–36). (Actually, it was probably his astonishing wife, Theodora, rather than he who was the Monophysite.) From then on, as though now taking human justice more seriously, he turned over military affairs to general Belisarius and devoted himself to simplifying and codifying Roman law, that classic instrument of world justice.

Justinian wants to show that the role of the Roman Empire in history is divinely willed and worthy of reverence. Its enemies are not only the anti-imperial Guelphs of Dante's day, allied with the "lilies of France," but also the supposedly pro-imperial but narrow-minded Ghibellines. (Only here in the poem are these two parties cited together by name.)

Employing the ancient symbol of the Roman eagle, Justinian himself next glides like an eagle over the history of the empire from its beginning with Aeneas, through the crucifixion of Jesus (under Tiberius) and the fall of Jerusalem (under Titus), to the championship of the Church by Charlemagne. Including some minor historical errors, this swooping summary aims to establish the link between the original empire and its current, fourteenth-century embodiment.

Turning to Dante's second question, the spirit explains that all the souls Dante sees in this little star of Mercury performed virtuous deeds on Earth but were taintingly spurred on by hunger for earthly honor and fame. Now freed from envious desire for greater reward and momentarily associated with a planet often obscured by the Sun, these souls actually rejoice in the justice of the inferior degree of happiness accorded them.

Among these souls, and in humble contrast to the great Justinian, is Romeo, once minister of Raymond Berengar at the court of Provence. (Provence, ironically, did not acknowledge fealty to the Holy Roman emperor.) When Romeo was slandered out of jealousy, he cited his good deeds—returning "twelve" for every "ten"—took up again his pilgrim's staff, and wandered off, poor and old. "If the world knew the heart he had as he begged his bread morsel by morsel, it would praise him more."

So much for the justice of the world's glory-giving. With this story of Romeo (which seems to be legendary), Dante the exile could identify his own experience at the hands of anti-imperial Florence.

Notes

This canto provides us with the first mention of Christ in the *Paradiso*. Also, though Justinian speaks of Cassius and Brutus as barking out in Hell, Dante in the pit of Hell spoke of Brutus as saying nothing, and mentioned no sound issuing from Cassius.

In canto 6 of the *Inferno*, we encounter the first discussion of Florence in the poem; in the sixth of the *Purgatorio* Dante discusses the state of Italy. In this sixth canto Justinian treats of the political condition of the whole empire.

In the last half of this canto there are four references to "justice," the root of Justinian's name and the ideal goal of any system of law.

Canto 7

SINGING A SONG based on a Mass hymn, Justinian praises the holy God of hosts, Who with His own brightness intensifies the happy fires of Heaven's realms. Radiant with both earthly and heavenly glory, the emperor uses both Hebrew and Latin, the languages of history's pivotal cities of Jerusalem and Rome.

As he sings, he and his fellow spirits present us with the first of many celestial dances. Then, like the swiftest flames, they hide themselves from Dante "with sudden distance." Thus these active spirits of Earth preserve even in Heaven their energetic ways.

In his account of the history of the empire, Justinian has said something that perplexes Dante. But even the syllables of Beatrice's nickname *(Bice)* now overawe this lover, so he finds himself unable to question her. But "with a smile that would make a person in fire happy," she answers his question with words that fill up almost all the lines of this canto.

How could God's just vengeance, which used one Roman emperor (Tiberius) to conspire with Jewish leaders in Jerusalem to put Christ to death, use another Roman emperor (Vespatian) to punish that same Jerusalem by destroying it? In answer to this dilemma, Beatrice promises her hearer the gift of a great doctrine.

She begins with the first man, directly created in body and soul, and therefore "never born." By refusing to be limited in his choices, Adam brought ruin upon himself and his descendants, who lay sick in great error for long centuries. Then, out of love, God's own Son united Himself with Adam's fallen nature. When Christ was crucified, the penalty was just with regard to the human nature that suffered it. But it was grievously unjust with regard to the divine person who endured it.

But for Dante (and many another), the further question, *cur crux?* arises: why did God choose this method of reconciliation with Himself? "This decree," says Beatrice, "is hidden from the eyes of everyone whose understanding has not matured within love's flame." When it was first created by God, human nature enjoyed the gifts of immortality and free will and hence a special likeness to God. When human nature sinned in Adam, it became unlike God and fell from its noble state. Mortality resulted, along with an impairment of freedom.

Now it would seem that humankind could have been reconciled either by a one-sided act of God's mercy *("cortesia")*, or by a full act of reparation by humankind. But humanity could never go so low in humble apology as to counterbalance the heights to which sinful pride had impelled Adam to aspire. Since a deed is more pleasing to the doer when it displays more of his or her heart's goodness, "God was more bounteous in giving Himself to make man sufficient to lift himself again, than if He solely of Himself remitted the sin."

To clarify her statement about the immortality of whatever proceeds directly from God, Beatrice notes that the corruptible elements of the universe (earth, air, fire, water) and all the compounds made from them receive their forms from created powers—namely, the basic stuff of the world combined with the molding influence of the stars and their angelic ministrants. The soul too of every beast and plant is drawn from its potential matter by the shining and the motion of these holy lights of Heaven. But without intermediary, the human soul is breathed forth by the Supreme Benefactor, Who so enamors it of Himself that it desires Him ever after.

Here, concludes Beatrice, is an argument for the resurrection of the body—it too was directly made by God in the case of our first parents. Hence it is touched with the promise of ultimate immortality.

Notes

The "paradise" mentioned twice in this canto refers to the earthly garden of delight from which Adam and Eve were expelled, not the heavenly goal toward which Dante is now traveling.

With a slight misspelling, Dante (who knew little Hebrew) probably borrowed *malacoth* in line three from the word *mamlacoth* (the Hebrew word for *kingdoms*) cited by Saint Jerome in his preface to the Vulgate Bible.

Canto 8

THE GODDESS VENUS was said to have been born on the island of Cyprus, hence she is "the Cyprian." Ancient people identified her with the planet Venus, which woos the Sun from in front as the morning star, from behind as the evening star. To their own detriment, pagans believed that from this planet she radiated insane love—as when her son Cupid inspired Queen Dido with a suicidal love for Aeneas.

Dante is not conscious of rising to the sphere of Venus, but the magnified beauty of Beatrice assures him that he has. He sees, as sparks within a flame, lights dancing within the planet's light. Leaving this dance, which originates among the highest angels in God's presence, some of these lights come as swiftly as lightning to the poet. They sing, "*Hosanna*" with unforgettable loveliness.

One of these spirits comes especially close, and the rest of this canto is a dialogue between Dante and this spirit of the French Angevan prince Charles Martel. Six years Dante's junior, Charles had visited Florence for several weeks in 1294, the year before his tragic death at age twenty-four.

Martel had met the poet during that visit. Giving the author a third chance to quote himself, the spirit now cites the first line of a sixty-one–line poem (a literary sensation in Florence at that time) that Dante addressed to the angelic forces that control this sphere of Venus: "You who move the third heaven with your minds." (This is another of the three canzones Dante explains at great length in *The Banquet*.) Apparently, their brief association on Earth was quite affectionate. "You loved me much and had good cause," Charles reminisces. If he had lived longer, he would have shown Dante "much more of my love than the leaves." (Charles is said to have admired the poet's perfect handwriting and offered him a secretarial job.)

Referring to various rivers and land boundaries, Charles speaks of territories that were to be his (Provence, Naples) or were his already (Hungary). He would have been heir too of the Kingdom of Sicily (Trinacria) had not his harsh grandfather Charles I caused the Sicilians to revolt and expel the French ("the Sicilian Vespers" of 1282). His younger brother Robert will become King of Naples after their father's death in 1309. Charles foresees trouble for Robert if he does not control his own greediness and that of his Catalan (Spanish) aides. Alas, that generous ancestors should have produced such a stingy heir!

Representing this planet of love, Charles began by saying, "We all stand ready to please you, that you may have joy of us....We are so full of love that to do you pleasure a little stillness will be no less sweet to us" than their customary dancing. Dante, who asked to know who they were, now says that he knows that thanks to his vision of God, Charles can see how much joy his words have given the poet and the even greater joy that Dante feels in knowing that Charles knows. But can Charles tell him how it happens that bitter fruit can come from sweet seed? How can noble fathers beget ignoble children?

Charles replies that temperament is not hereditary but is largely determined by the Providence that exerts its influence through heavenly bodies, giving individuals their specific natures and the inclination to develop them. Thus are produced those human variations that are needed as people enjoy the advantages of civil society. These different types are needed to perform various roles, such as legislators, warriors, priests, and artisans. (Dante's "master," Aristotle, taught thus about society.)

So it happens that Providence modifies heredity to make children different from parents. Nature too stamps out differences without regard to family background. Thus, even before birth the twins Jacob and Esau differed, and Quirinus (Romulus), who founded Rome, came from such an obscure background that people felt free to suppose that his father was Mars.

As a sign of his delight in Dante, Charles adds a practical corollary:

people should follow their temperaments, otherwise nature will be thwarted like a seed in hostile soil. Charles's own brother Louis, born to be a warrior, had entered the priesthood. His brother Robert, fond of theology and sermon-writing, had gone into kingship. Thus do human footprints wander off the road.

Notes

This Charles Martel should not be confused with the better-known one who defeated the Arab Muslims at the battle of Tours (732). This present Charles belonged to the French House of Anjou (Angevins). Dante had trusted the Angevins in his youth, but they helped defeat his later, dearest hopes by their opposition to Emperor Henry VII. Related to the Angevins by marriage was the Charles of Valois whose papally endorsed entrance into Florence led to Dante's exile and death sentence. Despite all his negative experiences of the Angevins, however, Dante could still regard Charles as a dear friend. Such are the variations of personality within family groups.

In this canto Dante reveals for the first time his belief that heavenly souls, by a kind of spiritual telepathy resulting from their vision of God, know what he is thinking and feeling.

Canto 9

IN THE OPENING LINE of this canto, Dante addresses beautiful Clemence, probably the wife of Charles Martel, but possibly his daughter. In any case, the poet refers to the wrongs that will be done to the son of Charles when Charles's brother deprives that son of the throne of Naples. Charles gives revelations to Dante about this matter but bids him keep silent. He can only say that deserved sorrows will avenge the treachery.

As Charles takes his leave, Dante refers to the presence of the saint as his "*vita* (life)"—a usage he will repeat five times in the *Paradiso*, and one that indicates the vital personality that the saints enjoy in Heaven.

In addition to his friend Charles (whose specific "Venereal" flaw the poet delicately leaves unmentioned), three other excessive lovers, now purified, occupy this last canto dealing with Venus. Two are women, one is a man. Dante asks the first woman, Cunizza (1198–1279), to show that she knows his question before he asks it. She says she was the sister of the horrible Italian tyrant Ezzelino (1194–1259) mentioned in the *Inferno* (canto 12). She was the lover of that Sordello we met in the *Purgatorio* (canto 6). He abducted her from her first husband. She had three other husbands and at least two other lovers.

Later she led a reformed life in Florence, living with Guido Cavalcanti's family and dying when Dante was about fifteen. Like Piccarda, she accepts her limited degree of bliss: "I gladly pardon in myself the cause of my lot and it does not grieve me." Translator Dorothy Sayers calls this one of the most joyous utterances in all the *Paradiso*.

Beholding as she does God's angels of justice (the "thrones" of Saturn), she forecasts the punishment of certain loveless sinners from her native northeastern section of Italy. Her references, including six rivers and six cities of the area, are a bit hard to follow. It may help to know that Realto refers to Venice; Padua (which claims to be the oldest city in Italy) was punished for resisting imperial authority; the bishop of Feltre betrayed to the city of Ferrara (from which the Florentine Alighieris may have come) a group of political exiles who had sought his protection; and there was in Malta a well-known prison for ecclesiastics.

In the midst of her prophecy, Cunizza—characteristically generous—refers to the fame of the precious jewel now shining close to her. Of this Folquet (*circa* 1160–1231) she says his fame will survive five more turns of the century. (Time's up!) Thus should a man excel in his mortal life and lead a life of worthy fame afterward.

Dante now sees Folquet shining as a fine, sun-struck ruby. Referring to the saint's past as a troubadour, our poet teasingly asks why he has not yet heard Folquet's famous voice. Finally speaking, the saint reveals that he was born at Marseilles (the oldest city in France), whose waters were once muddied by a battle between Caesar's fleet and local supporters of Pompey.

He claims that love for women made him suffer torments equal to that of three classic lovers: Dido, whose love for Aeneas wronged her dead husband and led to her suicide; a princess who hanged herself when she thought her lover had abandoned her; and Hercules (Alcides), whose wife caused his death when he made Iole his mistress. After his repentance, Folquet persuaded his wife to join a convent with their two children and became a Cistercian monk and later the bishop of Toulouse (where, alas, he passionately persecuted heretics).

Yet here we do not repent, but rather smile—not for our fault, which escapes our mind—but for the power that ordained and foresaw everything. Here we ponder the art that beautifies the lofty outcome of it all. Here we discern those good results for which the world above makes the world below revolve.

Just as Cunizza sang Folquet's praise, he lauds his companion, Rahab, the harlot who helped Joshua conquer Jericho and who was an ancestor of the Christ who won salvation for her. Not so caring about the land of Joshua are those Vatican officials who study papal decrees as a way of making money—epitomized by the devil-minted florins of Florence. (Here occurs the poem's first and only use of the word *Vatican*—the section in pagan Rome where the "vates" [prophets] lived and where Saint Peter was buried.) As a result, no crusade has been summoned to rescue the Holy Land after the last Christian government there was destroyed at Acre in 1291. Folquet concludes by prophesying that by leaving Rome for Avignon (1309), the papacy will soon cease defiling the burial place of Peter and other early Christian martyrs. (In point of fact, Clement V had been on the road since his election in 1305.)

Note

As Rome increasingly became the final court of appeal for Western Christianity, the financial cost of the growing bureaucracy became ever steeper. Until Dante was a teenager, the pope's official residence had been the Lateran Palace, donated by Constantine. Nicholas III (1277–80) was the first pope to make the Vatican his residence. The poet gave him his posthumous residence in the Hell of avarice.

Canto 10

DANTE HAS NOW ARRIVED at the Sun, the first heavenly sphere that is untouched by the Earth's shadow. From now on he will encounter saints who are briefly reflected in an appropriate sphere for a positive reason only. Thus with a speed that is outside of time Beatrice conducts him from good to better.

The Sun is an apt symbol of God's own brightness and that of those human beings who wisely labored on Earth to absorb and reflect the light of truth about God and His universe. Dante invites the reader to share in his admiration for the heavens, including the tilt of the Sun that gives Earth its change of seasons and a cyclical increase of generating warmth. For Dante, the God of Whom the Sun is image is a trinity consisting of the power of the Father, the wisdom of the Son, and the Spirit of love breathed forth by Each for the Others.

The circle, symbol of eternity, pertains to all the heavenly spheres. But it is heavily emphasized here with references to the equator, the ecliptic (the Sun's path through the zodiac), revolutions, the Moon and its girdle, a garland, a wreath, a clock, and a wheel.

When Beatrice urges Dante to give thanks for his arrival, he is so moved with love for God that even Beatrice is momentarily eclipsed in his thoughts. (An eclipse *in* the Sun!) She is not displeased, but smiles in such a way that the splendor of her laughing eyes recalls him to his surroundings. "There I saw many living and surpassing lights, sweeter in voice than bright in aspect, who made a center of us and a crown of themselves." (A neat image!)

This first circle of saints—there will eventually be three in this sphere—thrice dances around the poet and his guide. Beatrice, a symbol of wisdom, is thus surrounded by the wise. Though Dante compares them to women dancing, these dancers are all male. Like hours on a clock, this circle contains twelve scholars from whose writings Dante has personally reaped much wisdom. So bright are they that they stand out even with the Sun as a backdrop!

One figure speaks, identifying himself as Thomas Aquinas (1224–74), the masterful Dominican philosopher/theologian. He died when Dante was nine. Our poet here canonizes him before the Church did (1323), but not before the bishops of Paris, Oxford, and Canterbury (a fellow Dominican!) condemned some of his teachings. (He was judged to be too heavily influenced by "pagan" thinkers like Aristotle. Believing that natural reason was a "harlot," and that human nature was a damned and damnable mass, Martin Luther later held the same view of Aquinas and doubted the salvation of this "greatest of chatterboxes.")

Curiously, our poet doesn't mention any writings by Aquinas. A chief goal of these writings was to argue the basic compatibility between the discovered truths of reason and the revealed truths of the Bible. The commanding and newly available writings of the pre-Christian Aristotle made this task urgent. Among the Jews, Moses Maimonides (1135–1204) had the same task as regards Jewish tradition and Islamic thinkers with respect to the Koran.

Right off, this "Angelic Doctor" names his eleven companions in various indirect ways. These prove to be an international group spanning twenty-one centuries:

1. The Dominican Albert the Great (teacher of Aquinas), who died in 1280 when Dante was sixteen but wasn't canonized until 1932.

2. The Italian Gratian, the shadowy father of canon law, whose harmonizing collection of Church and civil laws appeared about 1150. It was named *A Concordance of Discordant Regulations,* or *Gratian's Decretals.*

3. Peter Lombard (*circa* 1100–1164), bishop of Paris and "the master of opinions," who wrote four *Libri Sententiarum (The Books of Opinions),* bringing together the views of the Church Fathers on four key subjects; he called his writings his "widow's mite."

4. King Solomon, David's son by Bathsheba, the most beautiful of the group, though Saint Augustine believed him to have been damned.

5. Dionysius the Areopagite, Saint Paul's first-century Greek convert, to whom was falsely ascribed a highly influential fifth- or sixth-century opus about angels, *On the Heavenly Hierarchy.*

6. Probably the Orosius who was a Spanish cleric and historian, and a fifth-century contemporary of Saint Augustine. He wrote seven books that aimed to disprove the pagan claim that the world had grown worse since Christianity arrived.

7. Boethius (*circa* 480–524), Roman-born and a favorite of our poet. Written in jail before his execution for treason, his *On the Consolation of Philosophy* consoled Dante greatly after the death of Beatrice. The Middle Ages widely regarded him as a martyr under the name Saint Severinus, his full name being Anicius Manlius Severinus Boethius.

8. Isidore of Seville (*circa* 570–636), archbishop and highly influential author of encyclopedic works.

9. The Venerable Bede (*circa* 673–735), Anglo-Saxon monk and father of English history.

10. Richard of St. Victor (died 1173), perhaps a Scotsman, chief of the twelfth-century mystics, prior of the illustrious Augustinian monastery near Paris.

11. Siger of Brabant (died *circa* 1284), a shadowy Belgian whose brilliance caused jealousy and who died under a ban of heresy, was actually a philosophic adversary of Aquinas; but Heaven has reconciled them.

After Aquinas has finished doing the honors, the whole group revolves like a clock wheel (which goes, *"tin, tin"* on Earth) and sings with a sweetness that can be known only where joy is eternal.

Notes

After making his introductory and complicated astronomical observations, Dante has blunt advice for the reader: "Now stay on your bench...I have put food before you; now feed yourself."

Aquinas implies Dante's eventual salvation by affirming that no one descends these heavenly stairs without climbing them again.

The poet pointedly mentions the Parisian street in the Latin Quarter where Siger taught (before he fled to Italy and was stabbed to death by a mad cleric). Some see this as a sign that Dante himself visited Paris and perhaps studied there. Today that Straw Street is named Rue Dante.

Canto II

ONCE AGAIN WE HAVE a canto that is almost entirely a quote from one person. In this case the Dominican Thomas Aquinas sings the praises of Francis of Assisi, the founder of the Franciscan order, to which Aquinas did not belong and whose novices were for awhile forbidden to study Thomas's writings. In Heaven there is no room for professional jealousy between various religious fraternities. There is room, though, for Aquinas to lament that his own fraternity on Earth has declined from the ideals of its early days not that long ago.

But first Dante thinks of the various earthly activities, both good and bad, that distract human beings from the deeper concerns of the spirit.

Dante delights to recall that while earthlings were wasting their time in diverse ways, "I, set free from all these things, was high in Heaven with Beatrice."

In his previous remarks, Aquinas made two statements that puzzled the poet. The mind-reading saint now proceeds to deal with one of the puzzlements: what he meant by saying that Saint Dominic leads his holy flock on a path that fattens if they do not stray. (It is hard to see why Dante, of all people, would have found this imagery obscure.)

The saint explains that Providence, in its inscrutable manner, raised up two princes to help make Christ's bride (the Church) more faithful to Him. These were Dominic of Spain and Francis of Assisi. Dominic stressed the gifts of the mind and reflected the angelic rank of the bright Cherubim. Francis stressed devotion of the heart and reflected the ardent Seraphim. Courteously, Aquinas chooses to expand on the life of Saint Francis (*circa* 1181–1226) and his Christlike devotion to Lady Poverty.

In terms thick with Italian geographical references, Aquinas (who traveled around Europe mostly on foot) tells of Assisi, the birthplace of a spiritual sun who rose to soften and fructify the dormant Earth. While still a youth, Francis abandoned the pursuit of possessions, stripped himself before his father and his bishop, and chose the company of Lady Poverty, "to whom, as to death, no one willingly unlocks the door."

That Lady, who joined the dispossessed Christ on the cross, had since His time gone without an ardent suitor. People had not learned the lesson that even the poor pagan fisherman Amyclas had taught when he refused to be intimidated by the mighty Julius Caesar. A certain security lies in having little to lose.

The barefoot Francis soon attracted followers like Bernard, Giles, and Sylvester. Though a Church council in 1215 had forbidden the establishment of any new religious orders, in 1223 Pope Honorius III put his seal of approval on the Franciscan brotherhood that developed. Innocent III had given preliminary approval in 1210.

Heaven itself put a final seal on the very body of Francis when the wounds of Christ crucified (the stigmata) were miraculously imprinted there two years before his death. (Francis was one of the very few males known to have exhibited these marks, and possibly the first of any.) Earlier, Francis had bravely gone to Egypt in an effort to convert the Moslem sultan, who received him respectfully. At his death the saint commended his Lady to the care of his followers and asked to be placed in her bosom (the Earth) and to have no other covering. He was canonized less than two years later. His early disciples, at least, continued to court Lady Poverty. The first Franciscan foundation in London was in the slums at a place called "Stinking Alley."

Aquinas ends this discourse by referring to the founder of his own order, the patriarch Dominic, who strove to keep Peter's barque (the Church) on the right course. But his followers now seek worldly fame and gain. The number who stay close to the original ideals are so few that only a little cloth would be needed to make their religious garb. As though making subtle fun of Aquinas's style, Dante has him say in his conclusion: "if my words were not obscure, and if you have listened with attention, and if you recall what I said...."

Note

The 1893 *Life of St. Francis* by Calvinist pastor Paul Sabatier sparked a renewal in our century of interest in Francis and Franciscan studies. Though warmly sympathetic to the saint, it was judged too liberal by Vatican authorities and promptly placed on the Roman Index.

Canto 12

AS AQUINAS ENDS his first clarification, the circle of saints starts another revolution. Before it concludes, it is joined by an outer circle that is synchronized with it in motion and song. The result reminds the poet of a double rainbow. The outer circle is like an echo of the inner. Suggesting the coordination of a single pair of eyes, both stop at the same instant.

Then, from the heart of one of these new lights, Dante hears a voice that draws him like a needle to a magnet. It is the "life" of Saint Bonaventure, who died as superior of the Franciscan friars in 1274—the year of Aquinas's death and of Dante's first glimpse of Beatrice. Prompted by "the love that makes me lovely *(l'amor che mi fa bella)* [feminine *bella* to agree with *vita*]," the saint says he will speak of another great founder, Saint Dominic *(circa* 1170–1221).

Bonaventure's eulogy of Dominic closely parallels Aquinas's of Francis, though there is a greater emphasis on the miraculous—prophetic utterances and foreshadowing dreams. As Francis was like the Sun "ascending" (Assisi) in the east, Dominic, born in Spain "near" the Atlantic, was like the enlivening west wind. His baptismal name indicated that he belonged to the Lord *(Dominus)*. His father, Felice, was indeed felicitous; his mother, Giovanna (Yahweh gives), was indeed a channel of "God's giving."

Like Dante's mother, she had a prophetic dream before her son was born. In it she gave birth to a dog whose mouth held a black and white torch that set the world aflame. (The dog appears in the statue of the saint near the main altar of the Vatican's St. Peter's.) Black and white are the colors of the Dominican habit. *Canes* meaning "dogs" in Latin, the Dominicans have been called hounds of the Lord. In their less inspiring moments, as inquisitors who violated their founder's belief in sharp arguments rather than sharp swords, they hounded heretics and supposed heretics mercilessly.

Like Francis, Dominic was genuinely concerned about the poor, not about Church honors or alms diverted from the needy. He wanted to crusade for the Gospel, not to study worldly textbooks by Ostian (law) and Taddeo (medicine). In this he was following Christ's "first" command (probably "Go, sell what thou hast, and give to the poor" [Matthew 19:21]). Founding his order in 1215, the same year in which he accompanied the fierce ex-troubadour Bishop Folquet to the Fourth Lateran Council, he received approbation within a year from the seat (the Chair of Peter), which, in principle, is kind to the poor, though the present incumbent (Boniface VIII) is degenerating. Dead in 1221, Dominic was canonized in 1234. The canonizing pope said he no more doubted Dominic's sanctity than that of Peter or Paul.

Calling Francis and Dominic the two wheels of the chariot we saw in the pageant in the Forest of Eden, Bonaventure describes Dominic in imagery that is a riot of mixed metaphors: a soldier, an athlete, a gardener, a torrent. (Is Dante ribbing the lush style of some spiritual authors?) Like the backsliding Dominicans deplored by Aquinas, current Franciscans do not follow in the tracks of their founder; indeed, they go backward. Some friars observe the rule too laxly, others too narrowly. The names of friars who keep the rule correctly would require only a single page in a book.

Bonaventure ends, as Aquinas began, by naming himself and his companions. These twelve too form an international, all-male group spanning twenty-two centuries. They are

1, 2. Two early Italian Franciscans, Illuminato and Augustine.

   3. Hugh of the Abbey of St. Victor near Paris (*circa* 1097–1141), an influential mystic and theologian who was hailed as a second Saint Augustine, his very tongue.

   4. Peter the Eater (of books, not pumpkins); born in French Troyes, he died in 1179.

   5. Peter the Spaniard (*circa* 1225–1277), who was actually from Portugal. As John XXI he became the only Portuguese pope. Against the dangers of Aristotelianism he issued a decree that spurred the bishop of Paris to condemn nineteen positions of the newly deceased Aquinas. After only nine months in the papacy, he was killed by the falling ceiling of a cell hastily built at the rear of his palace. There he planned to continue his scholarly pursuits while leaving decision making to advisers. Son of a doctor, he was a doctor himself and the personal physician of Pope Gregory X. He wrote a widely used book on logic and a popular book on the eye. Canonized by the poem but not by the Church, he is the only contemporary pope mentioned by Dante as being in Paradise. (In his various writings, the Florentine mentions or alludes to twenty-eight popes.)

   6. The Hebrew prophet Nathan, who was not afraid to chastise the mighty King David for arranging the death of Bathsheba's husband ("Thou art the man!").

   7. Saint John Chrysostom (*circa* 345–407), the Syrian, "golden-mouthed" patriarch of Constantinople; he was justly famous for his honesty, self-denial, and tactlessness. The last quality led to his exile.

   8. Saint Anselm (1033–1109), Italian archbishop of Canterbury, famous for his "Ontological Argument" for God's existence. Aquinas and Kant criticized it; Descartes and Hegel defended it.

   9. Donatus, the fourth-century Roman author of a famous Latin grammar (an odd choice, except that Dante loved language).

  10. Rabanus/Hrabanus (*circa* 776–856), abbot and archbishop of his native Mainz, who was regarded as one of the greatest scholars of his day.

  11. Finally, just as Aquinas has his adversary Siger on his left, so Bonaventure has on his left the Abbot Joachim of Flora (died

circa 1220). This Cistercian monk predicted an approaching final age of history, the age of the Everlasting Gospel. The Church would then be superseded by the individual perfection and freedom conferred by the Holy Spirit. The abbot triggered an extremist spiritual movement among the Franciscans. (See the book and movie *The Name of the Rose*.) Bonaventure strove to combat it.

Notes

Born Giovanni de Fidanza, Bonaventure was blessed by Francis of Assisi during a childhood illness. When Francis heard of the boy's remarkable recovery, he gave thanks for the *buona ventura*—the good outcome—and inspired a new name for the future saint, who wrote one of the first biographies of Francis. Like Roger Bacon and William of Ockham, Bonaventure was one of the early Franciscans who did not inherit their founder's disdain for book learning.

Back in the 1960s when the flower children were speaking of a new age, Joachim of Flora made the cover of *Time* magazine. Joachim's stock fell when the year 1260 passed without the cataclysm that he had foretold would usher in a new age. Yet Bonaventure still says Joachim was endowed with a prophetic spirit.

Though Franciscans and Dominicans were discouraged from seeking Church offices—Francis was not a priest, and Dominic thrice refused a bishop's miter—before their founding century was over, the papacy would have its first Dominican (Blessed Innocent V, 1276) and its first Franciscan (Nicholas IV, 1288.)

In line seven, for the first time in the poem, the word "Christ" is used to end a line. As though to indicate that *Cristo* has no worthy rhyme (though in a youthful sonnet he rhymed *Cristo* with *tristo*), Dante uses it twice again to round out his terza rima. This unique rhyme scheme occurs three more times in the *Paradiso*. (At times in *The Comedy* he occasionally rhymes a word with itself. But these literal "triple rhymes" are unique.)

Line 104's "Catholic garden" gives us the only use of the word "Catholic" in the poem. "Christianity" appears twice, and "Christian" thirteen times.

Canto 13

DANTE INVITES THE READER to imagine twenty-four stars arranged as two concentric circles. Let these stars be the fifteen considered to be of the first magnitude, plus seven from the Big Dipper (the Wain) and two from the Little Dipper (the Horn). All this would give the reader a pale idea of the saintly circles he saw in the sphere of the Sun.

Once again these solar saints circle about at a speed that is as far beyond human experience as the swiftest heaven exceeds the speed of the sluggish Tuscan stream known as Chiana. Not about gods like Bacchus and Apollo does this spiritual constellation sing rapturously, but of God as three-personed and of Christ as double-natured.

When the circling and the singing stop again, Aquinas out of sweet love resumes his discussion. He notes Dante's belief that God's light shone brightest in Adam and in Christ. Therefore, the poet is puzzled by Aquinas's earlier statement that Solomon has no equal in his wisdom. The saint proceeds to show that both he and Dante are correct.

Creating out of love and through His Son the Word, God mirrors His reality through the nine choirs of angels. These in turn transmit divine energy down through the heavenly spheres to the pure potency of prime matter. Variations in the receptive matter and in the imprinting forms of things produce a variety of effects and degrees of perfection. Nature may be defective on occasion, like an artist with trembling hands. (A bold statement about God-created nature!) But when God acts directly, the result is perfect. Such was the case in the creation of Adam and in the conception of Christ.

What Aquinas meant about Solomon was that he was without equal in the gift of the kingly wisdom that he asked and received of God at the dedication of the Temple (1 Kings 2). Aquinas itemizes some of the merely speculative questions for which Solomon did not seek an answer when God offered him anything he wanted. Aquinas recalls that he had used the verb *rose* of Solomon and was thus putting him in the category of men who rose to kingly power. Of kings, the saint notes, there are many, though the good ones few.

These verbal distinctions will strike many a reader as much ado about nothing. But the saint ends his disquisition with some picturesque advice against hasty judgments and the neglect of necessary distinctions.

(It has been said that a true scholastic seldom affirms, never denies, and always distinguishes.) He names some pagan philosophers and Christian theologians (like Arius) who failed in these respects. He also warns of the way in which pride can keep hasty persons from changing their minds.

"Let us not be too sure in judging," Aquinas summarizes. Seeming saints who donate money may stumble at the end of life, while seeming sinners who steal money may produce unexpected fruits of repentance. "I have seen a thornbush first show itself stiff and savage all winter long, and then bear a rose on its crown. I have before now seen a ship plow the sea straight and swift through all her course, then finally meet disaster at the harbor entrance." These warnings are intended for Dame Bertha and Squire Martin—his version of Jane and John Doe.

Thus the "dry" Aquinas, Dante's intellectual father, poetically ends his 287 lines of speech spread over three cantos. Apart from Virgil, Beatrice, and Dante himself, no one has more lines in *The Comedy*, except our poet's physical progenitor, Cacciaguida, who will speak 299 lines over four upcoming cantos.

Notes

The Franciscans and Dominicans, founded almost simultaneously, were mendicant, or begging, orders, true novelties in the Church. Unlike older orders and parish priests, they renounced property, often had no fixed address, went straight to the people, and depended directly on them. They were like medieval hippies and were quite popular. They aroused much jealously, not least of all when they diverted donations from other clerics, criticized the ecclesiastical status quo, and competed for teaching positions with the academic establishment.

Sharing common attacks from outside, the mendicant orders tended to stick together. So it is not surprising that in the *Paradiso* a Dominican lauds the Franciscan founder, and vice versa. In their litanies, each order uniquely mentions the two founders twice in a row. In the past, the "general" of each order has conducted the funeral of the "general" of the other. On each founder's feast day it is customary for a member of the opposite order to preach the eulogy at the community Mass.

This canto, in which Aquinas speaks of variations, has one line with only three words: "*etternalmente rimanendosi una* (eternally remaining one)"; and one with ten words, of which nine are necessarily monosyllables: "*e al si e al no che tu non vedi* (and to the 'yes' and to the 'no' that you do not see)."

Canto 14

WE HAVE BEEN in the heaven of the Sun for three cantos. We will leave it midway through this one, but not before Beatrice (silent since her arrival) addresses nine lines to the two saintly circles, vocalizing two more questions in Dante's mind: Will you saints always remain so bright; and if so, will not such blinding light harm your fleshy eyes when you have resumed your earthly bodies?

Rejoicing at the chance to answer such devout questioning, the saints revolve again and wondrously sing a threefold praise of the Blessed Trinity. Hearing it, Dante avows that those who lament the prospect of death can only be unaware of the celestial refreshment awaiting them. (Provided they get there!)

It is King Solomon who responds modestly—the reputed author of the Song of Songs, that hymn of bodily delight. He asserts that their saintly splendor will last as long as Paradise, since it is an expression of the ardor that results from their vision of God. Reunited with their bodies, they will be loved even more by God, Who will freely shed on them an even more bountiful degree of that light that enables them to see Him. From their increased vision will come increased ardor, which will heighten their joyous radiance.

The risen body will be like a hot coal manifesting its shape through flames and outshining them. Thus will the body's glory outshine even the spirit's! And the bodily eyes will be strengthened to do all that can delight them. Solomon's twenty-three companions instantly answer, "Amen," thereby manifesting their desire for their bodies, and perhaps for the bodies of their fathers and mothers and others who were dear before they became eternal flames. (No Gnostic, Manichean, or Albigensian rejection of the body here!)

Suddenly, Dante sees a third circle of light shining around the other two, faintly at first, then overwhelmingly. He calls this phenomenon the veritable sparkling of the Holy Spirit. It seems composed of new substances.

Is it meant to suggest that final Age of the Spirit predicted by Abbot Joachim? (At the time of the poem, it was embarrassingly forty years overdue.)

Beatrice now so grows in beauty that she too overwhelms Dante's sight, though actually fortifying it in the process. When his eyes recover, the poet looks up and sees that he has risen to a new sphere, for he perceives the fiery smile of the planet Mars, ruddier than usual.

Before he has finished expressing gratitude in his heart for this new grace, he beholds a gigantic cross of white light, within which ruddy splendors dart about like dust particles visible in a sunbeam shining into a darkened room. In some ineffable way, that cross radiates forth Christ Himself. From the splendors issues a melodious song that transports Dante, though he can make out only the words "Arise and conquer."

It seems that no sweetness has ever gripped him so completely. Not even Beatrice's eyes? True, they were even more enchanting at this fresh level, but he has not yet gazed at them.

Canto 15

WE ARE NEARING the central canto of the *Paradiso*. Dante makes ready for it by recounting a dramatic meeting with his great-great-grandfather, Cacciaguida, who died a martyr in the Second Crusade (1147–49). Given more lines than anyone except Beatrice, Virgil, and Dante, he will be the main figure of this canto and the two that follow.

Manifesting their gracious desire that Dante should question them, the saints reflected in this sphere of Mars grow silent. ("Rightly should that man grieve forever who, through love of things that do not last, robs himself of such amiable company!")

Racing like a shooting star, but without leaving the outline of the cross, one of the blazing spirits in the right arm of the cross moves close to the poet, who stands at its foot. Speaking in Latin, the spirit exclaims, "O blood of mine! O lavish grace of God! To whom as to you was Heaven's gate ever opened twice?" (Another prophecy of Dante's ultimate salvation!)

The spirit continues briefly in words too deep for human grasping. Then, relaxing the bow of its affection so that the poet can understand, it praises the Trinity for having been "so courteous to my seed." Finally, it addresses the poet as "my son," saying it has longed for this moment, foreseen in the book of destiny.

Though Dante knows that the spirit knows what Dante wants to ask, the spirit wants to hear the questioning words from his descendant's own lips. Though God and His saints have no wish that they lack the intelligence to fulfill, not so we tongue-tied earthlings. So Dante confesses that his words cannot match his gratitude for so paternal a welcome. He calls the spirit a living topaz and asks the inevitable: "Who are you?"

"O leaf of mine...I was your root!" He reveals that a son of his has been circling the pride-atoning first ledge of Purgatory for more than a century. That son, who gave Dante his family name of Alighieri, was the grandfather of the poet's father. Recalling his own baptism, the spirit reveals his name as Cacciaguida. Conceived after ardent prayers to the Madonna, he was born in a better Florence than Dante was.

Citizens dressed simply then. Dowries were not too high, nor the age of marriage too low. Homes were not wastefully big. People did not indulge in the kind of sexual excesses that made King Sardanapalus of Assyria infamous. (That king had not yet arrived in Florence to show what could be done in the bed chamber.) Women did not paint their faces nor dread being buried in exile or having their husbands away on long business trips to France. (Supposedly, *Francis* of Assisi was so called because of his merchant father's French connections.)

Fond parents handed down inspiring stories of patriotism to their children. The city's Mount Uccellatoio did not then look down on opulence greater than Rome's, nor on decay worse than Rome's. Citizens like Berti, de' Nerli, and del Vecchio were like the noble Romans Cincinnatus and Cornelia—not like Dante's corrupt contemporaries, Cianghella and Salterello.

Cacciaguida tells how he left his beloved Florence to follow the Emperor Conrad in a crusade against the infidel Muslims in the Holy Land—that land neglected by current popes. He was knighted by Conrad, and by a soldierly death he was "set free...from the entanglements of the deceitful world, the love of which perverts many souls, and came from martyrdom to this peace."

Note

Cacciaguida probably means "hunting guide," aptly so in this situation, in which Dante is hunting for guidance about his future.

Canto 16

THIS CANTO IS not of much general interest, crammed as it is with references to specific places and families in medieval Florence. It is a kind of melancholy meditation on the decline and fall of peoples and their cities. Dante begins by confessing that even in Heaven he feels a family pride in his knighted and bravely dying ancestor. Yet he realizes that nobility of blood is a mantle that quickly shrinks, so that "if we do not add to it day by day, time goes round it with a scissors."

When he addresses the self-identified Cacciaguida this time, he switches to the plural "you" of respect, which was supposedly first used in Latin by the Romans toward Julius Caesar—though Rome is now the last place to show such respect. Beatrice smiles at Dante's change of grammar.

Dante poses a quartet of questions: What was your ancestry? When were you born? How large was Florence then? Who were its outstanding families?

Sweetly and gently his ancestor replies in the old Florentine dialect— "not in this modern speech" (which our poet will help make dominant in Italy). He says that from the time of Christ's conception to his own birth, this planet Mars had entered the constellation of Leo (another symbol of soldierly courage) 580 times. That would make his birth year somewhere between 1091 and 1106.

As though refusing to encourage his progeny's "ancestor worship," he says that as to their who and when, "silence is more decent than speech." (Interestingly, Statius used almost the identical words in Purgatory when speaking of the organs of generation.) He does state that his ancestors were not newcomers to Florence. He reckons that the city was five times smaller in his day (that is, embracing some six thousand citizens, as opposed to thirty thousand).

His main complaint is against the influx of troublesome outsiders. "The mixture of peoples was ever the beginning of a city's ills." Much of this influx occurred because degenerate churchmen treated the Holy Roman emperor as a stepchild, and the resulting polarization caused the uprooting and decline of many families.

But such decline is a law of life, though it is a law that can be easily overlooked. "All your affairs are mortal, even as yourselves; but in some things that last long this fact is concealed because individual lives are short."

In his discourse, Cacciaguida mentions families that were patrons of the diocese of Florence. When the bishop died, they would take their time in looking for a replacement, since they could enjoy the Church revenues in the meantime.

He specifically laments the coming of the Buondelmonti family to Florence. Would that they had drowned in the stream Ema on their way! (Savage indignation seems a family trait.) When a member of that family jilted his fiancée, her family killed him and members of his family on Easter Sunday 1215, at the foot of a statue of Mars. Thus began the lethal Guelph/Ghibelline split in the city. How different are the brave and noble souls reflected in the heavenly sphere of Mars!

In his day, the old man concludes, Florence was a place of tranquillity. The lily/iris in its flag had never been turned upside down in defeat, nor had its white color been changed to red, as happened in 1251 when the Guelph faction defeated the Ghibellines and the white flower and red field were reversed. (Florence today gives an annual prize for the local iris closest in hue to the one on its flag.)

Note

In all of the poem, Dante employs elsewhere the respectful *you (voi)* only for Beatrice, Farinata and the senior Cavalcanti (*Inferno* 10), Brunetto Latini (*Inferno* 15), and Pope Adrian/Hadrian V (*Purgatorio* 29). He uses the intimate *tu* even with Virgil. More people get the honor in Hell than elsewhere!

Canto 17

THIS CANTO, in the exact center of the *Paradiso*, is a favorite of many. On his journey so far the poet has heard hints of a troubled future:

1. In Hell, Farinata said he would learn about the difficulty of returning from exile; Brunetto Latini warned of enemies in the dung heap of Florence; Vanni Fucci took delight in foretelling the expulsion of Dante's party from his hometown.

2. In Purgatory, Malaspina said that within seven years he would

know the need of hospitality; Salvani said he would experience the embarrassment of begging alms; Guido del Duca indirectly warned the poet of a fierce hunter in Florence who would sell the flesh of Florentines while they are still living.

Dante feels like the mythical Phaëthon, who had heard rumors that Apollo wasn't really his father, so he went to his mother to be reassured. Ask him for a favor that only a father would grant, she suggests. But disaster came upon him when Apollo let him borrow his chariot (the Sun).

Expecting a disaster of his own, Dante may be wondering whether by his courage he will prove a worthy descendant of his martyred ancestor. Beatrice, whom Virgil had erroneously said would clarify these hints, now encourages her protégé to ask Cacciaguida. The poet affirms his belief that the saints, gazing on that point of light that is God Himself, can foresee "accidental" things as clearly as earthlings can see geometric necessities. Dante, therefore, asks to know more specifics about his future, "since an arrow foreseen comes more slowly."

Cacciaguida answers in clear and precise words, not with the dark sayings uttered by pagan oracles before Christ was slain. (He was the sacrificial Lamb of God, the martyr most revered in this sphere of martyrs.) He states that the Divine Eye foresees all contingent happenings on Earth. This foreseeing, however, does not cause the events and thereby destroy human free will. Because the saints see history from a triumphant, divine perspective, even the trials awaiting Dante produce a sweet harmony in the ear of his ancestor. That ancestor now makes several predictions:

1. Dante will be driven from Florence. Even so was Hippolytus driven from Athens by his stepmother, Phaedra, when he refused her sinful advances. Dante's exile will be the work of Pope Boniface VIII, who is already plotting it in that city (Rome) where Christ is daily bought and sold. The victim will be blamed, as usual, but a vengeful fate awaits the guilty Boniface.

2. "You will leave everything loved most dearly." This may be Dante's tribute to his wife and children, otherwise unmentioned in the poem.

3. You will come to learn how salty [bitter] tastes
   another man's bread, and how rough is the road
   going down and up another man's stairs.

> *(Tu proverai si come sa di sale*
> *lo pane altrui, e come e duro calle*
> *lo scendere e 'l salir per l'altrui scale.)*

This is an unforgettable summary of the life of an exile begging room and board. Twelve verses after the mention of these alien stairs *(scale)*, Cacciaguida will refer to the hospitality of the della Scala (stairway/ladder) family.

4. The heaviest(!) burden will be the wicked and senseless companionship of his fellow exiles. They will prove themselves ungrateful and turn furiously against Dante. But in the end they will blush for their behavior. Instead of adhering to any political party, Dante will best honor himself by becoming a party of one.

But Cacciaguida has words of comfort too. The della Scala family (the Scaligers) of Verona will offer him refuge. This Ghibelline family shows its devotion to the emperor by the sacred eagle depicted above a ladder *(scala)* on its coat of arms. When Dante the exile first arrives in their city, Bartolommeo will head the family of these "Gentlemen of Verona," and such will be their mutual courtesy that the giving will precede the asking.

Bartolommeo's younger brother, Can Grande, is now only nine years old. But by the time (1312) that the Gaston pope, Clement V, deceives the noble Emperor Henry VII about the ardor of his support, Can Grande will be giving off sparks of heroism by his indifference to wealth. Born under the sign of Mars, he will perform such deeds of renown that even his adversaries will have to acknowledge them. "Look to him and to his benefits."

Concerning this exemplary man, Cacciaguida speaks incredible secrets that Dante does not reveal. (Are they about the mysterious hound of Heaven and the DVX?) In any case, Dante should not be hatefully envious of his own fellow citizens. His life (of fame?) will continue long after their treachery has been punished.

Now more certain of his future, the poet has a practical dilemma. He wants to write about what he has witnessed on his journey, otherwise (as a timid friend of truth) he will lose his life of fame in the future (which will call the present time "ancient"). But he may also thereby forfeit his welcome in places outside of the lost Florence.

(After all, in one way or another, the poet insults the vain French; the gluttonous Germans; the mad English and Scots; the tyrant-filled cities of Italy; the hopelessly wicked Florentines; the foul-sounding and foul-living Romans; the avaricious Bolognese; the grafting Luccans; the corrupt Genoese; the silly Sienese; the Pisans, who should be drowned; and the Pistoians, who should cremate themselves.)

Cacciaguida replies: "A conscience dark with its own or another's shame will undoubtedly feel your words to be harsh. Nevertheless, put aside every falsehood and make all your vision manifest, and let the scratching be where the itching (the scab) is. For if your voice is grievous at first taste, it will leave a vital nourishment after it has been digested."

Like the wind, Dante's revelations will strike against the treetops the hardest of all. He should gain honor for having the courage to reveal the truth about the world's lofty ones. Besides, well-known people will best engage the attention of his readers. (It has been drolly observed that most of its people are in the poem not because they are famous; they are famous because they are in the poem. In any case, some of them remain quite obscure.)

Canto 18

MUSING ON THE BITTERSWEET WORDS of his ancestor, Dante hears Beatrice comfort him and feels the inexpressible delight of her smile. She bids him look again at Cacciaguida, "for not only in my eyes is Paradise." His ancestor in turn bids him look at the arms of the galactic cross in the sky. As he names them, souls of great renown will flash like lightning.

These eight holy warriors are Joshua, successor of Moses and conqueror of the Holy Land; Judas Maccabaeus, the Jewish general who fought the Syrians in the second century B.C. (here he spins like a top that is topped with joy); Charlemagne, restorer of the Western Empire, who was locally canonized in 1165; his brave nephew Roland, who fought the Saracens in Spain; William of Orange, who fought them in southern France, and Renouard, the Saracen convert who fought at William's side; Duke Godfrey, leader of the First Crusade, who fought the Saracens in the Holy Land and became the first King of Jerusalem; and the eleventh-century Robert Guiscard, who fought the Saracens in Sicily and in southern Italy and founded the Norman dynasty there.

Cacciaguida, who has been with us for four cantos, now rejoins his heavenly companions and shows his descendant what a singer he is. Dante then looks again at his guide, finds her more lovely yet, and realizes he is circling in a wider arc and has joined the sixth planet, Jupiter. This star is "temperate" because it is located between hot Mars and cold Saturn. Passing from the ruddy planet to this pale one, the poet is reminded of a blush of modesty passing from a woman's face.

About to describe the marvel he sees there, Dante briefly invokes one of the Muses, calling her a Pegasian because the Muses drank from a spring that sprang from the hoof prints of the winged horse, Pegasus. Like birds forming patterns, the luminous souls in this sphere arrange themselves to spell, successively, the thirty-five letters of the Latin words "*Diligite justitiam, qui judicatis terram* (Love justice, you that are the judges of the Earth)." These are the opening words of the biblical book of Wisdom.

When the lights arrive at the final letter *(M),* other lights descend on its top. Joined by the "more than a thousand" lights already below, the group turns the *M* into the profile of the Imperial Eagle. Still other lights take the shape of a lily, the emblem of the Guelphs as well as of the French monarchy. Dante is perhaps seeing a symbol of the eventual merging of the French monarchy with the supreme *M* (*Monarchy,* the title of one of Dante's books) of the Holy Roman Empire. In any case, the divine wisdom that is at work in birds as they build their nests is at work in this heavenly design.

Dante addresses this "sweet star," Jupiter, acknowledging that justice is the effect on earthly affairs of this planet and its angelic agents. But the smoke of the papal court dims its beams. As Christ did in Jerusalem, may God once again grow angry at the buying and selling that goes on in that Roman "temple," that Church built upon miracles and martyrdoms. May the saints of this sphere pray for earthlings, all led astray by bad example.

The poet grieves that popes now make war not with swords but by refusing the sacramental bread that God meant for all. (Such, in one of Dante's few explicit references to the Holy Eucharist, was one effect of a papal interdict.) Addressing John XXII (1316–34), the pope who was reigning while Dante was composing these lines, the poet says that John writes only to cancel (by excommunicating). But Dante warns him that Saints Peter and Paul still live. This pope, however, is so preoccupied with the image of John the Baptist on the golden coins of Florence (florins) that he cannot say that he knows either Peter or Paul.

Note

Dante's patron and friend, Can Grande della Scala (1291–1329), mentioned in the previous canto, was excommunicated by this John XXII and died under the ban. Dante dedicated the *Paradiso* to him. Though Dante died eight years before him, perhaps della Scala found comfort in the words Dante attributed to Manfred:

> Through the clergy's curse no one is so lost
> That eternal love cannot come to him,
> So long as hope bears one green leaf. (*Purgatorio* 3:133–35)

Canto 19

DANTE CONTINUES TO STARE at the image of the Imperial Eagle formed by these souls who on Earth pursued justice. He is astonished to see and hear the Eagle's beak talk as if all these souls were one single soul. (Indeed, this is the only sphere in which no soul speaks individually.) Here is a striking symbol of the harmony of just souls and the ideal unity that a just empire would effectuate. The Eagle states that there are wicked people who laud the majesty of the Roman Empire but do not strive to prolong its virtue.

Dante now asks to be delivered from a great fast that has long held him hungering. Ever passionate about justice, he begs to be told how justice is served by the divine decree that makes faith in Christ necessary for salvation. What of the person in distant India who never hears of Christ, but who to all appearances lives a good life? (One thinks of Gandhi, though he knew Christ and admired Him much more than he did Christians.)

The Eagle first points out that God's designs are so profound that nothing created (such as the human mind) can adequately probe them. (At the shore you can see the bottom of the water, but not out on the open sea.) Even the supreme created intellect, Lucifer's, was by nature deficient for that task. So, proud Lucifer fell "unripe through not waiting for the light"— a supernatural gift of enlightenment that would have deepened his grasp of the divine design. Even more is such a design beyond human understanding. Without pure heavenly light, human answers are shadowed by ignorance and poisoned by sin.

The Eagle does not actually answer Dante's question but rather asks, "Who are you who would sit on the bench and judge" the eternal Justice, which is, itself, the ultimate measure of all justice? (Shades of the voice out of the whirlwind speaking to Job!) God has spoken in the Scriptures. Let that suffice.

The Eagle, which was earlier compared to a falcon eager for flight, now circles over Dante like a stork that has just fed its young. As it wheels above, it sings an incomprehensible song. "As my music is to you who cannot follow it, so is eternal Judgment to you mortals."

Pausing in its song, the Eagle continues, "To this kingdom none ever rose who did not believe in Christ, either before or after He was nailed to the tree. But note: many cry 'Christ! Christ!' who shall be far less near Him on Judgment Day than such as do not know Him. Heathen Ethiopians shall condemn such Christians when the two groups are parted, the first forever rich, the other poor."

The Eagle does not explain this seeming contradiction but does assert that heathens who know not Christ can somehow end up rich forever. Next, the Eagle names some of the unworthy Christian rulers whose evil deeds the heathens will one day see recorded in the book of Judgment.

Speaking of what that book will reveal, Dante begins the next three verses with the letter *L,* the next three with *V (U),* and the next three with *E.* These letters, *LUE,* spell the Italian word for pestilence and reflect the Eagle's (and Dante's) opinion of various contemporary rulers in Christendom. (This is the poem's second and final acrostic; see the one constructed from *omo* in *Purgatorio* 12:25 ff.)

In this roundup, the Eagle refers to the Emperor Albert's devastation of Prague (Bohemia); the money-debasing Philip the Fair, who died from a fall from his horse when a boar ran between its legs; and the mad English and Scottish leaders who can't stay within their own borders (the poet has his contemporaries Robert the Bruce and William Wallace in mind—see the Mel Gibson movie *Braveheart*). There are also references to Serbia, which then included Bosnia and Croatia; its king was the mentioned Rascia (alias Urosh or Milutin), who died a few weeks after Dante did. The cowardly and avaricious Sicilian, Frederick II, ruled in Sicily (the Isle of Fire thanks to Mount Etna), where the father of Aeneas died. His foul uncle is his *barba,* a dialect word still used in Italy for a parent's brother. The Eagle also uses an old word for Venice, *Vinegia.*

Canto 20

IN DANTE'S DAY it was believed that the stars that reveal themselves at sunset are reflecting the light of the Sun. When the Eagle "sets" into a brief silence, the individual lights composing it similarly shine more brightly and sing melodies that the poet's memory cannot retain. Thus does their love for God mantle itself in a smile of light and song.

From the depths of the Eagle he then hears a murmuring that becomes a voice. This Eagle, the emblem of the sixth heaven (Jupiter), is now going to name the six righteous rulers who compose its eye area as seen in profile. After each naming the voice will add, "Now he knows..." and itemize some new understanding gained in Heaven.

The pupil of the eye is King David, who in his psalms was the singer of the Holy Spirit. Now he knows his reward is in proportion to his merit.

The next five spirits, from the top of the beak outward, form the eyebrow. The inmost is the Emperor Trajan (died A.D. 117), who befriended a widow by justly punishing her son's murderers. Having been in Limbo before coming to this "sweet life *(dolce vita),*" he now knows how dear is the usual cost of not following Christ.

Next is King Hezekiah, whose penitential prayer caused his death to be postponed for fifteen years. Now he knows that God antecedently wills to be influenced by prayer, so that His basic will is not altered when He postpones His own decrees.

The next spirit is that of Constantine, who in deference to the papacy moved his capital to the East (Constantinople in 330) and so became "Greek." His (supposed) donation of power and property to the papacy was made with good intent, so now he knows that his gift does not harm him, even if the world be destroyed thereby.

The fifth spirit is William II, the Good, of Naples and Sicily (died 1189). The son of William the Bad and nephew of the Empress Costanza, he is the only contemporary ruler mentioned. Now he knows how Heaven is moved with love for a just king.

The final spirit is that of the pre-Christian Trojan Ripheus, who is mentioned a few times briefly in Virgil's *Aeneid* (2:426). There he was characterized as "most just" and "most zealous for justice." Though his grasp is still partial, he now knows much about divine grace that is beyond the world's ken.

Having finished this naming, the Eagle becomes like the lark that soars and sings, then silently savors having done so. Though Dante's puzzlement is as plain as the color painted on the other side of glass, he blurts it out in words: "How can this be?"—two pagans in Heaven!

Delighted at the chance to enlighten the poet, the Eagle produces a great revelry of flashing lights. "The kingdom of Heaven," he explains, "suffereth violence" (Matthew 11:12) when it is overcome by human love and human hope. Yet Heaven wishes to be thus conquered, and hence conquers by its own "defeat."

The Eagle explains: Trajan and Ripheus died not as pagans but as Christians—the one believing in Christ who had suffered, the other in Christ who was to suffer. Thanks to the fervent prayer of Pope Gregory the Great (died 604), the emperor was brought back to life long enough to accept Christ, die as a Christian, and come to this festival. Ripheus, a millennium before Christ, had such a love for justice that God led him to believe in the coming redemption. Such faith, hope, and love on his part served as his baptism.

Referring to the mystery of *"predestinazion,"* the Eagle concludes: "You mortals, keep yourselves restrained in judging, for even we who see God do not yet know all who have been chosen to be saved." But even this lack is sweet, because such is God's will.

At last, Dante has been given medicine for the absolutist judgment that afflicted him concerning good pagans. The poet can still recall that as the Eagle spoke of Trajan and Ripheus, these two blessed lights pulsed to its words. Such, after three cantos, is Dante's final remembrance of the sphere of Jupiter.

Note

If earnest prayer could save Trajan posthumously and Ripheus prematurely, one might justifiably wonder what other surprises Providence has in store for good souls of all places and all times—including Virgil and the suicide Cato, who has already risen from Hell as far as Purgatory. Some Christian mystics (like Julian of Norwich) and theologians (like Origen) believed that in the end, "all will be well," even for those now damned. This viewpoint would allow for the complete triumph of unconditional Love. It is called apocatastasis—from the Greek *apo* (away from), *kata* (down), *stasis* (set): away from what has been set down: that is, an upset verdict.

Canto 21

WHILE DANTE GAZES AGAIN at Beatrice (who has been totally silent in nine of the previous thirteen cantos, and has spoken a total of only twenty-two lines in the other four), they ascend another step of the eternal palace. So mighty has her beauty become that she does not smile, lest she pulverize the poet. (So was the mythical Semele incinerated when her lover Jupiter consented to reveal his full splendor.)

They have arrived in the cold sphere of Saturn, which was then in the warming constellation of Leo. This was the outermost planet known to Dante's world, and it is an apt symbol of "unworldly" contemplative souls. The planet's name also recalls the Golden Age when the mythical Saturn ruled a sinless world.

Beatrice directs Dante's eyes to a golden ladder rising beyond his ken. (He likes to gaze at her, but also to obey her.) Down its rungs come numerous splendors. One light comes closer than the others and grows in brightness. Dante thinks, "I know you are trying to indicate your love, but I dare not break this monastic silence." Beatrice, however, encourages him to address the spirit. So he asks why he can hear no heavenly music in this sphere, and why this spirit, out of all the others, has come forward to greet him.

According to the spirit, the silence indicates that Dante's mortal hearing has been altogether transcended. (In previous spheres his grasp of music had been slipping.) This spirit has welcomed Dante because divine Providence assigned him the task.

Yes, replies the poet, but my puzzle is, why were precisely *you* predestined for this role? Like a rapid millstone, the spirit whirls about its own center. Then, referring to the light within which it "en-bellies" itself, it explains, "Not even the angel who penetrates God most searchingly could answer that question in its ultimate roots. Report this fact on Earth, where minds much duller foolishly try to fathom these unfathomable depths."

Dante now abandons his deeper question and merely asks the saint who he is. The spirit says he once lived as a Benedictine monk in a mountain hermitage near Florence, which he calls Dante's *"patria."* There, his food leavened only with olive juice, he fasted and endured heat and cold while he pondered divine truths. Alas, no longer does that cloister send souls to this contemplative realm.

He gives his name as Peter Damian (1007–72). Toward the end of his life and against his will, he was given the cardinal's hat, "which now passes from bad to worse." Unlike the lean and barefoot Peter and Paul, modern shepherds are so fat that they need people to prop them up, while servants lead their horses or hold up their trains. These shepherds cover their horses with their mantles, "so that two beasts [!] go under one hide." "O Patience that endures so much!"

At these words, Dante sees many little flames spiraling down the stairs, lovelier at each turning. They gather about the saint and utter an unearthly shout, deeper than thunder. Dante does not understand its import, so overcome is he.

Notes

The cardinal's red hat did not actually come into use until first conferred by Innocent IV in 1252, 180 years after the saint's death.

Since the time of Jacob's dream in Genesis 28:12, the ladder has been a symbol of communication between the human and the divine. On it, prayerful souls ascend to contemplate God and descend to bring compassionate blessings.

In these three final planets (Mars, Jupiter, and Saturn) a trinity of colossal emblems is featured: the cross, the eagle, the ladder. These summarize the supreme medieval concerns: human salvation, earthly order, and spiritual vision. Dante, who bore many a cross, died the night prior to the feast of the Exaltation of the Holy Cross (September 14). That feast celebrated the 629 recovery of the "True Cross" from the Persians, who had seized it in 614. On this date in 335 was dedicated the Basilica of the Holy Sepulcher, built in Jerusalem by Constantine.

Canto 22

STUPEFIED BY THE FIERCE SHOUT of the contemplative saints, and like a pale and panting child running to its mother, Dante turns to Beatrice for reassurance. "This cry, which you do not understand, has moved you profoundly. What if you had heard the song of this sphere, or seen my smile? Consider, though, that everything done here springs from good will, so a well-intentioned person need not be afraid.

"The saints," she continues, "have prayed for the just punishment of outrages on Earth. You will see their prayers answered before you die. [An optimistic forecast!] The divine sword cuts exactly when it should, no matter how swift or slow it appears to earthlings. But now look again at the ladder and you will see many illustrious spirits."

Dante complies and sees a hundred little globes of light shining on one another. The largest and most lustrous of these "pearls" draws near. Once again, however, the poet fears to break the silence. Out of charity the pearl spontaneously identifies itself as Saint Benedict of Monte Cassino (480?–543?), the founder of Western monasticism. He in turn points out other contemplative spirits such as Saint Macarius (died 404) and Saint Romualdus (died 1027). The former had a powerful influence on Eastern monasticism; the latter, who was from Ravenna like Peter Damian, re-formed Benedictinism in the eleventh century. These Benedictines "stayed their feet" with the vow of stability, a vow that the wandering mendicants did not take.

Heartened by Benedict's benignity, and addressing him as "father," Dante asks whether he might see him more distinctly. Calling him "brother," the saint promises that he and all the other saints will be seen clearly in the ultimate sphere, which is not a space and does not revolve. There everything is blessedly at rest.

Benedict concludes by lamenting that his religious rule is now treated like wastepaper, monks no longer genuinely climb the ladder of contemplation, abbeys have become dens, monks' cowls are sacks full of bad flour, and love for money corrupts monasteries. (It's the old story: discipline creates wealth; wealth destroys discipline.)

But needed reforms will come. These will be even less miraculous than the crossing of the Red Sea and the Jordan; therefore, they are not too much to hope for. (Dante the pessimist regularly alternates with Dante the optimist.) Benedict then returns to his companions, and they rise up the ladder like a whirlwind.

With a mere signal, Beatrice drives Dante behind them, and he swiftly finds himself among the fixed stars. By a blessed coincidence he is in and revolving with the constellation Gemini, "to which I owe all my genius," since the poet was born between May 14 and June 13, when in his day the Sun was supposed to rise and set with the Twins in the background, and when first he felt the air of Tuscany. He now begs for special power from this constellation for the completion of his arduous poem.

Since he is now near the goal of his journey, Beatrice bids him look down through the seven spheres to the Earth and "see how great a world I have already put beneath your feet." He identifies the seven planets in terms of their mythological parentage. He comprehends now how great they are, how rapidly they move, and how they arrange themselves. When he sees the paltriness of the Earth he has to smile:

> There appeared to me, from its hills to its river mouths,
> all the little threshing floor that makes us so fierce *(feroci)*.

Then he raises his eyes yet once again to the fair eyes of Beatrice.

Notes

Though the contemplatives are otherworldly, in Heaven they obviously know and care about the progress or decline of holiness on the Earth.

Legend had it that Alexander the Great, lifted aloft, saw the world as "a threshing floor." Dante's word, *"aiuola,"* means "flower bed" in modern Italian. If our poet had that meaning in mind, his comparison would be ironic since we don't usually think of flowers as making people fierce in the way that a threshing floor would.

In line 106, Dante begins the last of his fifteen direct addresses to the reader (using the word *"lettor"* itself twice on this occasion) and also uses a second backward image called hysteron proteron (latter first): "quicker than you could have drawn out and put your finger into a fire." (See *Paradiso* 2:23–24 and 32:4–6.)

Canto 23

BEATRICE STANDS UPRIGHT and attentive, turned toward the zenith like a bird awaiting dawn so it can see the longed-for faces of its sweet brood and find the food with which to feed them. Seeing her thus, Dante too is filled with expectation. Suddenly she cries, "Behold the army of Christ's triumph, and all the fruit gathered from the circling of these spheres!" Here are the true heavenly stars! These are the souls who made good use of the angelic influences radiating from the various heavens.

Dante sees thousands of lights, and above them all a Sun whose gleaming substance his eyes cannot endure. Beatrice explains that light: it is Christ in His wisdom and power—He who opened for humankind the road from Earth to Heaven.

In this feast of the spirit, Dante's mind transcends itself, undergoing some kind of transport he cannot now remember. Beatrice affirms that he has now seen things that will permit him to endure her smile, so "open your eyes and see how I am." He gazes at that smile and finds that it is beyond description, even if all the Muses would come to his aid. Now that he has gained this anticipatory vision of the full heavenly court, his words must henceforth strain for new heights of sublimity:

> So, depicting Paradise, this sacred poem must make a leap, like a person who finds his way cut off. But whoever considers the weighty theme and the mortal shoulders that are burdened with it will not fault those shoulders if they stagger beneath it. This is no voyage for a small ship, this sea that my bold prow goes cleaving; nor is it one for a helmsman who would spare himself.

Beatrice urges him to look again at the beautiful garden that blossoms under the rays of Christ. So our poet resumes "the battle of the feeble brows [eyes]." Christ has courteously removed His blinding presence so that Dante's eyes can now behold many throngs of splendors, the brightest of which is Mary, the mother of Christ.

Gazing at Mary—the mystical rose, the greatest of the flames, the living star—Dante lauds the name of that lovely flower that he invokes every morning and evening. (So the Madonna's concern for Dante is not entirely unprovoked!) The archangel Gabriel now descends in the form of a torch, circles Mary like a halo, and sings lyrical words that crown "this fair sapphire by which the sky is so luminously ensapphired." Like an encircling melody, Gabriel says he will crown her until she follows her Son back into the highest heaven, which is made more divine(!) when she enters it. When he ends his words, all the other lights make Mary's name resound.

At this point Mary follows the path her Son took and passes beyond the poet's sight. Though the saints remain behind, their flames reach out toward her affectionately, like a child's arms reaching out to its mother as she removes her nursing breast. Dante, who early lost his own mother, has regained the power to contemplate Beatrice's smile and once again hears music as the saints sing to Mary the hymn "*Regina Coeli* (O Queen of Heaven)," the Heaven they gained with tears of exile in Babylon, where they felt contempt for earthly gold.

Notes

In the poem there are some twenty-three bird passages involving a score of different birds. In the three tercets that open this canto, many readers find the most charming passage of them all. For a study of the poem's one hundred references to birds, beasts, fishes, and monsters, see Richard Holbrook's *Dante and the Animal Kingdom* (AMS Press, 1902, 1966).

In lines 101–2, where "sapphire" appears both as a noun and a verb, we have our only reference in the *Paradiso* to blue sky.

Canto 24

STILL IN THE HEAVEN of the constellations, Beatrice addresses all the saints who remain after Jesus and Mary have departed. "Consider the immense longing of this man, and refresh him somewhat" with a deeper revelation of heavenly truth. In response, these happy souls, flaming like comets, make spheres of themselves and dance about at varying speeds.

From the circle that seems the richest, the spirit that appears most beautiful of all leaves its place and, while singing, circles thrice around Beatrice. Dante doesn't even try to describe that song—"my pen leaps and I do not record it, for our imagination, not to say our speech, is too light a color for such deep folds."

The circling saint tells Beatrice that her prayer has moved him. Knowing he is Saint Peter, the keeper of the heavenly keys, she asks him to test Dante on various aspects of that faith which once empowered him to walk on water. We first heard of these keys at the gate to Purgatory. With the questioners now facing him, Dante is, as it were, stopped at the inner gate of Paradise.

So, calling him a good Christian, Peter bids Dante tell him what faith is. (Beatrice signals Dante to start pouring out water from his inner fountain.) Citing the words of Saint Paul (Hebrews 11:1), the poet says that faith is what gives substance to hope. And though it deals with unseen

realities such as he has been witnessing in these heavens, faith also pro-
vides evidence for further reasoning on spiritual matters. The existence of
these matters is based on "*sola credenza* (faith alone)," a pre-echo of
Luther's celebrated phrase.

Peter replies: "The composition and weight of this money [faith] have
been well examined. But tell me if you have it in your purse."

Dante: "I do indeed. So bright and round is it that of its mintage I have
no doubt." (Speaking of the coin of faith, the poet coins a verb: he says
that the mintage of faith does not "perhaps-itself to me (*mi s'inforsa*—
from *forse* [perhaps])."

"Where did you get it?"

Dante: "From the Holy Spirit speaking through the Old and New Tes-
taments."

"Why do you believe the Scriptures?"

Because of the miracles they record, deeds "for which nature never
heated iron nor smote anvil."

"How do you know these miracles truly happened?"

If without them the world turned to Christianity as it did, that would
have been a hundred times more miraculous. For it was a poor and hun-
gry Peter that entered the field to sow a good plant (which has now be-
come a thorn).

At this point, the spirits sing a "*Te Deum* (We Praise Thee As God)."
(The melody is different from the chant used on Earth.) Then Peter con-
tinues: I approve of what you have said so far. But tell us what precisely is
your belief, and what caused it.

Dante believes in one God, sole and eternal, Who moves all things with
His love. For this, Dante claims proofs that are physical, philosophical,
and biblical. He believes as well in three eternal Persons comprising the
one Godhead, so that "is" and "are" are equally appropriate in speaking
of Them. The Gospel many times assures him of this belief. "This is the
beginning, this is the spark that then broadens to a living flame and shines
within me like a star [!] in Heaven." So pleased is Saint Peter with Dante's
words that he circles him thrice, singing benedictions upon his head.

Note

The interviews given in these cantos to Dante on the three theological
virtues of faith, hope, and charity parallel a medieval examination of a

bachelor *(baccialier)* going for his degree. Hence, the tone is formal and somewhat impersonal, especially on the part of the questioning saints. Thus the personal names of the saints are never used during the actual interviews, even as Dante recalls them.

The poet's profession of faith here is an abbreviated version of the one he composed, it is said, in response to a charge of heresy. (See the appendix.)

Canto 25

IN FOUR OPENING STANZAS, Dante voices the poignant hope—never to be realized—that his sacred poem may some day overcome his enemies in Florence and allow him to be crowned a poet at the baptismal font where he first received the Christian faith. He says that Heaven and Earth have set their hands on this poem that has kept him lean for many years.

Saint Peter has acknowledged Dante's faith by encircling his brow. When the saint ends his approving dance, another blinding light approaches, exchanges affectionate courtesies with Peter, and then stops in front of the dazzled Dante. Beatrice first tells her charge that this is the apostle Saint James, widely honored at his tomb in Santiago de Compostela in Spain. Recalling the hopeful promises the saint cited in his epistle, Beatrice entreats the saint to make hope sound forth here. She seems to regard James as a symbol of hope because of the special favors Jesus granted him: for example, witnessing the Transfiguration.

The apostle invites Dante to gaze at him again, thus to have his sight further ripened. Then, like Saint Peter, he asks three questions: What is hope? Does your mind blossom with it? Whence did it come to you?

Lest he should appear to be boasting, Beatrice answers the second question for the poet: "The Church militant has no son with greater hope, therefore he has been granted this journey." Dante then defines hope: it is a sure expectation of future glory, an expectation based on God's grace and the merits of the believer. "This light," he explains, "comes to me from many stars [!]." He especially finds the psalms and Saint James's own epistle drenched with hope—"so that I am brimming with it and shower your shower on others."

As though in response to these answers, sudden and repeated flashings come from that apostolic flame, that "son of thunder" (Mark 3:17). Tell me, continues this saint whose hope braced him for martyrdom, what does hope promise you?

Dante quotes the words of the prophet Isaiah (61:7, 10) to the effect that everyone will be clothed in his own land with a double garment. That garment is body and soul, one day to be reunited in the promised land—"this sweet life *(questa dolce vita)"*—of Heaven.

From above them, words from Psalm 9:11 are sounded: "Let them trust in Thee." The surrounding saints pick up the words and continue the psalm. Then a flame brightens in one of the other groups and joins Peter and James as they dance to the singing. Beatrice identifies him as the beloved apostle John, who at the Last Supper rested his head on the breast of Christ (the Pelican). The dying Christ chose him to look after His mother, Mary.

Dante was aware of the disputed tradition that the body of John was assumed into Heaven at the time of his death. To see whether this was true, Dante stares so intently at the blazing spirit that he is blinded. John tells him that his body is not there—only Jesus and Mary (and Dante!) came here bodily. Tell this fact back on Earth, the saint bids Dante, who turns toward Beatrice and grows deeply disturbed at not being able to see her.

Notes

After all the lamentations of the previous ninety cantos, it may come as a surprise to hear Beatrice (and the poet) describe himself as so hopeful. Still, throughout the entire poem, complaints and grievings are regularly followed by some promise of improvement.

A common belief of Dante's time was that the pelican wounds itself to feed its young with blood. It was an apt image for the self-sacrificing Christ.

In line thirty-three, the word *Jesus* makes its first appearance in the poem; in 31:107, the only other appearance occurs as *Jesus Christ.* The word *Christ* never appears in the *Inferno* but appears five times in the *Purgatorio* and thirty-four times in the *Paradiso.*

During the first month of winter, the constellation of Cancer (the Crab) rises at sunset and sets at sunrise. Dante says that if that constellation had a star as bright as Saint John, that month would be one long day.

Canto 26

SAINT JOHN ASSURES DANTE that his loss of sight is temporary. Ananias restored sight to Saint Paul (Acts 9:17); the glance of Beatrice will do the same for the poet. Meantime, the saint asks him to name the goal on which his soul is targeted. During the rest of this interview, Dante is blind as love is blind. (Unlike Peter and James, John does not ask for a definition of his subject, love; as, for example, *Amor significat nunquam dicendum erit "me poenitet"* ("Love is never having to say you're sorry"). Is love too mysterious to be defined by words? Yet Dante's mentor Aquinas tried: "*amare est velle bonum* [to love is to wish good upon].")

Recalling that it was through his eyes that Beatrice first entered with the fire that still burns in him, Dante declares that it is the same Goodness which satisfies Heaven that is the beginning and the end of all that love teaches him in whispers and in shouts.

Requesting the poet to be more specific, the saint wants to know who directed his arrow of love at such a target. Acknowledging the authority of reason and revelation, Dante first states his thesis: goodness when recognized begets love; the greater the good, the greater the love. Therefore, the Supreme Good, whom all other goods mirror, must be supremely loved. These ideas he attributes to the philosopher Aristotle, to the book of Exodus (33:17), and to Saint John's own Gospel. (The sublimity of this work caused John to be symbolized by a high-flying eagle.)

Are there other influences drawing Dante to God? "Name with how many teeth this love bites you *(con quanti denti questo amor ti morde)*." (You can almost hear the clicking of teeth in these seven Italian words.)

"Everything that could attract me to God has drawn me from the sea of perverse love and brought me to the shore of the love that is just." Eminent among these magnets are the world itself, Dante's own existence, Christ's death, and the hope of Heaven. Indeed, the leaves with which all the earthly garden of the eternal Gardener is embowered "I love in the measure of the goodness He has bestowed on them."

As soon as the poet finishes speaking, he hears the heavens sweetly sing, "*Sanctus, Sanctus, Sanctus*" (Isaiah 6:2), to which melody Beatrice lends her voice. He has passed the orals of his entrance exam! His guide now beams her brightness upon him as the Sun does upon awakening eyes as its beams go from tunic to tunic (membranes) of sleeping eyelids. His sight returns better than before.

In addition to the three apostles he now sees a fourth light, whom Beatrice identifies as Adam, the first man, and the first to be saved by faith, hope, and love. Dante bows before this ultimate ancestor (this is ancestor day!), this ancient father of whom every bride is both daughter and daughter-in-law. Somewhat indelicately, given Adam's bad luck with apples, he starts by calling Adam the only apple *("pomo")* that was produced mature. Typically, our poet seizes the occasion by asking Adam questions, which he answers out of order.

Sometimes an animal when covered up, like a pig in a poke, stirs so that its impulses are apparent. Just so, by the stirring of his radiance, Adam shows how glad he is to answer.

1. He was banished from Eden not for eating the forbidden fruit as such, but for disobedience.
2. He lived 930 years on Earth and 4,302 in Limbo.
3. He spoke in a tongue that was extinct before Nimrod and his race tried to build the Tower of Babel. "I" was the name for God in that tongue. Speech in itself is natural, but specific words are human coinages that keep changing.
4. He lived without sin only from 6 A.M. of the day of his creation until sometime between noon and 1 P.M. of that same day. Adopting the pessimistic estimate of Peter the Eater (canto 12 above), our poet has a dim view of the human ability to stay on the right path.

Note

I (J) is the first letter of Iahweh or Iehovah; maybe that's where Dante got the notion of God's original name. Here the poet corrects what he had written in *Eloquence in the Vernacular,* namely, that Adam's first word was God's name, *El,* and that after Babel only the Hebrews kept speaking the Adamic language. Some Dantean editors took the *I* to be the number one, as God is one.

Canto 27

DANTE AND HIS GUIDE have been in the eighth sphere (the Fixed Stars) since canto 22. Now, with the poet's "final exam" successfully concluded, they will advance to the outermost physical sphere (the Primum Mobile/ Crystalline).

First, however, after Adam has had his say, all of Paradise breaks out into an intoxicating song in praise of God the Father, the Son, and the Holy Spirit. "What I experienced seemed to me a smile of the universe *(un riso de l'universo)*." At this point the poet gives a compact definition of Heaven:

> O joy! O gladness unspeakable!
> O life brimming with love and peace!
> O wealth secure and free from greed!

The flame encasing Saint Peter begins to change from white to red as he thinks of those papal successors of his who have failed to show mankind the way to such a heavenly life. Usurpers have taken "*il luogo mio, il luogo mio, il luogo mio* (my place, my place, my place)," cries the first pope, who says that his place (currently occupied by Boniface VIII) is actually vacant in the sight of Christ, and that his Vatican burial site has been turned into a sewer ("*cloaca,*" reminiscent of Rome's Cloaca Maxima.) Lucifer can take comfort in that! (No Reformation figure ever spoke more condemningly.) All of Heaven, Beatrice included, blushes and darkens— as did the sky when Christ died. (Surveying history, the modern Catholic theologian Romano Guardini could assert: "The church is the cross on which Christ was crucified.")

The wrathful Peter insists that he and his early successors did not shed their blood for gold, nor play favorites with Christians for political reasons. The keys Christ gave him were not meant to adorn standards in papal wars against the baptized; nor was his figure meant to be stamped on seals profaned by unworthy documents.

God seems to sleep as future unworthy popes like Clement V (1305–14) and John XXII (1316–34) wait in the wings. But the Providence that saved Rome from Hannibal will soon bring aid to His Church. Peter tells his son Dante to reveal these things when he returns to Earth.

At this point all the saints rise upward and out of sight, like the reverse of those snowstorms that come when the Sun is in Capricorn (December 21–January 20). When he is finished looking up, Beatrice tells her poet to look down a second time. Before, he was over Jerusalem. Now he is over Spain and can look west to the path that the foolish Ulysses took beyond Gibraltar, and as far east as Phoenicia, whence Europa set out for Crete on the back of Jupiter disguised as a bull. Dante has, therefore, traveled ninety degrees, or six hours, in the constellation of the Twins, whose parents were Leda and that same Jupiter (disguised as a swan).

By her glance Beatrice now drives Dante into the final physical sphere, whose parts are so uniform that he cannot tell exactly where he is. Knowing his desire to know more, she tells him that in this sphere the material world finds its starting point. All other spheres receive their motion from this transmission belt—hence it is the Primum Mobile, the first movable thing. This sphere in turn takes its origin in the Divine Mind, which encircles it with light and love, and shares divine energy with it. Here is the inverse model for the universe that holds the center (the Earth) quiet and moves all the rest around it. (One thinks of T. S. Eliot's "the still point of the turning world.") This sphere is the flowerpot of time; the other spheres bear the leaves of time.

Saint Peter excoriated the Church shepherds. Beatrice now blasts the sheep. Thinking of the vile greediness that keeps human beings from rising to these heights, Beatrice condemns it and notes how childhood faith and innocence flee before a boy's cheeks are covered (with peach fuzz). The lisping child who loves its mother will long to see her buried by the time its speech is perfected. A youngster keeps the Church fasts but then will devour any food in any season.

Thus does the alluring Circe, daughter of the Sun, turn humans into beasts. But no wonder! The Earth is not rightly governed, so people go astray. Take heart, though! Human affairs will be righted before the lagging Julian calendar (which slips behind nature's cycle about 1/100th of a day each year) "unwinters" January and makes it come when the calendar indicates spring.

Notes

Line fifty-eight's reference to the pope from French Cahors, John XXII, shows that Dante, who died in 1321, was composing or editing this section after this pope's election in 1316.

It was a future pope, Gregory XIII (1572–85), who in 1582 would promulgate a more accurate calendar. By dropping ten days and making a new rule for leap years, the Gregorian reform aimed to correct Julius Caesar's calendar.

Canto 28

LINGERING IN THIS NINTH SPHERE, where only the "imparadising" Beatrice speaks to him—a unique situation—Dante first sees reflected in those lovely eyes, which Love made a rope to capture him, a sight that will appear wherever he peers deeply in this temple of the angels: a blinding point of light, a pure spark, around which nine circles of fire whirl with varying speed, the closer to the point, the faster. The smallest star we can see would seem like a moon compared to this infinitesimal point. (A modern will think of the "almost nothing" that produced the Big Bang.) Beatrice explains:

> On that point Heaven and all nature depend.
> *(Da quel punto / depende il cielo e tutta la natura.)*

(We've already heard of this point from Cacciaguida in canto 17. There is an Einsteinian flavor to this image of God as a point of light. Not for Dante an enthroned old man with a beard, though in the opening canto Virgil referred to God's "high chair.")

In his last direct words to Beatrice, Dante voices his puzzlement that this image seems the reverse of nature, where the Earth is at the center and the encircling spheres become more divine and swifter as they move away from the center. Beatrice says that his Earth-centered viewpoint is an inside-out copy of ultimate reality.

In reality, God is at the center of reality, and groups of angels circle about Him with a closeness and vitality that depend on their capacity to know the Divine Center and hence to love it and hence to be enraptured by it and hence to wish to resemble His power more energetically.

Moreover, there is a marvelous correspondence between the size and the speed of each material sphere of the universe, and the closeness to God of the type of angels that exercise their power through that particular sphere. Thus the seraphim, who are most like God in knowledge and love, transmit their benevolent energy through the largest and speediest of the spheres—the Primum Mobile, where Dante and Beatrice now find themselves. All nine choirs of angels thus "gaze up" at God, but "prevail down" in the communication of their energies. Hence, it is toward God that all draw and all are drawn.

As though in confirmation of Beatrice's words, the angelic circles sparkle like molten iron. They all sing, *"Hosanna"* to God at their center. These angelic sparks are greater in number than would be obtained by doubling the number one as many times as there are squares on a chessboard. (This would amount to about eighteen and a half billion billion!)

These angels are delighted to the extent that they penetrate that Truth in which every intellect finds rest. Thus the state of blessedness is founded on an act of seeing, not on an act of loving, which follows afterward. (Here our poet follows Aquinas with respect to the primacy of the Beatific Vision, as opposed to the Augustinian-Franciscan tradition that located the essence of bliss in loving.)

Beatrice terminates her comments in this canto by naming the choirs of angels in three sets of threes: the seraphim, cherubim, and thrones; the dominations, virtues, and powers; the principalities, archangels, and angels.

Dante says that in his [supposed] writings, Saint Paul's Athenian disciple Dionysius gave the proper order of these pure spirits. He learned this order from Saint Paul, who had been lifted to Heaven in his lifetime (2 Corinthians 12:1–4) and told Dionysius what he saw. Pope Saint Gregory the Great (590–604) had listed them differently, but when he arrived in Heaven he realized his mistake and smiled. Dante too must have been smiling as he wrote this, because in *The Banquet* he followed Gregory's arrangement.

Notes

The names of nine categories of angels occur in one place or another in the Bible, but never at one time, and without any implication of an interlocking system. Saint Paul names five of them (Ephesians 1:21 and Colossians 1:16).

Much of medieval thought on angels was based on a fifth- or sixth-century treatise, *On the Heavenly Hierarchy,* attributed by the anonymous author himself to Saint Paul's convert Dionysius. This "mystical" book was one of the chief forces countering the scholastic tendency to excessive rationalism. Nowadays, the author is called Dionysius the Pseudo-Areopagite, since he's not the one who heard Saint Paul preach at Athens' "Mercury Hill" (Areopagus).

The constellation of the Ram (alias Aries in line 117) appears at sunset during the first month of winter and hence signals the falling of leaves in central Italy—an event that has no seasonal parallel among the angels.

Canto 29

WITH THIS CANTO Dante will end his visit to the ninth sphere, and Beatrice will end her revelations about the world of angels. In the previous canto she explained the interlocked functioning of the nine choirs of angels. In this canto—which is almost entirely in her words—she will discuss the creation of angels (why, where, when, and how), the fall from Heaven of some of them, and the faculties and numbers of the unfallen. In the midst of these elucidations she will make a fifty-six–line digression to attack earthly teachers and preachers who fail to declare and maintain the spiritual values represented by the angelic orders.

Before the second part of her discussion, Beatrice was silent for just a moment and gazed at the Light-Point that is God. In that Point every where *("ubi")* and every when *("quando")* are centered. In His eternity, beyond all time and space, the eternal Love revealed itself in new loves. That is, He created reflections of Himself—the immaterial spirits of angels—that were so like Him that they too could affirm "I exist."

But along with these "pure forms," God simultaneously and instantaneously created pure matter and forms mixed with matter. This latter category includes the heavenly spheres, through which as through bodily organs the angels exercise their natures. So Saint Jerome (*circa* 340–420) was wrong in supposing that the angels were created long before the rest of the universe. (They would thus have been professionally unemployed.)

Before the count of twenty after their creation, some angels sinned by pride and fell to the Earth. (So angels were even less resistant to temptation than Adam was—possibly because they saw the ultimate point quicker than he did.) In *The Banquet* Dante suggested that the number who fell was about one out of every ten.

Since the angels have always seen everything in God, Beatrice rejects the theory that angels have need of memory. She denounces those fanciful teachers and preachers who, believing or not believing, "dream without sleeping," are inconsistent, and are guilty of the love of show. Heaven is especially angered by the neglect or perversion of the Scriptures. Irrelevant issues are preached about in greater number than certain common names in Florence (namely Lapo and Bindo—we would say Smith and Jones.) The poor, ignorant sheep return from pasture fed with wind.

Christ did not enjoin His followers, "Go and preach idle tales to the world." Yet men now preach with jests and gibes, and "if only there is a good laugh the monk's cowl inflates and he requires no more." But Satan is the bird who nests in that cowl. He is behind all those foolish and unauthorized promises of pardon that permit certain "sacred" swine to eat anywhere, and provide a sinful income for people who are even more swinish.

Beatrice concludes by asserting that when the book of Daniel (7:10) speaks of many thousands of angels, it means that their number is countless. But each of them expresses its individuality by mirroring the eternal Goodness to a different degree.

Note

In this canto the lower clergy gets its comeuppance. In 1445, for the library of the King of Naples, the Sienese illuminator Giovanni di Paolo produced a series of stunning miniatures for the *Paradiso*. One scene shows a monk preaching with a monkeylike devil hanging onto his cowl. The nearest parishioner is having a good chuckle at something the preacher has just said.

Canto 30

NOW WE LEAVE the material world entirely and enter into the tenth and final sphere, the Empyrean (the Mind of God). As stars fade before the dawn, so does Dante's vision of the blinding Point of Light and the nine angelic circles whirling about it.

Dante looks again at Beatrice and finally finds her beauty hopelessly beyond the telling. Only her Maker can enjoy her fully. From the first time that ever he saw her face, until now, his song of praise has never ceased; but now it must, as with any artist at his utmost. For her part, speaking like a guide whose task is done, she announces: We have come

> ...to the heaven that is pure light—
> *light* intellectual, full of love,
> *love* of true goodness, full of joy,
> *joy* surpassing every sweetness. [Emphases mine.]
> (*...al ciel ch'e pura luce:*
> *luce intellettual, piena d'amore;*
> *amor di vero ben, pien di letizia;*
> *letizia che trascende ogne dolzore.*)

After this miracle of melodious description she tells him that here in their true home he will see, along with the angels, the saints in bodily form as they will appear, and he will see them, after the Last Judgment.

Suddenly, he is briefly blinded by a flash of light that is meant "to prepare the candle for its flame." As vision returns he feels that there is now no light he cannot bear. First, he sees a river of light (*"vidi lume in forma di riviera"*). Living angelic sparks fly up from the river, settle like rubies on the golden saintly flowers lining the banks, and then fall back into the tawny waters as though drunk with perfume. These angels are bringing graces *from God* and returning with praises.

Beatrice tells him that he must now literally drink of that water with his eyes if he wishes to see beyond the shadowy preface of its symbolism. He instantly complies, and the river of horizontal time now becomes a luminous ocean of circular eternity. Reflected in that ocean, like a blossoming hillside admiring its own loveliness in a lake, more than a thousand tiers of saints appear to him. They encircle the mirroring center and rise above it, like the crowd at an amphitheater. The pool of light at the center derives from the ray of light that strikes the convex top of the Primum Mobile. Thus the horizontal river of light has now become an upward cascade of reflected light drenching the blessed for Dante's viewing. He estimates that the lowest and smallest tier of this amphitheater has a circumference greater than the Sun's. The number of the blessed must thus be almost incalculable.

The poet now gazes up directly at this assembly of saints. He discovers that distance does not diminish the clarity of his sight. Inventing an image all his own in its detail, he compares what he sees to a white rose that eternally expands its petals and emits its fragrance of praise to a Sun that creates a perpetual spring.

The circle of golden light at the floor of the amphitheater he compares to the yellow center of a rose. Into this center Beatrice now draws Dante as she bids him take in this vast white-robed assembly, this City of God. He has just drunk with his eyes; now he will walk with them.

Only a few seats remain to be filled, and one of these—a throne with a crown above it—is meant for the Emperor Henry VII, who will try to reform an Italy that is unripe for his efforts. (How striking to find an emblem of earthly sovereignty in the heaven where God is sovereign and has no throne!) Blind greed will keep people from the help they most desperately need. The double-crossing Pope Clement V will make matters worse. But he will die soon after Henry does and help to push his own predecessor Boniface VIII more deeply into the Hell of the simoniacs. Thus terribly does Beatrice utter her final words in the poem.

Notes

The thirty-eight-year-old Henry VII died on August 24, 1313; Clement V on April 20, 1314. Legend has it that when Jacques de Molay was dying at the stake as the head of the condemned Knights Templar, he issued a curse on Clement V, predicting that he would die within forty days. The pope obligingly died thirty-three days later. The scheming, Clement-dominating King Philip the Fair of France, limited to a year by the curse, died that November 29. Within fourteen years his three sons were crowned and buried, and the dynasty of Hugh Capet fizzled to an inglorious end (987–1328).

On a more positive note, this canto supplies two final indications of Dante's ultimate salvation: Beatrice says he will see the saints now in their bodies as he will at the Last Judgment (line 45) and speaks of the time when he will sup at Heaven's wedding feast (line 135). She thus confirms the implications of earlier remarks by Charon, Virgil, Aquinas, and Cacciaguida. The alert reader will not forget that Dante himself made all these prophecies.

Canto 31

DANTE HAS ALREADY COMPARED the saintly throng to a rose. Now he compares the angelic throng to a swarm of bees moving between flower and hive. Their faces are living flames, their wings golden, and their robes a peerless white. But this multitude casts no shadow and obscures no vision. In a reversal of nature they bring down to the saints the nectar of peace and ardor. They then bring back to God the praises of His holy ones.

In this secure and joyful kingdom, all seeing and loving is fixed on one mark: the three-in-one light of God. The poet begs that light to shine down on the stormy darkness of Earth. When the barbarians of the northland first gazed on the grandeur that was Rome, they were no more amazed than Dante, who has come from the human to the divine, from the temporal to the eternal, and "from Florence to a people just and sane." (Thus Dante's final, stinging reference to the city that deprived him of his earthly, temporal home.)

Content to be silent and hear no word from Beatrice, the poet sweeps his eyes over the blessed multitude, finding there "faces surrendered to loving, adorned with Another's light, with their own smiles, and with gestures graced with every dignity."

Inevitably, he has questions for Beatrice, but when he turns, he sees instead a fatherly old man dressed like the saints. "Where is she?" Dante blurts out.

"To crown your quest, Beatrice sent me from my place," the sire replies. "Behold her in her place on the third-highest tier." Dante looks at once and sees her clearly, though she is immensely far away.

In a prayer of praise, he addresses his beloved for the final time, but for the first and only time with the familiar "thou" of the Italian: "By thy potent goodness thou has delivered me from slavery to freedom. Mayest thou preserve thy good work by seeing that my soul dies in favor with thee." Smiling, she gazes at him, and then turns her eyes again to the eternal Fount, acknowledging thereby the source of her own power and goodness.

The old man identifies himself as the contemplative Saint Bernard of Clairvaux (1091–1153), "one of the most prominent figures of the history of his time." Renowned for his devotion to the Virgin Mary, he secured the condemnation of Héloïse's Peter Abélard (1079–1142), whom he found too rationalistic in his explanation of religious mysteries. Canonized twenty-one years after his death, this was the man who preached the disastrous Second Crusade, in which Dante's Cacciaguida died. The saint never recovered from the debacle.

Dante now looks at him with wonder, like some pilgrim from Croatia peering at the veil of Veronica on which the suffering Christ reputedly imprinted His image. "Child of grace," the saint continues, "if you seek supreme joy, look not only at me, but at all the saints, up to the Queen at the farthest rim."

Climbing with his eyes, as if rising from valley to mountaintop (as he tried to do in the poem's opening canto), the poet sees Mary glowing like a perpetual sunrise, with "more than a thousand angels" playfully rejoicing about her. A delight to all the saints, she smiles at their sport and their singing. Bernard too looks toward her with an ardor that intensifies Dante's own. Yet even if our poet had words as rich as his imagination, he would not dare attempt to describe the least of her delights.

Notes

Despite his devotion to Mary, Saint Bernard (like Aquinas later) opposed the idea of her Immaculate Conception. She too needed first to be "born in sin" if Christ was to be the universal Redeemer. Still, "You can never say enough about Mary."

Saint Bernard supposedly had a mystical experience (the Lactation), in which he nursed at Mary's breast. Saint Clare did him one better: she dreamed she nursed at Saint Francis of Assisi's breast! These medievals were no prudes.

Canto 32

AS HE NEARS THE CLIMAX of his journey, Dante stands beside the last of his trinity of guides: Virgil had symbolized the light of Reason; then Beatrice, the light of Revelation; and now Bernard, the light of monastic Contemplation. Bernard has told Dante that by studying this scene of saints and angels he will ready his sight to probe even deeper. So the poet spends this penultimate canto following with his eyes as Bernard explains the arrangement of the spirits who compose the white rose of Paradise.

This whole rose is a marvel of balance, thanks to divine foresight. A completed half is made up of pagan and Old Testament souls who in some way had faith in the coming of Christ. So, apart from some presumably few pagans, half of Heaven must be Jewish. A nearly completed second half contains souls who believed in the Christ Who had come. (As Abbot Joachim had predicted, the end must be near!)

These halves are arranged as semicircles. At the summit of a divider row separating B.C. from A.D., the Virgin Mary crowns a line of Hebrew women who believed in the Messiah to come. She is the reversing "Ave" who closed and anointed the wound that "Eva" opened and pierced (a final and double hysteron proteron). Beneath her, in chronological sequence, are that selfsame Eve, Rachel, Sarah, Rebecca, Judith, and Ruth (the great-grandmother of King David, who in sorrow for sin cried, "Have mercy on me" [Psalm 50/51—the first spoken words of the poem, repeated now near its end as the penultimate Scripture quotation]).

On the top row, to Mary's own left, are Adam (with his wife just below to his right) and then Moses; to her immediate right are Peter and then Saint John the Evangelist. Beatrice is two places below Saint Peter.

Exactly opposite Mary's divider row is a corresponding row of A.D. saints. John the Baptist is in the top place. (Both he and Mary span B.C. and A.D.)

Beneath the Baptist sequentially but in reverse chronological order are Saints Francis of Assisi, Benedict, and Augustine of Hippo (who is astonishingly underplayed in the poem, gaining mention elsewhere only in *Paradiso* 10:120).

To the Baptist's own right (B.C.) is Saint Anne, the mother of the Virgin; to his left (A.D.) is Dante's patron, Saint Lucy.

Apparently, only in these two opposing divider rows are all the seats down to the bottom occupied by adults. Otherwise, around the entire rose there is a horizontal midpoint, below which all are children. These were redeemed either before Christ by the faith of their parents or their own circumcision, or after Christ by baptism. (Bernard invites Dante to note their childish voices, so the acoustics must be extraordinary.)

Though saved without personal merit, even these children (who compose half of Heaven) have a higher or lower rank depending on the variations in their original God-given capacity to receive grace. These variations are as real and mysterious as the differences of hair color in the twins Jacob and red-headed Esau, who struggled with each other even in Rebecca's womb.

Interestingly unmentioned in this celestial tour are Abraham; David; Solomon; the Evangelists Matthew, Mark, and Luke; Saint Paul; Cacciaguida; and Saint Dominic.

At the beginning, middle, and end of this canto, Saint Bernard refers to Mary as to a starting point. Since hers is "the face that most resembles Christ's...only its brightness can fit you to see Christ" (whose human face we never see described in the poem).

In the middle reference, the archangel Gabriel relives the moment of the Annunciation, singing again his *"Ave Maria"*—the final Bible quotation—while the saints and other angels do honor to the humble handmaid of the Lord. This moment is reminiscent of the earthly custom of praying the *Angelus* (The angel of the Lord declared unto Mary) daily at dawn, noon, and sunset.

Because the time is flying by that keeps Dante from returning to the quasi-slumber that is earthly life, Bernard ceases his naming—"like a good tailor who cuts the garment according to the cloth." (Even for the sublimest heights our poet resorts to the humblest imagery. This was a sharp break from the classical tradition, and an example of "vulgar [vernacular] eloquence.")

It is time for Dante Alighieri of Florence, Italy, to look upon the Archetypal Love, God Himself. As noted, for this final grace he will need help from Mary. Bidding the poet to follow with his heart, Saint Bernard prepares to begin his lyrical prayer to Mary on Dante's behalf. (In the Godly world everybody helps everybody else.)

Notes

Line sixty-eight's words about Jacob and Esau and Rachel's womb provide another of the mother/baby images in the poem. The final canto will begin with the words "Virgin Mother" and make reference to the womb in which divine love was rekindled on Earth. On its last page will appear an infant who still bathes its tongue at the breast. It is remarkable how many times this image of infancy appears in the final cantos: a child reaching out its arms after the mother who removes her breast; a mother bird feeding her chicks; the pelican that feeds its young with its own blood; children once innocent turning on their mothers; the child dying of hunger who repels the one who would nurse it; a late-waking baby desperate for its milk. (Is it that we are all "babes in Paradise?")

Dante follows a minority opinion when he presents saved children as remaining children in Heaven. It is ironic that Saint Bernard (who is represented realistically as an old man and not as a handsome youth) is here made to say that after Christ's time unbaptized children are confined to Limbo. In his own life he had written of such: "It is in God's hands. Let it not be mine to set the limit."

By Dante's reckoning no more souls (and relatively fewer children!) were to be saved after Christ's coming than before—a rather narrow, perplexing, and idiosyncratic view of "abounding grace." Perhaps he succumbed to the seduction of symmetry.

Saint Anne, the Virgin's mother, is charmingly shown to be gazing with love at her daughter opposite her, while all the other saints are gazing at God. Everywhere in Dante's other world, even in Hell, souls vividly retain their earthly characteristics. These are not the pale, washed-out ghosts of earlier traditions. Visiting Achilles in the realm of the dead, Odysseus tried to console him for dying by noting that he ruled mightily over a crowd of specters. Famously, Achilles retorted that he would rather be alive on Earth as the hireling of a landless, hard-pressed master than be king of all the undone dead (*Odyssey* 11:488).

Canto 33

THE FINAL CANTO of this poem, embracing the longest time span of any, may well contain the last words that Dante ever wrote in a lifetime of writing. It records two prayers uttered twenty years apart, and the answers to those prayers. The first prayer is Saint Bernard's in heaven on behalf of Dante; the second is Dante's own on Earth.

The first answer—a glimpse of Absolute Goodness—comes in total silence, during which neither Dante nor anyone else speaks. When he is in their presence, Dante ascribes no words to God, to Mary, or to Christ (except as a griffin repeating a single sentence from Matthew's Gospel [3:15. See *Purgatorio* 32:48]). With respect to this total silence, the climactic moment of the *Paradiso* parallels the climactic moment in the *Inferno*—which was a glimpse of Absolute Evil who speaks no words.

The first fourth of this one hundredth canto contains Saint Bernard's celebrated prayer to the Virgin. (Chaucer, who was born twenty years after Dante's death and who wrote of "the grete poete of Itaille, that highte [lofty] Dante," adapted much of it in the "The Second Nun's Tale" of his *Canterbury Tales*.) In the intimate form of *you (tu)* that everyone seems to use in this Heaven of heavens, Bernard begins with a trinity of paradoxes:

> Virgin Mother, daughter of your son,
>> lowliest and loftiest of creatures....
> *(Vergine Madre, figlia del tuo figlio,*
>> *umile e alta piu che creatura....)*

After singing other praises and noting that Mary often helps without being asked—as she has already done in Dante's case (though he does pray to her daily)—the saint tells her that "this man now begs of thee by thy grace for such a surge of power that with his eyes he may rise still higher toward the ultimate, saving vision, the bliss supreme...keep his emotions sound after so great a vision...guard his human impulses." (The saint may be thinking of the axiom See God and die, and of Dante's admitted inclination to pride.) Bernard adds his prayer to Dante's and notes that Beatrice and many other blessed ones support his petition. (This is our farewell glimpse of Beatrice.)

Thus far in this highest heaven Dante has seen everything by reflected light. Now, with utterly simple dignity, the Mary who initiated Dante's whole journey now crowns it by moving her eyes from Bernard to the Source of all light. Imitating Mary and anticipating Bernard's instruction, Dante now visually mounts to that eternal Light for the first time and struggles with his utmost energies to plumb the depths of these heights.

Suddenly, we are back on Earth with Dante the exile (from Florence and from Heaven). He is straining to recall his overwhelming vision and to find the least useless words with which to describe it. That vision, granted some twenty years earlier, now seems like a dissolving dream, like melting snow, like the scattered prophecies written on leaves by the Sibyl.

(His beloved Virgil, hovering here at the end, had written about this prophetess in the sixth chapter of the *Aeneid*. Sibyl was a generic name, but this one was called Cumaean because she lived in a cave at Cumae, near Naples/Vesuvius. She would transcribe her prophecies on fragile leaves, a few words per leaf. If a wind scattered them, she wouldn't try to recover and reorganize them.)

So now we have the second prayer, but not to Apollo or any Muse. His last poetic plea is to the Supreme Light for some gleam of remembrance, some verbal power on behalf of readers yet to be born. (Thus, nearly seven centuries later, we ourselves become part of this final canto.)

Having prayed, the poet embodies the answer by proceeding to tell of a trinity of sights he saw in those blinding but compelling depths: creation, the Creator, and the Christ Who is the bridge from One to the other:

1. At the heart of the divinity, Dante saw the whole of creation like a book with all its unbound leaves stitched together again:

In its depth I saw that, within, there internalized itself,
bound with love into one volume,
that which throughout the universe unbinds itself.
*(Nel suo profondo vidi che s'interna
legato con amore in un volume
cio che per l'universo si squaderna.)*

It is worth reading the entire poem just to arrive at this miraculous terzine with its unforgettable and strikingly literary image. It is an image that reverses the sibylline scattering and replaces written-on tree leaves with book leaves! (Revealingly, our English word "book" comes from a tree—the "beech," whose bark was good for writing on.) Will our poet try to detail his cosmic vision? No, for at that moment when he [the poet] looked up at God amazed, he has done more forgetting than has the world in the twenty-five centuries since that first sea voyage—when the god Neptune looked up astounded to see the ship of Jason and the Argonauts. (This is the poem's fourth reference to Jason and his Argonauts. Their story, the oldest in Western literature, is especially apt as the last literary reference in the poem: it tells of a man going as a pioneer on a perilous journey to gain the golden fleece.)

2. What he saw next he is less able to express than an infant who still bathes its tongue at the breast. To say that he remembers little is to say too much. For he saw a glimpse of God Himself, a brightness from which this time he would have found it impossible to divert his hungry eyes. Though God remained unchanging, as Dante was transformed he saw the single Light change into three circles of different color but of equal magnitude. One (the Father) seemed reflected by the Other (the Son),

and the third (the Spirit) seemed to be fire breathed forth by each. The One was the Knower, the Other was the Known, and the Third was loved and smiled on by Both.

3. His final focus fixed on the second circle. There the poet seemed to see a human image. Trying to grasp how in the everlasting Son human nature "where-ins" itself (*s'indova*, his own coinage), he wrestled in vain, like a geometer trying to square the *circle.* Suddenly, however, he was gifted with a flash of understanding. Back on Earth, his speech fails him and his memory fails him. But on the original occasion he experienced a failure of even his "lofty imagining *(alta fantasia)."* For what he saw was utterly beyond his mind's capacity to make an image of it.

Even so, because the unified Christ unifies, the split between the poet's spiritual will and his carnal desiring, as also between his desire to know and his ability to will what he desires, was healed in that blessed instant. Like a single wheel, will and desire were sent into harmonious circling by

the love that moves the Sun and the other stars.
(L'amor che move il sole e l'altre stelle.)

Thus instantaneously and at the last moment does the poet's journey achieve its goal. No longer need he lament with Saint Paul: "The good which I will I do not; but the evil which I will not, that I do" (Romans 7:19).

Notes

The supreme love *moves* in two ways: it moves created things by imparting its energy to them and by making them yearn to *move* closer to it.

The opera *Pagliacci* ends with the ironic words *"La commedia e finita."* It ends tragically. Not so the most famous *Comedy* as a poem. But in many ways Dante's personal life and his dreams for a purified Church spiritualizing a united Empire were tragic. Indeed, his poem was a swan song for the vision of Church-state harmony that was born with Constantine's Edict of Milan in 313 (making the Christian religion permissible) and died exactly a thousand years later with the death of Emperor Henry VII of Luxembourg in 1313. Even more broadly, "the *Divine Comedy* is the swan song of the Middle Ages" (Giuseppe Antonio Borgese).

Paradoxically, though, with *The Comedy,* "poetry in the fullest sense of the word is reborn in Europe" (Francis Fergusson).

The *Paradiso,* which took Dante through the circling spheres and showed him the Trinity as three circles, ends with the image of a smoothly turning wheel. Also, unlike the *Inferno* and the *Purgatorio,* the *Paradiso* as a unit circles upon itself. For it begins by speaking of "the glory of Him Who moves all things" and ends with that activating glory revealed as love.

Finally, the whole poem comes full circle. It began, 14,233 lines earlier, with the poet struggling upward toward the redeeming light. In the meantime, he descended the shrinking circles of Hell, mounted the contracting circles of Purgatory, and cut across the expanding circles of the heavens.

The pitchy black of Dante's nights no doubt made him more aware of the stars than most moderns are—he mentions them on the average more than once every other canto. Each part of the journey has ended with the word *stelle,* a glowing tribute to those blazing emblems of divinity that tug at the mind, heart, and soul of the creature with "upturned eyes" (as *anthropos,* the Greek word for *man,* has been decoded), who beneath their mystery exults and agonizes on the tiny threshing floor that makes it so fierce.

As in the last line of the poem we read of the Sun and the other stars—those extremes of stellarity for a human being—we can feel Dante tumbling full-circle back to Earth. God's Trinitarian love, manifested through the devotion of a trinity of women, has brought the lost Dante back to himself, through the encircling gloom to the light that he had "loved long since and lost awhile."

The very second chapter of the Bible refers three times to a garden—the garden of Eden. (Eden meant a "fertile plain" somewhere in the Tigris-Euphrates area, the homeland of the patriarch Abraham.)

When the Hebrew Bible was translated into Greek (the Septuagint), the Greek word *paradeisos* was used for the Hebrew word for garden *(gan).* (As mentioned, the Greek word itself came from a Persian word meaning "a walled-around place.") So it is actually redundant to speak of the garden of paradise. The prophets Isaiah and Ezechiel promised the Jewish people a return to this ideal garden of the Lord (51:3; 35:36, respectively).

There are three uses of *paradise* in the Greek New Testament: the dying Jesus tells the good thief, "This day thou shalt be with me in paradise" (Luke 23:43); Saint Paul says he was "caught up into paradise" (2 Corinthians 12:4); and in the second chapter of the very last book of the Christian Bible, "The Spirit sayeth...to him that overcometh, I will give to eat of the tree of life, which is in the paradise of my God" (Apocalypse 2:7)

Appendix

Other Poems by Dante

OTHER POETIC WORKS attributed to Dante are

1. A paraphrase in Italian *terza rima* of The Seven Penitential Psalms (Psalms 6, 31, 37, 50, 101, 129, and 142, according to the Catholic numbering).
2. *A Profession of Faith*, consisting of an Italian paraphrase in eighty-three terza rimas of the Apostles' Creed, the Ten Commandments, the Our Father, and the Hail Mary, along with reflections on the Seven Sacraments and the Seven Deadly Sins. There's a story that this profession was Dante's response to being accused of heresy.
3. Two eclogues, four sestinas, eleven ballads, twenty-two canzones, and eighty-one sonnets. About 23 of these 118 have been regarded by some experts as doubtfully genuine or genuinely spurious.

Usually listed as the first of Dante's major sonnets is the first one to appear in his *La Vita Nuova*: "*A ciascun' alma presa e gentil core* (To every captive soul and courtly heart)."

Dante addresses it to the devotees of Love, that is, to his fellow love poets. He asks them to interpret a dream he had about his Lady (Beatrice). He tells of suddenly seeing horrific (!) Love in the middle of the night. In his hand Love carries Dante's heart; in his arm he carries the sleeping Beatrice. Love awakens her, and despite her fear he proceeds to nourish her humbly with Dante's burning heart. Then Love tearfully departs.

We still have the reply of one of Florence's poets, Guido Cavalcanti, who was Dante's elder by fifteen years or so. In his sonnet 37, "*Vedeste, al mio parere, onne valore* (You saw, it seems to me, every power [of Love])," Cavalcanti says of Dante's Love: "He comes so sweetly to sleeping souls, that he takes away the heart without causing pain. He took your heart away, because he saw that your Lady was slipping toward death. Dreading that, he fed her with your heart." Love seemed to depart in tears because wakefulness was about to conquer it—a rather prosaic explanation.

As a result of this famous poetic exchange, Cavalcanti became Dante's "first friend," a friend whose death the politician Dante would indirectly cause in A.D. 1300. Dante dedicated his *La Vita Nuova* to him and mentions him also in the *Inferno* and the *Purgatorio,* in several sonnets, and in his *De Vulgari Eloquentia.*

There is almost a score of Guidos in Dante's writings, thirteen in *The Comedy* alone, and three within twenty-five lines in canto 14 of the *Purgatorio.* As mentioned, Guido Cavalcanti was Dante's "first friend"; Guido da Polenta was his host in Ravenna, and in that sense his "last friend"; and the Guido Guinizelli whom he will meet in Purgatory he calls his poetic "father" (though a younger Guido—Cavalcanti—is replacing him as "the glory of our tongue").

Although Guinizelli is regarded as "the first complete master of the Tuscan vernacular," the younger Guido is called by critic Francesco de Sanctis "the first Italian poet worthy of the name, the first to have a sense and feeling of the real." Earlier love poets in Provence and Sicily had celebrated love and other concerns among the select at court. The poets of Florence more narrowly focused philosophically on "the phenomenology of love" in a blossoming urban environment—one that was rife with political and personal hatred.

Among the singers of what Dante will call the "sweet new style" (*"dolce stil n[u]ovo": Purgatorio* 24:57), Cavalcanti was unique in emphasizing the built-in frustrations of not-so-sweet human relationships. Guido explored the conflicting moods and lower depths of love. Unlike Dante, he held the Averroist belief that the human person briefly shares in a universal soul. At death, the individual dies for good. During life our individuality comes from the body, whose passions war against body-soul harmony. Moderation in satisfying the natural but malign and Mars-inspired desire for love is impossible. Relationships can only lead to one death after another.

"Dante and the *stilnovistic* rejection of the pretensions of literary Latin in favor of something more 'natural' signals a new age for European literature." By his personal rejection of Dante's belief in an ideal, spiritual fulfillment of eros in this world and the next, Cavalcanti was undeniably universal when he suffered, "but peculiarly modern in that he doesn't like it." (See *Guido Cavalcanti* by Marc A. Cirigliano, New York: Italica Press, 1992.) A peculiarly modern poet, T. S. Eliot, began his poem *Ash Wednes-*

day (1930) with the opening line of a canzone that Guido wrote in exile shortly before his death, "*Perch'io no spero de tornar giammai* (Because I do not hope to turn again)."

Guido lurks, by the way, in a very popular American word. Guido became Guy in English. Though as a personal name Guy is relatively rare in the States, as an informal word for "person" (even female), "guy" is very common. This latter use may be jokingly linked with a grotesque effigy of Guy Fawkes, the Gunpowder Plot conspirator (1605), used in British parades. The Yiddish word *goy* (all non-Jews) may also have exerted some influence. It isn't clear what *Guido* means. Some connect it with "guide," as in Dante's ancestor, Cacciaguida ("hunting guide").

La Vita Nuova (The New Life)

The title of this "little book" (ninety pages in one modern translation) literally means, "The New Life" and can mean, "My Young Days" or, more likely, "My Life Made New" by love for Beatrice (who speaks of Dante's *vita nuova* in *The Comedy* and is mentioned twenty-three times by name in this earliest volume). Considered the first autobiographical work of modern literature, it was written in Italian before Dante was thirty and covers his life from age nine (when he first saw Beatrice) through age twenty-five, when Beatrice died, to a year or so afterward, during which he felt guilty for being attracted to a gentle lady, young and very beautiful, who showed him compassion in his grief.

The book contains thirty-one poems: twenty-five sonnets, five canzones ("odes"), and one ballad. Dante wrote them before and after the death of his secret, unsuspecting beloved. The forty-three brief prose sections serve to give the background, general and specific, of the individual poems. There is also given an account of seven visions, his interest in drawing, and the weighty significance of the number nine as pertaining to Beatrice. As for the latter, Dante first sees Beatrice when they are both in their ninth year; he sees her again nine years later and receives her first greeting at the ninth hour of the day; his subsequent first vision comes during the last nine hours of the night; the third one, at the ninth hour of the day; the last one, at the hour of nones; her death (June 8, 1290) occurs on the ninth day of the Arabic calendar (whose days start at sunset), in the ninth month of the Syrian calendar, and at the start of the ninth decade of the Roman century. Why all these nines? Because Beatrice was herself "a 'nine,' that is to say, a miracle, whose root is no other than the marvelous Trinity" (30:37–41). He ends the book by saying that if God prolongs his life,

> I hope to say of her that which has not ever been said of another [woman].
> *(io spero di dire di lei quello che mai non fu detto d'alcuna.)*

Of *La Vita Nuova*, translator Charles Eliot Norton has said, "So long as there are lovers in this world and so long as lovers are poets, this first and tenderest love story of modern literature will be read with appreciation and responsive sympathy."

A 1576 printed edition was vetted by the Inquisition. Many passages or phrases considered offensive to the Church or to religion were altered or suppressed. The book's deification of Beatrice can still shock.

Il Convivio (The Banquet)

Plato wrote his *Symposium,* a famous account of the philosophical conversation at a banquet whose guests drank their potions *(posium)* together *(sym)*. Dante put on his own banquet, called it *Il Convivio* ("living [it up] together,") and did all the talking himself. He modestly proposed himself as the waiter, but the fourteen-course feast was to consist of fourteen of his own canzones (odes) and his lengthy philosophical commentary on them.

In the book he mentions Beatrice and his *Vita Nuova*. The compassionate woman who consoled him upon Beatrice's death is revealed to have been philosophy, which he does not here renounce. (The philosopher Aquinas, by the way, is simply "Thomas.") He hopes to write a book on vernacular eloquence. There are numerous persons, episodes, and themes in this book that reappear in *The Comedy,* in which he changed his views expressed here on the cause of the moon's spots and the arrangement of the angelic orders.

Since he mentions his exile and refers to the Emperor Albert as though still living (he died in 1308), scholars suppose that *Il Convivio* was written between 1302 and 1308. Though it is three hundred pages long in one English translation, Dante wrote only three of the fourteen proposed "books," with an introduction explaining why it was permissible for him to speak of himself, and why he wrote it in the "rye" of Italian instead of the "wheat" of Latin.

The three canzones treated are "You [angels] who by thought move the third heaven" (Venus); "Love, who converses with me in my mind"; and "The sweet rimes of love which I used [to seek]." He spends about 220 pages explaining these 297 lines! We don't know what the other eleven canzones were going to be, but nineteen more are attributed to him. By 1723 the common word for banquet in Italian had become *convito*, and some editors began using that word instead of Dante's own word *convivio*. (For a similar reason, *Comedia* became *Commedia*.)

Here are some flavorsome quotations not already mentioned in this guide:

> I have seemed vile in the eyes of many....I fear the reproach of having yielded to passion [in view of a misreading of his *Vita Nuova*].

> I feel not only love, but most perfect love for my native tongue....A faint-hearted man always thinks meanly of himself...and therefore despises his mother tongue.

> Philosophy is the daughter of God, the queen of all things, most noble and beautiful....He who is a lover of wisdom for the sake of advantage ought not be called a true philosopher: such are lawyers, doctors and almost all who are vowed to religion, who study in order to gain money or rank.

> The youth who enters into the bewildering forest of this life could not keep the right path unless it was pointed out to him by his elders.

> There are many so presumptuous as to believe they know everything; they never ask questions, they never listen.

> No nature ever was or will be gentler in bearing rule, or stronger in upholding it, or keener in acquiring it than that of the Latin race.

> In order to replace [the fallen angels] mankind was created...Human nobility, when its importance is measured by the number of fruits it bears, surpasses that of angels.

A man should show himself moderate in merriment, laugh with becoming restraint and with little movement of his arms.

First a child wants an apple most of all, then, growing older, he wants a little bird, then fine clothes, then a horse, then a wife *(donna)*, then modest wealth, then great wealth, then more of the same.

It is most false that "noble" comes from *nosco* [I know]; it comes from *non vile* [not vile]. [Here Dante is most wrong; *noble* does come from *nosco* and refers to the "knownness" or fame of nobility.]

If Christ had not been crucified he would have lived to his 81st year. [See Psalm 89/90:10.]

Aristotle says one swallow does not make spring.

Long chapters are the enemies of memory.

De Vulgari Eloquentia (Eloquence in the Vernacular)

Dante was, of course, intensely interested in language, especially poetic language. He recognized at least fourteen current Italian dialects. In this unfinished book, which its author considered a pioneering work, he judged that none of these dialects was worthy to be *the* Italian language, which must be, among other things, an illustrious vernacular capable of the three great themes: love, virtue, and *"salus"* (probably security provided by warriors). What was needed was a vernacular that belonged to all the Italian cities but was peculiar to none. A few poets rose above the limitations of dialect, including an unnamed one from Florence. (Three guesses!)

This Latin work was meant to have four sections, but stopping in midsentence, it has only two parts with a total of thirty-three chapters (about forty pages in print.) In it Dante mentioned being "unjustly exiled," and scholars date it from 1302–5. Notable aspects of this work:

- Dante says his fatherland is the world, as a fish's is the sea.
- The Roman accent is the worst: a dismal, disagreeable noise. And no wonder! It matches the deformity of Roman manners and customs.

- His fellow Tuscans, mired in their vast stupidity, consider their dialect the best, but it is foul.
- If the Genoese were to mislay the letter Z, they would have to become totally mute or find themselves a new language.
- Bolognese is probably the sweetest dialect, but even Bologna's greatest poets have found it deficient.

De Monarchia (Monarchical Rule)

Dante wrote this political treatise in Latin. Scholars date it from as early as before his 1302 exile to as late as just before his 1321 death. In any case, it was written around the time (1302) that his favorite enemy, Pope Boniface VIII, issued his infamous bull, *Unam Sanctam,* which declared that it is "necessary to salvation that every creature be subject to the Roman Pontiff." In the book, claiming to demonstrate facts that no one else had considered, Dante stated that since the truth about papal political claims "can scarcely be brought to light without putting certain people to shame, it may give rise to anger against me." Soon after his death the book was publicly burned by the papal legate in Lombardy, who had to be talked out of trying to burn its author's bones. It became famous when Emperor Louis IV of Bavaria used Dante's ideas to justify his creation of the anti-pope, Nicholas (1328–30).

The book consists of three sections divided into forty-four chapters and comprising about ninety printed pages. Dante argued three main points:

1. Monarchy is the rightful form of government;
2. Universal dominion rightfully belongs to the Romans (though none of the Holy Roman emperors were technically Romans!);
3. Imperial authority is directly given by God and not through the papacy—so it's a case of two suns, and not of a moon totally dependent on one sun.

Hence: Constantine's Donation was illegal (and eventually proven fraudulent), and Pope Leo III exceeded his authority in conferring the imperial crown on Charlemagne in 800.

The temporal power of the papacy can have been given neither by natural law, nor by divine ordinance, nor by universal consent: indeed, it is against its own form and essence, the life of Christ, who said, "My kingdom is not of this world."

(It isn't surprising that this book was one of the first to be put on the Counter Reformation's *Index of Prohibited Books* when it was established in 1557. In the next century, papalist Jesuits began a relentless attack on Dante, which persisted through later centuries.)

Quaestio de Aqua et Terra
(A Question about Water and Land)

Quaestio de Aqua et Terra is the Latin text of a physics lecture given by Dante, four months before his death, in Can Grande's Verona on Sunday, January 20, 1320. Unique for its precise dating, it deals with this problem: if the whole universe is concentric, containing sphere within sphere, how is it that the sphere of water is invaded from place to place with elements from the sphere of earth (for example, islands rising above the sea)? The point was important, because God is perfect and His universe is an arrangement of those perfect forms called circles.

Calling himself the least of philosophers, Dante argues that while nature is most fond of concentricity, she also likes a little variety. So, to actualize other potencies, she allows some mingling of the sublunar elements of earth, air, fire, and water. This lecture shows a master poet's interest in details of physics. Not in him will you find a split between the "Two Cultures," of the poetic and the scientific. The lecture is also notable for the remark that "from my boyhood I have been continuously nurtured by love for the truth."

Letters

Though Dante was an avid letter writer, only ten Latin letters survive that are generally regarded as genuine.

1. A thank-you letter to a cardinal for trying to persuade Florence to let her exiles return (1304?).
2. A sympathy letter to two counts upon the death of their father (1304?).
3. A brief epistle to a marquis, describing how he himself had once been gripped by a terrible and imperious love. Still, "let love reign in me without pulling any of its punches." He encloses a poem of his (1307?).

4. A brief letter to a fellow exile, answering his question about love. He includes one of his own sonnets (1308).

5. An enthusiastic letter to the princes and people of Italy, urging them to welcome a visit from Emperor Henry VII (1310).

6. A violent direct attack on the wicked Florentines for resisting the emperor (1311).

7. An urgent appeal to the emperor to hasten and crush the Florentines (1311).

8. An appeal to the Italian cardinals at the 1314 conclave, urging them to elect an Italian who would return the papacy from Avignon to Rome, now deprived of both its suns. (The young emperor had died suddenly in 1313.)

9. An explanation to a Florentine friend (a priest?) as to why he rejects the degrading conditions under which he would be allowed to return home (1316): "...No, my father, not by this path will I return to my native city. If some other path can be found...which does not detract from the fame and honor of Dante, that I will tread with no halting steps. But if Florence cannot be entered by such a path, then never will I enter. What! Can I not gaze on the face of the sun and the stars from any place? Can I not ponder the most precious truths under any sky?...Surely bread will not fail me!"

10. A lengthy technical letter (1318?) to his patron, Can Grande (to whom he dedicates, offers, and recommends *Il Paradiso*), explaining the subject, form, language, title, and meaning of *La Comedia*. As for the title, in it he famously described himself as Florentine by birth but not by behavior. Experts argue about the authenticity of this key letter, or about parts of it. Today, Dante is generally viewed to be substantially its author.

Last Poems, Last Letters

Given Dante's supreme regard for Virgil, it is poetic that his last poems were in the form of two letters written to a Giovanni del Virgilio, a professor of poetry at the University of Bologna. A keen admirer of Virgil himself, Giovanni had written him a "carmen" expressing regret that Dante had been neglecting Virgil's Latin and writing poetry for the common herd.

That's like casting pearls before swine, he said, and restricts his non-Italian readership.

Imitating Virgil's pastoral eclogues perhaps in response to the words "herd" and "swine," Dante replied in Latin that he would send Virgilio ten vessels of milk from his favorite ewe—the *Paradiso,* presumably.

Dante deferred accepting Virgilio's offer to crown him poet laureate in Bologna. In addition to having enemies in Bologna (perhaps created by the *Inferno*), Dante would rather wait and be crowned poet laureate in Florence first.

Boccaccio quotes a fourteen-line epitaph that Virgilio submitted for Dante's tomb, but it seems never to have been used.

Bookends

Like bookends for *The Comedy,* there is an intriguing tradition about its first seven cantos and its last thirteen. As mentioned, the eighth canto begins with the curious phrase, "I say, continuing...." Early commentators like Boccaccio, who was eight when Dante died, related the story that Dante had already begun the poem when he was suddenly exiled while out of town. The homes of exiles being in danger of looting and their property of confiscation and destruction, his wife hid his manuscript with a friend. It finally caught up with the wanderer four years later. He had abandoned his project but now took it up again. So we may owe this imperiled classic to the wife he never saw again, and who goes unmentioned in any of her husband's surviving works.

Dante's biographer Boccaccio also told the story that upon the poet's sudden death, no trace could be found of the last thirteen cantos. His family and friends were "mortified" that God had not allowed him to complete his great religious work. Upon persuasion, his rhymester sons Jacopo and Pietro succumbed to the "presumptuous folly" of planning to finish the masterpiece. Then, exactly eight months after his demise, Dante appeared to Jacopo di Dante in a dream. Clothed in purest white, he revealed that his final cantos were hidden by bricks behind a wall mat. Rising in the middle of the night, Jacopo hastened to his father's former residence, roused its new occupant, and found the moldy cantos exactly as dreamed. Jacopo sat down at once to transcribe the crumbling pages. As we owe the beginning cantos and perhaps the whole poem to the unmentioned wife, we may owe the concluding ones to the unmentioned son.

Dante's Remains

Without success, Florence tried five times to have Dante's remains returned from Ravenna to the town that exiled him. Some saw in this fact a fulfillment of Brunetto Latini's words in the *Inferno*, canto 15: "Far from the goat [Florence] will be the grass [Dante]."

With Michelangelo promising to carve a worthy monument, the Florentine pope, Leo X, in 1519 authorized a mission to go fetch his relics. They found his sarcophagus empty, except for a few bone fragments and some withered laurel leaves. Guarding the secret, they surmised that since he had already visited the next world in his body, he had done so again.

In fact, alarmed at the prospect of losing their illustrious guest in 1519, the Franciscan superiors in whose church he laid buried quietly hid his remains. They hid them so well that they were not discovered until workmen removed some wall stones in 1865 and found a wooden box marked, "The bones of Dante." Unaware that the sarcophagus was empty, the workmen had been renovating the chapel for Dante's six-hundredth-birthday celebration. It is hard to believe that no Franciscan knew the truth, but once the workmen knew, the secret was out.

It was for Dante's host in Ravenna, Guido da Polenta, that the poet went on his fatal diplomatic mission to Venice. This Guido proposed to build the dead poet a splendid tomb and sought epitaphs from eminent poets, including Virgilio of Bologna (see above). But ill fortune soon overtook this nephew of Francesca Polenta da Rimini, and the plans were abandoned. But by 1378 there were two inscriptions on the tomb, one by a Dante friend and associate, Menghino Mezzano of Ravenna.

These six lines disappeared when the deteriorating tomb was restored in 1483, 1692, and 1780, the last two times by cardinals! The remaining epitaph that now adorns it was written by a certain Bernardo Canaccio, who may have known Dante personally. It alone may have survived because for many years Dante himself was supposed to have composed it, as the large introductory letters maintain: S.V.F. (*Sibi Vivens Fecit*—"He wrote it for himself when he was still alive." [How else? one wonders.])

The Latin tribute translates

Wandering about as long as the fates permitted, I sang of the rule of monarchy [on Earth], the lofty beings above, and the rivers and lakes [of the underworld]. But since part of me has departed [to be] a guest in better quarters, and I have sought my Author amidst happier stars, I, the wounded Dante, lie here, an exile from my father's shores, and the son of Florence, a mother of little love.

Bibliography

THE TRANSLATIONS ALREADY mentioned contain very useful information. Here is a basic library of other introductory works:

Auerbach, Eric. *Dante, Poet of the Secular World*. Chicago: University of Chicago Press, 1961.

Barbi, Michele. *Life of Dante*. University of California Press, 1954.

Barolini, Teodolina. *The Undivine Comedy*. Princeton: Princeton University Press, 1992.

Bergin, Thomas. *Dante*. New York: Orion Press, 1965.

Chubb, Thomas C. *Dante and His World*. Boston: Little, Brown, 1966.

Clements, Robert J., ed. *American Critical Essays on the Divine Comedy*. New York: New York University Press, 1967.

Collins, James. *Pilgrim in Love: An Introduction to Dante and His Spirituality*. Chicago: Loyola University Press, 1984.

Cosmos, Umberto. *Handbook to Dante Studies*. Oxford: Blackwell, 1950.

Fergusson, Francis. *Dante*. New York: Collier Books, 1966.

Freccero, John. *Dante: A Collection of Critical Essays*. Englewood Cliffs, N.J.: Prentice-Hall, Inc., 1965.

————. *Dante: The Poetics of Conversion*. Cambridge: Harvard University Press, 1986.

Gardiner, Eileen. *Visions of Heaven and Hell Before Dante*. New York: Italica Press, Inc., 1989.

Gilbert, Allan. *Dante and His Comedy*. New York: New York University Press, 1963.

Gilson, Etienne. *Dante the Philosopher*. London: Sheed and Ward, 1948.

Grandgent, Charles H. *Companion to the Divine Comedy*. Cambridge: Harvard University Press, 1975.

Huntington, George P., ed. *Comments of John Ruskin on The Divine Comedy*. Boston: Houghton, Mifflin and Co., 1903.

Jones, Alan. *The Soul's Journey: Exploring the Three Passages of the Spiritual Life with Dante as Guide*. San Francisco: HarperCollins, 1995.

Kay, Richard. *Dante's Swift and Strong*. Lawrence: Regents Press of Kansas, 1978.

Moore, Edward. *Studies in Dante*. 3 vol. New York: Greenwood Press, 1968.

Palacio, Miguel Asin. *Islam and The Divine Comedy*. New York: E. P. Dutton, 1926.

Slattery, John T., ed. *My Favourite Passages in Dante*. New York: Devon-Adair, 1928.

Smith, James R., trans. *The Earliest Lives of Dante [Boccaccio and Aretino]*. New York: Frederick Ungar Publishing Co., 1963.

Took, J. F. *Dante: Lyric Poet and Philosopher: An Introduction to the Minor Works*. Oxford: Clarendon Press, 1990.

Toynbee, Paget. *Dante Alighieri: His Life and Works*. New York: Harper Torchbooks, 1965.

Vossler, Karl. *Medieval Culture: An Introduction to Dante and His Times*. New York: Frederick Ungar Publishing Co., 1958.

Williams, Charles. *The Figure of Beatrice*. New York: Noonday, 1961.

For information on any particular item in *The Comedy*, these books are invaluable:

Singleton, Charles. *Commentaries on The Divine Comedy: Inferno* (1970); *Purgatorio* (1973); *Paradiso* (1975). Princeton: Princeton University Press.

Toynbee, Paget. *Concise Dictionary of Proper Names and Notable Matters in the Works of Dante*. New York: Phaeton, 1968.

Wilkins, Ernest, and Thomas Bergin. *A Concordance to the Divine Comedy*. Cambridge: Harvard University Press, 1965.

Index

A

A Concordance of Discordant Regulations, 153
A Question about Water and Land, 210
Abel, 59, 89
Abélard, Peter, 194
Achan, 99
Acheron, 12, 13, 22
Achilles, 15, 29, 100, 198
"Acquainted with the Night," xx
Acre, 151
acrostic, 86, 172
Adam, 14, 73, 114, 124, 146, 147, 160, 185, 190, 196
Adonis, 57, 116
Aeneas, 7, 9, 14, 18, 94, 96, 101, 120, 121, 144, 147, 150, 172
Aeneid, xix, xxi, 7, 18, 31, 42, 43, 51, 79, 94, 100, 101, 103, 104, 115, 120, 121, 173, 199
Agamemnon, 142, 143
Age of the Spirit, 163
Agent Orange, 90
Aglauros, 89
Agnello, 50
Agnus Dei, 91
Albert, Emperor, 79, 172, 206
Albert the Great, 153
Alberto della Scala, 95
Albi, 113
Albigensian (Catharist/Manichean), 113, 162
Alcides, 150
Alcmaeon, 141
Alessio, 40
Alexander the Great, 29, 178
Alighiera degli Alighieri, xv
Alighieri, 164
Alighiero degli Alighieri, xv
Allegorical Portrait of Dante, xxv
Allegory of Love, The, 113
Amata, 94
American Heritage Dictionary, 50
amor, 8
Amphion, 59
Amyclas, 155
Ananias, 99, 184
angels, 189, 190, 207
Angelus, 197
Annas, 47
Anne, Saint, 196, 198
Annuit Coeptis, 104
Anselm, Saint, 158

Antaeus, 58
Antenora, 60
anthropos, 202
anti-Semitism, 48
Antigone, 103
Antony, 104
Aphrodite, 112
apocatastasis, 3, 174
Apollo, 22, 38, 134, 135, 160, 199
Apostles' Creed, 203
Aquinas, Thomas, xii, 11, 14, 43, 99, 102, 109, 152, 154, 156, 158, 161, 189, 195, 206
Arabic calendar, 205
Arachne, 86
arch-heretics, 25
Arezzo, 56, 89
Argonauts, 40, 200
Ariadne, 30
Aristotle, 14, 27, 76, 109, 136, 138, 148, 152, 184, 208
Arius, 161
Arnaut Daniel, 102, 112, 113
Arno River, xxv, 31, 89
Arthur, King, 16, 59
Arthurian legend, xxi
Ascension, 126
Ascension Thursday, 135
Ash Wednesday, 204
astrology, 43
Athens, 45
Atropos, 102
Attila the Hun, 29
Auerbach, Eric, 23
Augustine of Hippo, Saint, 114, 124, 126, 140, 153, 196
"Ave Maria," 139, 197
Averroës, 14, 110
Averroist, 204
Avicenna, 14
Avignon, 41, 125, 151, 211

B

Babylonian Captivity, 99
Bacchus, 95, 160
Bach, 31
Bacon, Roger, 159

Banquet, The (Il Convito, Il Convivio),
   xiii, xviii, xxiii, 10, 25, 53, 74, 75,
   123, 137, 148, 189, 191, 206
Baring, Maurice, 139
Barolini, 37
Bartolommeo, 168
Basques, 60
Bathsheba, 153, 158
beard, 122, 123
Beatific Vision, 132, 189
beatitudes, 70
Beatrice (Portinari/de' Bardi), xvi, 10, 121–27,
   199, 205–6, and *passim*
Beccheria, Abbot, 60
Belacqua, 78
Belisarius, 144
Bella Abati, xv
Benedict, Saint, 177, 196
Benevento, 76
Benvenuto da Imola, 113
Berengar, Raymond, 144
Bernard of Clairvaux, Saint, 127, 194, 195, 197,
   198, 199
Bernardo Canaccio, 213
Bertran de Born, 54, 55, 102, 113
Besterman, Theodore, xi
Bible, xii, 7, 27, 152, and *passim*
Big Bang, 188
Big Dog, 9
Birth of Purgatory, The, 71
"Black" Guelphs, 19, 49, 99
Blake, William, xxiv
Bloom, Harold, xi
Bocca, 60
Boccaccio, xv, xviii, 19, 38, 81, 123, 212,
Boethius, 112, 153
Bologna, 40, 47, 89, 111, 209, 211, 212
Bolognese, 209
Bonagiunta da Lucca, 102, 107
Bonaventure, Saint, 156
book, the word, 200
Borgese, Giuseppe Antonio, 201
Bosone d'Agubbio, 48
Botticelli, Sandro, xxiv
Branca d'Oria, 62
Braveheart, 172
Briareus the Hundred-Handed, 58, 86
Browning, Robert, 80
Brunetto Latini, 34, 166, 213
Brutus, 64, 74, 93, 145
Bucolics, 104
Buddha, 119
bulls, 30
Bunyan, xxi
Buonconte da Montefeltro, 78
Buondelmonti, 166
Buoso, 49
Byron, Lord, xiii, 82

C

Cacciaguida, 161, 163, 167, 168,
   169, 170, 188, 195
Cacus, 49
Caesar Augustus, 100, 104, 120
Caesar, Julius, 14, 24, 54, 56, 64, 73, 74, 92,
   93, 95, 99, 112, 150, 155, 165, 188
Caiaphas, 47
Cain, 59, 89, 137
Caina, 59
Calliope, 73
Camicion de' Pazzi, 59
Campaldino, battle of, xvi, 16
Can Grande della Scala, xxi, 9, 95, 168, 171,
   210, 211
Cana, 87, 104
Cancellieris, 49
cannibalism, 61
Canterbury, 158
Canterbury Tales, xxi, 199
"Canticle of the Sun," 102
Capaneus, 32, 37
Capocchio, 56
Capulets/Cappalletti, 79
cardinal sins, 73
cardinal virtues, 73
cardinal's hat, 176
Carlyle, Thomas, xxii
Casella, 75, 101
Casentino, 89
Cassius, 64, 74, 145
Catalano, 47
Catholic, 159
Cato the Younger, 73, 74, 75, 98, 174
Cavalcante de' Cavalcanti, 26, 166
celibacy, 110
centaurs, 29, 108
Cerberus, 18, 25
Cervantes, xxi
Charlemagne, 60, 125, 144, 169, 209
Charles I, King of Sicily, 148
Charles of Anjou, 99
Charles of Valois, 99, 149
Charon, 12
Chaucer, xxi, xxiii, 198
chessboard, 189
Chiron, 29
Christ (Jesus), 17, 100, 118, 124, 145–46, 159,
   178–79, 183, 200–201, and *passim. See also*
   griffin
Christ-figure, 120
Church of Rome, 93
Churchill, Winston, 43
Ciacco, 18
Ciampolo of Navarre, 46
Cianfa, 49
Ciardi, John, xxiv, 19
Cimabue, 19, 85

Cincinnatus, 164
Circe, 51, 187
Cirigliano, Marc A., 204
City of Dis, 21
Clare, Saint, 139, 195
Claudel, Paul, 120
Clemence, 149
Clements, Robert J., xxiii
Cleopatra, 15
Clotho, 102
Cocytus, 22, 33, 59, 63
Colonnas, 53
"Come, Sweet Death," 31
comedy, the word, 45
comedy (humor), 101
Concerning Monarchy (Monarchical Rule, De
    Monarchia), xxiii, 9, 20, 93, 209
Confessions of St. Augustine, The, 140
Conrad, Emperor, 164
Consolation of Philosophy, The, 127
Constance, Empress, 139, 140, 173
Constantine the Great, 41, 125, 144, 151, 173,
    176, 201
Constantinople, 158, 173
contrapasso, 55
Convito, Il. See Banquet, The
Convivio, Il. See Banquet, The
Cornelia, 164
Corpus Christi, 119, 120
correspondence with contrast, 131
Corso Donati, 107, 138
cortesia, 146
Counter Reformation, 210
courtesy, 36
courtly love, xxi, 113
Crassus, 99
Crete, 30, 33
Croatia, 195
crucifixion, 44
Crusades, 100, 163, 195
Cumaean, 199
Cunizza, 149, 151
Cupid, 116, 147
Curio, 54
Currado da Palazzo, 93
Currado Malaspina, 81
Cyprus, 147
Cyrus the Great, 86

D

da Vinci, 19
Daedalus, 39
Damian, Peter, 175
dances, 145, 182
Daniel, 33, 104, 140
Dante: dates, name, parents, xv; youth, wife,
    children, Beatrice, xvi; political office, death
    sentence, exile, xviii; The Comedy, xviii-
xxv, 212; other works, xxiii, 203–12; death,
    176; remains, tomb, 213–14; ultimate
    salvation, 12, 124, 154, 163, 192; and
    passim
Dante and the Animal Kingdom, 180
Dante Symphony, xii
Dante: The Poetics of Conversion, 61
Dante's Swift and Strong, 35
Danube, 59
Daphne, 134
Das Kapital, xxii
David, King, 14, 84, 102, 153, 158, 173, 196
De Monarchia. See Concerning Monarchy
De Profundis, 21
De Vulgari Eloquentia. See On Eloquence in the
    Vernacular
Decameron, The, xv
della Scala, 9, 168
Delphi, 134
demons, 39
Descartes, 158
devils, 39
Diana, 110, 143
Dickinson, Emily, 21
Dido, 15, 99, 121, 147, 150
Die Gottliche Komodie, 39
Diomedes, 51, 62
Dionysius the Pseudo-Areopagite, 153, 189, 190
Dis/Satan, 21, 29, 63
Dives, 21
Divine Comedy, The, xviii-xxv; length of poem,
    line, terza rima, xix; purpose, xxi;
    excellence, xxii; difficulty, xxiii; transla-
    tions, xxiv; inconsistencies, 79, 101, 103;
    "lost" cantos, 212; and passim
Dolce stil n(u)ovo / (sweet new style), 108, 204
dolce vita, 140, 173, 183
Dolcestilnovisti, 108
Dominic, Saint, 155, 156
Don, the river, 59
Don Giovanni, 75
Don Juan, 82
Don Quixote, xxi
Donati family, 49, 106. See Gemma Donati,
    Nella Donati, Piccarda Donati
Donation of Constantine, 42, 125, 209
Donatus, 158
Doré, Gustave, xxiv
Dorian Gray, 18
Douay-Rheims, xiii
dreams, 51, 82, 97, 114, 157, 191
Duomo, 42
Durante Abati, xv
DVX or DUX (Duce), 126, 168

E

eagle, 136, 144, 170, 171, 172, 184
early-morning dreams, 51

Eclogues, 21, 104
ecstasy, 135
Eden, 185
Edict of Milan, 201
Einstein, Albert, 188
Eleanor of Aquitaine, 55
Eliot, T. S., xi, xiii, 13, 53, 113, 187, 204
Elizabeth II, Queen of England, xvii
Elizabeth, Saint, 95
Eloquence in the Vernacular. See On Eloquence in the Vernacular
Emerson, Ralph Waldo, xxii
Enciclopedia Dantesca, xii
Encyclopedia Judaica, 48
Ephialtes, 58
Epicurus, 25
Erichtho, 24
eros, 204
Erysicthon, 105
Esau, 148, 196, 197
Essay on Man, 98
Ethiopians, 172
Eucharist-figure, 120
Euclid, 138
Eunoe, 115, 117, 126, 127
Euphrates, 127
Europa, 30
Europe, 30
Eve, 73, 114, 118, 121, 147, 196
Everlasting Gospel, 159
evil claws, 44
evil pouches, 39
Exaltation of the Holy Cross, 176
Ezzelino, 29, 150

F

faith, 180
fallen angels, the, 12, 23
Fano, 54
Farinata degli Uberti, 26, 27, 47, 119, 166
Fates, 102
Faust, 54, 63, 78
Fawkes, Guy, 205
Fergusson, Francis, 201
Ferrara, xv, 150
fides quaerens intellectum, 109
fig, 49, 50
Filippo Argenti, 22, 41
First Circle, The, 14
First Crusade, 169
first friend, 204
Florence, xv, xviii, 18, 19, 26, 31, 36, 49, 51, 60, 89, 99, 106, 107, 147, 165, 167, 182, 194, 197, 204, 208, 210, 213
Florenskij, 138
Florentine dialect, xxii
Florentines, 18, 19, 22, 26, 31, 34, 38, 139, 211
Folquet, 102, 113, 157

Foreigner, 96
Forese Donati, 102, 105, 138
Forest of Eden, 69
Fortune, 35
fortunetellers, 42
Fourth Eclogue, 7, 103, 104
Fra Angelico, 19
Francesca da Rimini, xii, 16, 17, 62
Francesco de' Cavalcanti, 49
Francesco de Sanctis, 204
Francis of Assisi, Saint, 53, 102, 154, 159, 164, 195, 196
Freccero, John, 61
Frederick Barbarossa, Emperor, xvii, 95, 139
Frederick II, Emperor, xvii, 27, 31, 76, 93, 139
French, 56
French Revolution, 99
Friar Alberigo, 62
Frost, Robert, xx, 90
Furies, 24

G

Gabriel, 55, 84, 179, 197
Gaddo, 61
Gaea, 59
Galeotto, 16
Galileo, 19
Gandhi, 171
Ganelon, 60
Garden of Eden, 127
gargoyle cantos, 45
Gemini, xv, 177
Gemma Donati, xvi, 105, 139
Genoa, 62
Genoese, 209
Gentucca, 107
Geri del Bello degli Alighieri, 55
Germans, 39
Geryon, 37, 38, 73
Gherardo, 93
Ghibellines, xvii, 20, 26, 27, 54, 60, 81, 88, 144, 168
Ghiberti, 42
Gianciotto, 17
Gianni Schicchi, 57
giants, 58
Gibraltar, 51
Gibson, Mel, 172
Gideon, 108
Giotto, xxii, 19, 85
Giovanni de Fidanza, 159
Giovanni del Virgilio, 211
Giovanni di Paolo, 191
Giovanni Villani, 53
Giraud of Limoges, 112
Glaucus, 135
"Gloria in Excelsis Deo," 99
Gnostic, 162

Gnosticism, 125
God: Point of Light, 188, 200–201, and *passim.*
    See also Trinity
Godfrey, Duke, 169
Golden Age, 33
Gorgon, 24
Gounod, 78
goy, 205
Gratian's Decretals, 153
Gray, Thomas, 82
Great Schism, 125
Great Seal, 104
Greeks, 51, 60
Gregorian calendar, 188
Gregory of Nazianzus, Saint, 139
Gregory the Great, Saint, 189
greyhound, 8
griffin, 118, 119, 122, 123, 124, 198
Guardini, Romano, 186
Guelphs, xvii, 19, 26, 36, 49, 54, 60, 81, 88,
    99, 144, 170
Guido Cavalcanti, 26, 85, 111, 150, 203, 204
Guido da Castel, 93
Guido da Montefeltro, 53
Guido da Polenta the Younger, 16, 204, 213
Guido del Duca, 89
Guido Guinizelli, 85, 102, 111, 204
Guido, the name, 204
Guinevere, 16
Guiscard, Robert, 169
Guittone d'Arezzo, 102, 112
Gunpowder Plot, 205
guy, the word, 205
Guy de Montfort, 30
Guy, the name, 205

H

Hadrian, Emperor, 104
Hail Mary, 203
Haman, 94
Hamlet, xix
Hannibal, 186
Harpies, 30, 31
Hebrew, 147
Hecate, 24
Hegel, 158
Helen of Troy, 15, 60
Heliodorus, 99
hellfire, 23
Héloïse, 194
hendecasyllabic, xix
Henry II of England, 54
Henry IV, Emperor, 117
Henry of Cornwall, Prince, 30
Henry of England, Prince, 54
Henry V, Emperor, 117
Henry VII, Emperor, 126, 149, 168, 193, 201,
    211

Hepburn, Katharine, 55
Hercules/Herakles, 24, 29, 37, 59, 150
heresy, 25, 182, 203
heretics, 25
hermaphrodite, 112
Hermes, 112
Hero, 116
Hezekiah, King, 173
Hippolytus, 167
History of Animals, 136
Hitler, 43
Hohenstaufens, xvii
Holbrook, Richard, 180
Holofernes, 86
Holy Eucharist, 170
Holy Grail, xxi
Holy Roman Empire, 99
Holy Year, xxi
Homer, xv, xix, xxi, 7, 14, 60, 97, 102, 103
homosexuality, 32–38, 111–12
hope, 182
Hopkins, Gerard Manley, 138
Horace, 14, 102
Hosanna, 189
Hound of Heaven, The, 8
Hugh Capet, 98, 100, 193
Hugh of St. Victor, 158
Hungary, 148
Huse, H. R., xiii, xxiv
Hypsipyle, 40
hysteron proteron, 178, 196

I

Iahweh or Iehovah, 185
Icarus, 39
Il Convito. See Banquet, The
Il Convivio. See Banquet, The
Il Poeta, xxii
Il Trovatore, 113
Iliad, xix
Immaculate Conception, 195
Immanuel ben Solomon, 48
In the Middle of This Road We Call Our Life, 9
Index of Prohibited Books, xxiii, 156, 210
Inquisition, 113, 206
Iphigenia, 143
Isidore of Seville, 153
Islam, 14, 23, 54, 125
Islam and the Divine Comedy, 55
Israel: See Jacob
Italian dialects, 208
Italian flag, 121
Italian language, 208

J

Jacob/Israel, 14, 65, 114, 148, 176, 196, 197
Jacopo del Cassero, 78

Jacopo di Dante, 212
Jacopo Rusticucci, 36
Jacques de Molay, 193
James, Saint, 119, 182
Jason, 40, 136, 200
Jehoshaphat, 25
Jephthah, 142, 143
Jericho, 61, 151
Jerome, Saint, 76, 147, 190
Jerusalem, 15, 25, 55, 64, 101, 105, 145, 146, 169, 170, 176, 187
Jesuits, 210
Jewish, 196
Jewish ghettos, 65
Jews, 48, 142
Joachim of Flora, Abbot, 158, 159, 163, 196
Job, 172
John Chrysostom, Saint, 158
John the Baptist, 31, 95, 104, 170, 196
John the Evangelist, Saint, 118, 119, 183, 184, 196
Jones, James W., 9
Joseph of Egypt, 57
Joshua, 151, 169
Jove, 32, 33, 58, 80, 125
Jovial Friars, 47, 62
Jubilee Year 1300, xxi, 40
Judah, 65
Judaism, 69
Judas Iscariot, 64
Judas Maccabaeus, 69, 169
Jude, 119
Judecca, 63, 64
Judgment Day, 25, 172
Judith, 196
Julian calendar, 187
Julian of Norwich, 174
Juno, 43
Jupiter, 43, 175, 187
Justin, Emperor, 144
Justinian, 143
Juvenal, 102

K

Kant, Immanuel, 136
Kay, Richard, 35
Kennedy, President, 13
King James Bible, 75
Kiss, The (Rodin), 17
Knights Templar, 100, 193
Koran, 55, 153

L

La Chanson de Roland, 60
"La donna e mobile," 81
La Pia, 78, 88
La Vita Nuova (My Life Made New/My

Young Days), xvi, xx, xxiii, 10, 108, 117, 203-7
Lachesis, 102
Lackland, John, 55
Lady Poverty, 155
Lancelot, 16
landslide, 17, 29
Last Judgment, 19, 31, 192, 193
Lateran Council, Fourth, 157
Lateran Palace, 151
Latin Quarter, 154
Latin race, the, 207
Lavinia, 94
Lawrence, Saint, 140
Lazarus, 21
Le Goff, Jacques 71
Leah, 114
Leander, 116
Lebanon, 120
Lepa, xvi
Lethe, 33, 116, 117, 122, 126, 127, 139
Letters, 210
lettor (reader), 23
Levites, 93
Lewis, C. S., 113
Libri Sententiarum, 153
Life of Dante, xviii
Life of St. Francis, 156
Limbo, 10, 13, 76, 102, 103, 173, 185, 198
Lion in Winter, The, 55
Liszt, Franz, xii
Loderingo, 47
Lombard, Peter, 153
London Bridge, 30
Longfellow, Henry Wadsworth, xii, 82
Lord's Prayer. *See* Our Father
Lorenzo Valla, 42
Lot's wife, 83
Louis IV of Bavaria, Emperor, 209
"Love Song of J. Alfred Prufrock, The," 53
Lucan, 14, 42, 102
Lucca, 44, 107
Lucifer, 86, 171, 186
Lucy, Saint, 9, 83, 196
Luke the Evangelist, 118, 119
Luther, Martin, 9, 152, 181
Lyons, Second Council of, 99

M

Macarius, Saint, 177
Maccabees (Machabees), 61, 67, 69
Machiavelli, 19
magician, 41, 42
Maimonides, 153
Mainz, 158
Malacoda, 44
Malaspina, 166
Malebolge, 39

Malebranche, 44
Malta, 150
Mandelbaum, Allen, xxiv
Manfred, 76, 77, 139, 171
Manfred Symphony, 77
Manichean, 113, 162
Manto, 42, 103
Mantua, 42, 79
Marcia, 73
Marco, 91
Mark the Evangelist, 118
Maro, 8
Mars, 22, 31, 148
Marseilles, 150
Marsyas, 135
Martel, Charles, 147, 149
Marx, Karl, xxii
Mary (Mother of Christ), 10, 70, 78, 179, 195–
99, and *passim*
Master Adam, 57
Master of the Disgusting, 45
Matilda (Matelda/Maud), 114, 116, 117, 122,
123, 124, 127
Matilda, La Gran Contessa, 117, 125
Matthew the Evangelist, 118
Mechthild, 117
Medici, 19
Medusa, 24
Meleager, 109
mendicant orders, 161
Menghino Mezzano, 213
Mephistopheles, 63
Mercury, 112
Merton, Thomas, 84
Metamorphoses, 42
Michal, 84
Michel Zanche, 62
Michelangelo, xxiv, 19, 213
Midas, 99
Milan, 95
Milky Way, 38
Milton, 64
Minerva, 135
Minos, 30, 31
Minotaur, 29, 30, 111
Monarchical Rule. See Concerning Monarchy
Monarchy, 170
Monophysite, 144
monosyllables, 141
Montagues/Montecchi, 79
Montaperti, battle of, 26
Monte Cassino, 177
morally neutral, 12
Mordred, 59
Mosca, 54
Moses, 14, 96, 169, 196
Moses Maimonides, 153

mosques, 54
Mount Parnassus, xxv, 103, 134
Mozart, 75
Mucius Scaevola, 141
Muhammad/Mahomet 54, 55, 65
Muses, 10, 59, 73, 103, 119, 134, 170, 179,
199
Muslims, 14, 37, 149, 164. *See also* Saracens
Myrrha, 57

N

Name of the Rose, The, 159
Naples, 99, 101, 104, 148, 199
Narcissus, 138
Nathan, 158
National Gallery, xxv
Nebuchadnezzar, King, 140
Nella Donati, 106
Neptune, 200
Nessus, 29
New and Revised National Gallery of Art, xxv
*New Grove Dictionary of Music and Musicians,
The,* 65
Newton, Isaac, 136
Nicholas, anti-pope, 209
Nicholas, Saint, 98
Nichomachean Ethics, 55
Nimrod, 58, 60, 86, 185
nine, the number, 205
Nino Visconti, 81
Niobe, 86
Noah, 14
Norton, Charles Eliot, 206
Novus Ordo Seclorum, 104

O

"Ode to the West Wind," xx
Oderisi, 85
Odysseus. *See* Ulysses
Odyssey, xix, xxi, 7, 101, 198
Old Man of Crete, 33
Omberto Aldobrandesco, 85
*On Eloquence in the Vernacular (De Vulgari
Eloquentia),* xxiii, 107, 185, 204, 206, 208
On the Consolation of Philosophy, 127, 153
On the Heavenly Hierarchy, 153, 189
Ontological Argument, 158
Orestes, 87
Origen, 174
Orosius, 153
Ostian, 157
O'Toole, Peter, 55
Otto the Great, 125
Our Father, 85, 112, 203
Ovid, 14, 33, 42, 102

P

P, the letter, 70, 83
Padua, 38, 150
Pagliacci, 201
Palacios, Miguel Asin, 55
Paolo Malatesta, 16, 17, 62
papacy, 92, 125
Paris (person), 15; (city) 85, 154
Parodi, E. G., 43
Pasiphaë, 30, 111
Pater Noster. See Our Father
Paul, Saint, 9, 104, 111, 119, 135, 153, 170, 176, 180, 184, 189
peccatum, 83
Pegasus, 170
pelican, 183
Penelope, 51
Peneus, 134
Pepin, 125
Persephone, 24
Peter, comb-seller named, 88
Peter, Saint, 41, 83, 97, 103, 119, 125, 151, 170, 176, 180, 181, 182, 186, 187, 196
Peter the Eater, 158, 185
Peter the Spaniard, 158
Petrarch, 19
Petrus Sabbatius, 144
Phaedra, 167
Phaëthon, 38, 167
Pharsalia, 24, 42
Philip IV (the Fair), King, 41, 99, 100, 125, 172, 193
philosophy, 207
Phlegethon, 22, 29
Phlegyas, 22
Phrynichus, 45
Piccarda Donati, 107, 138, 139, 140, 150
Pier da Medicina, 54
Pier della Vigne, 31, 32
Pietole, 96
Pilgrim's Progress, The, xxi
Pinsky, Robert, xxiv
Pisa, 61, 89
Pisistratus, 91
Pistoia, 19, 49
Plato, 14, 76, 140, 206
Pluto, 20, 24
poets, 102
Poitiers, 62
Pollio, 104
Polymnestor, 99
Pompey, 24, 95, 99, 150
ponte vecchio, 40
Pope, Alexander, 98
Popes: Adrian/Hadrian V, 97, 98, 107, 166; Agapetus, 144; Anastasius, 27; Benedict XV, xxiii; Boniface VIII, 12, 18, 19, 35, 41, 49, 53, 99, 125, 157, 167, 186, 193, 209; Celestine V, 12; Clement IV, 30, 76; Clement V, 41, 125, 151, 168, 186, 193; Gregory the Great, 69, 174; Gregory VII, 117; Gregory X, 158; Gregory XIII, 188; Honorius III, 155; Innocent III, 155; Innocent IV, 176; Innocent V, 159; John XXI, 158; John XXII, 170, 171, 186, 188; John XXIII, 43; Leo III, 209; Leo X, 213; Martin IV, 107; Nicholas III, 41, 151; Nicholas IV, 159; Paul VI, xxii
popes, 27
Portugal, 158
Potiphar, 57
Pound, Ezra, 77, 113
Prague, 172
Priam, King, 99
Procne, 93
Profession of Faith, A, 203
Promised Land, 96
Proserpina, 24, 116
Provençal, the language, 112, 113
Provençal poetry, xx
Provence, 113, 144, 148, 204
Provenzan Salvani, 86, 88
psalms, 75
Puccini, Giacomo, 57
Puccio the Cripple, 49
Pygmalion, 99
Pylades, 87

Q

Quaestio de Aqua et Terra, 210
Quirinus (Romulus), 148

R

Rabanus, 158
Rachel, 114, 196, 197
Rachmaninoff, Sergei, xii
Rahab, 151
Raphael, xxiv
Rascia, 172
Ravenna, xv, xviii, 16, 89, 177, 204, 213
Realto, 150
Rebecca, 196
Reformation, 186
"*Regina Coeli,*" 180
Rehoboam, 86
Renouard, 169
retribution, 54
Rhône, 125
rhyme, xix
Richard of St. Victor, 154
Richard the Lion-Hearted, King, 55
Rimbaud, Arthur, 3
Rimini, 16, 54, 89
Rinier da Calboli, 89

Ripheus, 173, 174
Robert the Bruce, 172
Rodin, Auguste, xii
Rodin's *The Kiss,* 17
Roland, 60, 169
Roma, 8
Romagna, 52, 89
Roman accent, 208
Roman Empire, 7
Rome, xxi, 9, 33, 40, 92, 126, 141, 144, 145, 148, 151, 167
Romena, 57
Romeo and Juliet, 79
Romualdus, Saint, 177
Romulus, 9, 148
Rubicon, 54
Rue Dante, 154
Ruggieri, Archbishop, 61, 62
Ruskin, John, xxii, 45, 132
Ruth, 196

S

Sabatier, Paul, 156
sacrament, 120
Saladin, 15
"*Salve, Regina,*" 80
Sanctus, Sanctus, Sanctus, 184
Sanhedrin, 47
Santa Croce, xv
Santiago de Compostela, 182
Sapia, 88
Sapphira, 99
Saracens, 60, 169. *See also* Muslims
Sarah, 196
Sardanapalus, King, 164
Sardinia, 106
Sassol, 60
Satan/Lucifer/Beelzebub, 21, 63, 65, 191
Saturn, 175
Saul, King, 86
Savonarola, 19
Sayers, Dorothy, xxiv, 38, 45, 52, 113, 117, 120, 150
Scaligers, 168
Schwartz, Delmore, 85
"Second Nun's Tale, The," 199
Semele, 175
Sennacherib, 86
Septuagint, 75
Ser, 34
Serbia, 172
sestina, 112
Seven, the movie, 69
Seven Deadly Sins, 203
Seven Penitential Psalms, The, 203
Seven Sacraments, 203
Seven Storey Mountain, The, 84
Severinus, Saint, 153

sex, 110
Shakespeare, xi, xv, 79, 93
Shelley, Percy Bysshe, xx, 132
Sibyl, 199, 200
Sicilian Vespers, 148
Sicily, 96, 148, 169, 172
Siena, 56, 86, 88
Sienese, 56
Siger of Brabant, 154
silence, 198
Silver Age, 100
Silvius, 9
Simon de Montfort, 30
Simone de' Bardi, xvi
Simon Magus, 41
Sinclair, John D., xiii, xxiv, 120, 138
Singleton, Charles S., xiii, xxiv, 9, 37, 61, 92
Sinon, 57
siren, 97, 122
Sisson, C. H., xxiv
Socrates, 14
Sodom and Gomorrah, 111
Solomon, King, 14, 120, 153, 160, 162
Solomon's Temple, 100, 126
Solzhenitsyn, Alexander, 14
Song of Roland, The, 60
sonnets, 203
Sordello, 79, 83, 101, 102, 113, 150
Sortes Virgilianae, 104
southern hemisphere, 64, 69
Spendthrift Club, 56
St. Peter's Basilica, 40, 117, 157
Stanza della Segnatura, xxv
stars (*stelle*), 64, 127, 201–2, 211, 214
Statius, 42, 100, 101, 102, 103, 109, 111, 114, 116, 124, 127, 165
Stephen, Saint, 91
stigmata, the, 155
Styx, 21, 22, 25
sullenness, 21
sultan, 155
Summa Theologiae/Theologica, xii
Summae Deus clementiae, 110
sweet new style, 108, 204
Symposium, The, 206
Syrian calendar, 205

T

Taddeo, 157
Tchaikovsky, Peter, xii, 16, 77
"*Te Deum laudamus,*" 83, 181
"*Te lucis ante terminum,*" 81
Tegghiaio Aldobrandi, 36
Ten Commandments, 203
Tennyson, 51, 138
terza rima, xx, xxiv
terzine, xix, xx
Thais, 40

Thames, 30
Thebaid, 42
Thebes, 33, 59, 95, 100
Theodora, 144
Theseus, 24, 30, 108
Thinker, The, xii
third eye, 119
Thompson, Francis, 8
threshing floor, 178, 202
Tiber, 75
Tiberius, 144, 146
Tigris, 127
Timaeus, 140
Time magazine, 159
Tiresias, 43, 103
Titus, Emperor, 101, 144
Tolomea, 61
Toulouse, 150
Tours, battle of, 149
Tower of Babel, 58, 185
tragedy, 45
Trajan, Emperor, 84, 173, 174
translations, xiii
Treasury, The, 35
Trent, 43
Trinity, xx, 11, 64, 122, 152, 201, 206
Tristan, 15
Trojan War, 51
Trojans, 52, 57, 60, 96
Trotsky, Leon, xxii
troubadour, 80, 102, 112, 113
Troy, 86
Turkey, 144
Turnus, 94
Tuscany, 19
Twins/Gemini, 177

U

Ugolino, Count, 61, 62
Ulysses, 51, 52, 54, 62, 97, 101, 187
Unam Sanctam, 209

V

Vanni Fucci, 49, 166
Vatican, xxv, 151, 186
Vatican Council, Second, xxii, 43
Vatican Gardens, 58

vendetta, divine, 28; private, 55
Venedico Caccianemico, 40
Venerable Bede, 153
Venice, xviii, 150
Venus, 57, 73, 74, 112, 116, 147
Verdi, 81, 113
Vergil, the spelling, 24
Verona, 95, 168, 210
Veronica, 195
Vespatian, 146
Vesuvius, 199
"Vexilla Regis," 62
Vietnam, 90
Virgil, 7–8, 24, 104, 115, 121, 174, 199, and
    passim
Virgilio of Bologna, 212, 213
vita, 149
vita n[u]ova. See La Vita Nuova
Viterbo, 30
vows, 142
Vulgate Bible, xiii, 76, 147

W

Wallace, William, 172
Waste Land, The, 13, 113
Western Canon, The, xi
"White" Guelphs, 19, 49
white rose, 193, 195
Wife of Bath, Chaucer's, 16
Wilde, Oscar, 18, 21
William II, the Good, 173
William of Ockham, 159
William of Orange, 169
William the Bad, 139, 173
William the Conqueror (alias the Bastard), 117
William the Good, 139
Wordsworth, William, xix
World Bibliography of Bibliographies, xi

Y

Yahweh, 143
Yugoslavia, 144

Z

Zerubbabel, 126
Zeus, 30, 39
zodiac, 135

About the Author

ORDAINED A CATHOLIC PRIEST in 1955, Joseph Gallagher has taught at St. Mary's Seminary, Johns Hopkins University, Notre Dame College, and Loyola College in Baltimore, at St. Ambrose College at Davenport, Iowa, and at Oxford University, England. His subjects have been preaching, philosophy, and poetry and other literature, especially Dante's *Comedy*. He wrote the entry on Dante in the 1994 *Modern Catholic Encyclopedia*. He has written several hundred articles for the Baltimore

Photo by John Abrahams

Sunpapers and published in half a hundred other publications. His books include *The Documents of Vatican II* (translation editor); *Painting on Silence* (poems); *The Pain and the Privilege: The Diary of a City Priest; The Christian under Pressure* (reprinted as *How To Survive Being Human*); *Voices of Strength and Hope for a Friend with AIDS;* and *The Business of Circumference: A Kaleidoscope*. His poetry has been published in several anthologies. He has also worked as a "buddy" for persons with AIDS, written and lectured on the disease, and helped conduct a number of retreats for persons suffering from it. Retired, he lives in his native Baltimore.